ARNAUD DESPIERRE

Happy Grow Lucky
Build a Thriving Career and Find Happiness at Work. For Life.

Routledge
Taylor & Francis Group

LONDON AND NEW YORK

Designed cover image: Sharon Koh

First published 2026
by Routledge
4 Park Square, Milton Park, Abingdon, Oxon, OX14 4RN

and by Routledge
605 Third Avenue, New York, NY 10158

Routledge is an imprint of the Taylor & Francis Group, an informa business

© 2026 Arnaud Despierre

The right of Arnaud Despierre to be identified as author of this work has been asserted in accordance with sections 77 and 78 of the Copyright, Designs and Patents Act 1988.

All rights reserved. No part of this book may be reprinted or reproduced or utilised in any form or by any electronic, mechanical, or other means, now known or hereafter invented, including photocopying and recording, or in any information storage or retrieval system, without permission in writing from the publishers.

For Product Safety Concerns and Information please contact our EU representative GPSR@taylorandfrancis.com. Taylor & Francis Verlag GmbH, Kaufingerstraße 24, 80331 München, Germany.

Trademark notice: Product or corporate names may be trademarks or registered trademarks, and are used only for identification and explanation without intent to infringe.

British Library Cataloguing-in-Publication Data
A catalogue record for this book is available from the British Library

ISBN: 9781041132820 (hbk)
ISBN: 9781041132806 (pbk)
ISBN: 9781003669005 (ebk)

DOI: 10.4324/9781003669005

Typeset in Joanna MT
by codeMantra

Happy Grow Lucky

Careers are like relationships; they are complex, critical, and you don't often get a second chance to get it right. *Happy Grow Lucky* will give you that chance.

Happy Grow Lucky's insights are built on in-depth interviews with 45 global Chief Human Resources Officers from some of the biggest companies on the planet, from adidas to Vodafone, totalling over $1 trillion in revenues. It showcases these senior leaders' life-tested career stories as they candidly share their mistakes, learnings, and best practices, giving readers an unprecedented look into their career journeys.

Along the way, this book's research busts conventional career management myths and lays out best practices that will drive your long-term professional success. It introduces the concept of Career Health and provides a practical and actionable method to help you (re)build a successful and fulfilling career at any stage of your life.

Happy Grow Lucky is for readers who want to play the long game and build a Thriving Career over years and decades. It is a book that you come back to every couple of years for a lifetime, even as you get into your legacy years. It is also a book you gift to your junior colleagues to set them on the right path and to your friends to help inspire them.

Happy Grow Lucky is a Masterclass in career-building. It will give you value immediately and continue to grow on you throughout your life.

Arnaud Despierre is a thought-leader on global career management issues. He is a former partner with Spencer Stuart and consultant with McKinsey & Company where he led organisational development work for clients in North America and Asia. When he is not writing about careers topics, Arnaud spends an inordinate amount of time on endurance sports, particularly long-distance running and triathlons, which gives him plenty of time for creative thinking and soul-searching.

Luck is what happens when preparation meets opportunity.
Seneca the Younger, First century AD

Contents

Kind Words about *Happy Grow Lucky* — ix
Acknowledgements — xii
Foreword, by Varun Bhatia — xiv
Introduction — xix
Meet our Fearless Leaders — xxvi

The curious case of the lucky career **One** — 1

Activating your Awareness **Two** — 17

Betting on Bravery **Three** — 35

Cultivating Connectivity **Four** — 51

Driving Delivery **Five** — 68

Managing your career flow **Six** — 86

Mastering pivotal HR career moments **Seven** — 113

Your career (re)starts here **Eight** — 146

Conclusion **Nine** — 169

Kind Words about *Happy Grow Lucky*

Career journeys often make more sense when we look back. As you reach critical decision points in your own career journey, wouldn't it be helpful to tap into the experiences of leaders who have built successful international careers? *Happy Grow Lucky* is the book for you – full of very personal individual stories expertly woven together to create valuable insights. Read it, reflect on it, and it will help you along your own way in life.

Lucien Alziari, EVP, former Chief Human Resources Officer, Prudential Financial

Happy Grow Lucky is a refreshing reminder that growth doesn't have to come at the cost of joy – in fact, the two are deeply connected. Arnaud invites us to rethink how we lead, live, and learn in a world that often prioritizes speed over substance. With clarity and heart, this work encourages us to embrace curiosity, cultivate resilience, and lead with intention – not just in our organizations, but in our lives. A thoughtful and timely read for anyone passionate about people, purpose, and progress.

Morten Enggaard Rasmussen, Executive Vice President of People & Stakeholder Relations, Novonesis

Happy Grow Lucky offers a very practical roadmap for people who have the ambition to reach the Chief HR Officer level. The "fil rouge" from the 45 CHROs interviewed is extremely valid and backed by concrete examples. It gives a sense of the elements the next generation of aspiring CHROs should look at to get there. In this book, you have an invaluable compass to guide your steps toward your dream job. I wish I had it for myself a few years back!

Roberto Di Bernardini, Former Chief HR Officer, Danone and Banco Santander

Happy Grow Lucky is a thought-provoking read that stays with you. It is filled with insights that linger and models that challenge you to think – about success, fulfilment, and the kind of career and life worth building. It reminds us that playing the long game is essential: true career satisfaction comes not from short-term wins but from nurturing long-term career health. It's a book that I will be gifting my young adult children as they embark upon their careers in the hope that it serves as a helpful, smart, soulful guide to building a career that's not just impressive on paper, but deeply meaningful in life. Margins of the book will be covered with your thoughts, quotes will be circled and sentences underlined. Get your pens ready!

Salima Shariff, Chief People Officer, Infineum

An important book full of career best practices and actionable insights on how to become "intentionally lucky". A fun and practical read. I strongly recommend this book to current and future HR leaders.

Tony Verbraeken, International HR Director, and Senior Advisor (former EVP HR, Shell)

Human Resources professionals spend much of their time providing career advice to others outside the function while failing to apply their expertise to themselves. In *Happy Grow Lucky*, Arnaud Despierre reminds us of best practices in what we profess to others while offering a comprehensive and practical framework for advancing our careers as HR professionals.

Alan R. May, Affiliate Professor, Foster School of Business, University of Washington, and former Chief People Officer, Hewlett Packard Enterprise

Happy Grow Lucky is the career playbook I wish I'd had years ago. With remarkable access to some of the world's most influential HR leaders, it offers a behind-the-scenes look at their triumphs, failures, and the lessons they learned along the way. The book's unique Career Health framework makes it a practical manual and a source of long-term inspiration. I will be recommending *Happy Grow Lucky* to colleagues, friends, and anyone serious about building a resilient, fulfilling career that stands the test of time.

Danielle Pallin, Chief People Officer, Hakluyt & Company

In today's fast-evolving business landscape, *Happy Grow Lucky* offers a timely and insightful guide to navigating your career with intention and resilience. Candid reflections, combined with practical tools, make this book a powerful asset for professionals at any stage seeking to future-proof their careers.

Allison Pinkham, Chief Human Resources Officer
and Executive Committee Member, Galderma

Happy Grow Lucky offers invaluable career insights that truly resonate. Through inspiring CHRO stories and practical frameworks like the ABCD traits (Awareness, Bravery, Connectivity, Delivery), it shows how to build success without sacrificing authenticity. More than climbing the ladder, this book teaches how to construct a career aligned with your values. A powerful toolkit for purposeful professionals at any stage.

Wendy Ng, Former Group Chief HR Officer

Happy Grow Lucky is an amazing guide for HR leaders to living the life they want, written with real inputs from CHROs themselves. It is also a powerful reminder of the need to make your own career choices, regardless of your profession. This book can literally change the trajectory of your life.

Mike James Ross, Former Chief HR Officer of La Maison Simons. Author of
Intention: The Surprising Psychology of High Performers

Happy Grow Lucky is more than a career guide: it is a mindset reset, which is far more powerful. Arnaud shows that luck in careers isn't random, but earned through awareness, bravery, connection, and delivery. A must-read for anyone who wants to thrive in their professional journey.

Daniel Strode, Culture & Innovation Strategist, Author of The Culture
Advantage, The Innovator's Edge, and From Web 1 to Web 3

Acknowledgements

I owe an immense debt of gratitude to all those who helped turn this ambitious project from a wild idea to an actual book on an actual shelf. You all helped bring a great deal of happiness and fulfilment into my life, for which I am grateful.

First and foremost, I wish to thank my wife Wang Yi for frequently reminding me that I should "write a book" each year, for 20 years, and for believing, against my own instincts, that I would be up to that daunting task. It took only two decades of her challenging me to put pen to paper. Well done for not giving up on me through that journey and for seeing in me what I could not see in myself.

Obviously, I owe a great debt of gratitude to all the Chief HR Officers who have selflessly and enthusiastically agreed to "open the kimono" on their career journeys with me and made this endeavour possible. Spending time with you and learning about your experiences was a true gift I will forever cherish. I have learned so much from each one of you, and I am really humbled that you put your trust in me to share some of your stories.

A few other HR leaders helped connect me with the right people along the way, and they ought to be acknowledged. I send a big hug to Amit Mittal, Jingqing Xia, Manish Verma, Nina Grosse, and Soorya Themudu for their friendship and support during this project.

The Routledge team has been a great partner to work with, and this book would not exist in its current form without them. My editor Kendrick Loo put his faith in my idea and, I fear, part of his own career on the line to support a new author with an ambitious project. Chelsea Low Yingqi has also been a force to be reckoned with, and I was glad to have her on my side. You are both great partners and a pleasure to work with.

On a personal note, I wish to thank 王阳北 for showing me the way of the writer, and that it is possible to reinvent yourself, at any age, with enough intention and commitment. I am amazed by what you have achieved in the first eight decades of your life and can't wait to see what will come out of your many more years to come. You are truly an inspiration.

I must tip my hat off to my go-to-market partner-in-crime, and all-round marketer extraordinaire, Sharon Koh. Sharon was instrumental in shaping the book's positioning and some of its key messages, particularly on the topic of executive branding. I also owe the catchy words Thriving Career to her. May her successful executive branding business keep on thriving.

This book makes the case for finding meaningful and inspirational mentors, and I wish to thank Shahrukh Marfatia, former VP HR, Global Commercial in Shell, and a long-time mentor. Shahrukh is one of the few HR leaders who retired from HR to become a successful commercial leader. He has always been a great source of energy and inspiration to me and to many others. I greatly value our professional and personal friendship, and I will not give up on our table tennis rivalry.

I wish to thank my beta readers – in addition to many who are already mentioned above: Kaifeng, Kini, Timon, Tony, Vivian, and Wendy. Thank you for bearing with my clumsy prose and feeding me with your "constructive" feedback, big and small. It made all the difference, and I greatly appreciated your candour and insights.

And finally, I must thank YOU, dear reader. Thank you for putting your trust and a few hard-earned dollars into this journey with me. I hope you find the book's ideas to be both meaningful and valuable as you seek to develop your own career. If you want to pursue this conversation, drop me a line on LinkedIn, and I will try my best to help.

Foreword, by Varun Bhatia

If you're holding this book in your hands right now, let me start by saying: lucky you. However, as you will discover, don't just count yourself lucky; invest time wisely and with intent.

Begin by reading this unique book. While it focuses on the pragmatic realities of building and navigating a career in Human Resources, its principles will resonate for careers across all functions and industries.

In *Happy Grow Lucky*, Arnaud Despierre tackles something every ambitious professional quietly battles, especially in Human Resources: the illusion of career control. For decades, we've been taught that if we tick all the boxes, play the game, and keep our heads down, we'll be rewarded with growth. But what happens when the rules of the game change mid-career, or worse, when we realise we were playing the wrong game all along?

I've had the privilege (and at times, the pressure) of operating on both sides of that equation – as a young professional seeking growth, and later, as a global or regional CHRO of companies like Levi Strauss, AirAsia, Kraft Foods, and Gillette, responsible for enabling the growth of others. Along the way, I've learned this unshakable truth: careers aren't ladders anymore – they're landscapes. You don't climb; you navigate. And without a compass, you drift.

This is what makes this book so essential. Arnaud doesn't offer a formulaic ten-step plan to career success because those will be quickly outdated. Instead, he offers a framework for Career Health, which I believe is the career compass we've all been waiting for.

CAREER HEALTH: THE OXYGEN MASK WE FORGET TO WEAR

Just like our physical or mental health, career health needs attention, investment, and above all – Awareness. This is where *Happy Grow Lucky* begins – with an honest look in the mirror.

Chapter 2, which dives into Awareness, brought me right back to a conversation I had with a young HR manager at Gillette in Boston. He was whip-smart, globally mobile, and full of fire. But he was unsure. His feedback? "I'm doing everything right, but it's not adding up". What he lacked wasn't ambition; it was alignment. He didn't know his intrinsic drivers. He was managing output, not energy. That's the power of Awareness: without it, even the best talent runs out of gas.

This concept is exactly what we've operationalised at eVolv, the company I founded a couple of years back after a long and fulfilling career in the trenches. Our diagnostics help employees and managers understand their purpose, energy, and values – not just what they do, but why they do it, how it fuels them, and where they're likely to burn out. That shift from role-fit to resonance aligns perfectly with what *Happy Grow Lucky* advocates.

THE MYTH OF THE LINEAR PATH

In a world obsessed with performance reviews and promotion cycles, Arnaud has the courage to say: "Let's stop idolizing linear success". Amen.

I recall a moment during my tenure as CHRO of AirAsia when we brought in a young man from the Flight Operations department into Recruiting. He had no prior HR experience but understood the work done in Flight ops, particularly with pilots and cabin crew. Traditionalists scoffed. However, he had something others didn't: a high sense of Delivery, a key dimension of Career Health. In that role, he didn't just grow, he thrived, because he wasn't stuck chasing titles. He was chasing impact.

This kind of thinking is deeply embedded in *Happy Grow Lucky*. Whether it is leaning into learning curves, pivoting into the unknown, or building your tribe along the way, this book is filled with real-life insights that challenge convention. Growth here isn't about outpacing others – it's about outgrowing your past self.

WHAT MAKES *HAPPY GROW LUCKY* STAND OUT

Let me be blunt: the self-help career genre is overcrowded. But most books are either too aspirational ("follow your passion!") or too tactical ("optimise your LinkedIn profile"). This book does neither. It sits in the sweet spot between insight and action. It offers frameworks, but they aren't checklists; they are reflection tools. It gives you stories, but they aren't sugar-coated; they are unvarnished truths.

And best of all? It invites HR professionals to see themselves not as talent stewards but as talent architects. Builders of their own blueprint. Influencers of their own trajectory.

MY OWN "HAPPY GROW LUCKY" MOMENTS

I will share some anecdotes from my own career, reflecting on some of the key sections in this book.

In Chapter 4, *Happy Grow Lucky* details the Connectivity practice of "Appreciate unfamiliar cultures". When I took the role of Chief People Officer in Malaysia for AirAsia, a totally new industry for me, and then later at Reali, a Tech Real Estate early-stage company, I faced new and alien cultures. However, I brought my own learnings from previous roles, tested them in these new cultures, adapted them, and still pursued what I believed was at the core of having an impact on both the business and the people.

In Chapter 5, *Happy Grow Lucky* discusses the Delivery practice of "behaving as an owner". To me, this is one of the most fundamental building blocks of a Human Resources career. In my case, it was about owning not only HR initiatives but the business impact and designing initiatives with the business end-goals in mind. I got an opportunity to do this globally at Gillette when I was asked to design and deliver a Global HR shared services model to lower HR costs while improving HR delivery and impact. We started from scratch, as if it were a business start-up. We designed the structure, staffed it, created and funded the budgets, allocated resources, invested in technology, and created a global organisation with about 150 employees across 14 countries, saving the company $13 million annually.

Reflecting on Chapter 7, where Arnaud shares mastering pivotal HR moments, I have a few career and life pivotal moments I am sharing below, in the hope they may guide the younger generations.

For my first job out of XLRI, I went into TCS, an amazing Tata company doing management consulting. However, I wanted to move into core HR and interviewed with Indian Shaving Products, a Gillette joint venture in India. I was immediately taken in by the head of HR, who was an older gentleman, close to retirement but with a wealth

of HR experience. I decided to risk moving from an established and iconic company to a totally unknown small joint venture because I felt I could learn a lot from him. The bet paid off. My career took off and as Gillette acquired a greater stake in the JV, I grew with it and got multiple international assignments.

Another pivotal moment was at Mondelez (Kraft Foods) when I was offered the role of the International Head of HR based in Chicago. At the same time, I was approached for the global CHRO role for Levi's. One was a familiar company and industry, and the other was a new industry but with the role at the helm of HR. I chose the more uncertain path – the Levi's role – an amazing opportunity.

Let me end with a story. At exactly 50, after having been in a couple of CHRO roles for global companies and experiencing two critical life moments – losing my mother to cancer and becoming an empty nester – I decided I wanted to define my own destiny and be an entrepreneur. Not because I was burned out, but because I was finally tuned in. I had helped shape thousands of careers but had never paused to audit my own. That pause became a pivot. I went back to the basics – what energised me, what gave me purpose, what values I could no longer compromise on. This journey of discovery led to the creation of eVolv.

WHO NEEDS THIS BOOK?

If you're early in your career and feeling overwhelmed by options, this book will ground you.

If you're mid-career and wondering, "Is this it?", this book will challenge you.

If you're a senior executive who has grown externally but shrunk internally, this book will humble you.

And if you're an HR leader looking to guide others through the fog of modern work, this book will equip you.

We live in a world where job titles change faster than job satisfaction. Where LinkedIn is a highlight reel, and burnout hides behind productivity metrics. Arnaud calls time on this madness. He's not just giving us a new lens – he's giving us new language.

It's what we, at eVolv, call "co-evolving" – where people and organisations evolve in sync, not in conflict.

FINAL WORD

If you're serious about your growth – not just professionally but as a whole person – read this book. Then reread Chapter 2. Then hand it to someone you mentor. Then revisit it the following year.

Because thriving isn't a destination. It's a journey.

And *Happy Grow Lucky* is your compass.

Varun Bhatia, Founder & CEO, eVolv,

Former Global and Regional CHRO – AirAsia,
Levi Strauss, Gillette, P&G, Reali, Kraft Foods/Mondelez
LinkedIn: linkedin.com/in/varunbhatiahr

Introduction

Your career stakes have never been higher. Consider the tumultuous events of recent years: global pandemics, economic swings, and rapid technological advancements. After years of unbridled growth, executives in leading technology firms had to learn to navigate a sudden and prolonged "tech winter" when the tide turned on years of mass-hiring by the industry. More broadly, every one of us should be worried about facing our own career winter. Artificial intelligence is automating tasks, creating both exciting new opportunities and anxieties as entire professions are under threat of being profoundly transformed, some even vanishing.

Each career choice we make, each conversation we have carries potentially monumental consequences for our future professional trajectory. I know of an ambitious leader who decided to move across continents for a new role only to find themselves in a hostile work environment. What seemed like an exhilarating leap turned into a lesson in navigating corporate politics and cultural nuances. Every opportunity you chase requires taking calculated risks. Whether through global events or from our own doing, our career landscape isn't just rocky; it's shifting beneath our feet.

Despite these momentous challenges, some executives appear to glide effortlessly through flourishing careers. What sets these Thriving Career builders apart from others who struggle to progress? This question has haunted me for two decades and sparked a series of enlightening career conversations with 45 of the most successful global Chief Human Resources Officers (CHROs[1]) on the planet. Through these discussions, I aimed to distil their career best practices into actionable insights that we, common mortals navigating our own career paths, can apply to drive our growth.

Through my 20 years as a management and executive search consultant advising senior executives on their professional journeys, many leaders have asked me for advice as they were looking for a career change. More often than I care to admit, I have given them rather generic advice that offered limited insights but, I hoped, would make them feel good and give them confidence that the future would be bright.

Being honest with myself, as I usually am, the question kept gnawing at me: what distinguishes executives who build amazing careers from the others? Were they born with the ability to make better career decisions? Did a happier childhood or better educational environment give them an unfair advantage? Were they simply more intelligent, harder-working individuals? Were they better at company politics and managing their bosses? Or did they possess an unrelenting ambition, a ruthless determination to "get there"? The desire to develop definitive, actionable answers led to this book.

I took the leap of faith to write this book with the goal of providing a guiding light to those in need of career clarity. However, after over two decades of counselling senior executives, I recognise my personal experience as a corporate executive is a big fat zero. Being aware of the inescapable threat of AI (Arnaud's Ignorance), I recognised early on that I needed help. It quickly became obvious that HR professionals who have achieved outstanding global careers who would be most thoughtful on career-building. As a result, I set out to gather their wisdom. The rationale for focusing on global CHRO careers was fourfold:

1. HR executives who have ascended to the top in large organisations must possess valuable insights, whether consciously or not, that could benefit others.
2. Career insights should be universally applicable across cultural contexts, so I needed individuals who had lived abroad and demonstrated an ability to adapt to different cultures.
3. HR professionals are deeply involved in talent management and career development issues and likely spend time reflecting on career pathing – if not for themselves, certainly for their organisations.
4. Focusing on a specific functional area like HR enabled my research to be more targeted, allowing for a more rigorous analytical comparison of the diverse experiences of the executives interviewed.

Powered by this intuition, I set off to study the career patterns of CHROs who got to the top in large organisations and spent meaningful time working outside their home country. As a result, the insights from this book will be immediately relevant to HR professionals wanting to accelerate their careers. It will also be valuable for any professional in a non-HR role, as many of the findings from the research can be easily extrapolated to any other corporate function. Throughout the book, I will consistently use HR examples to support my arguments, but attempt to step up to a broader, more generic view when providing overarching frameworks or action tips, to benefit any professional who wants not just to survive, but to thrive in their career.

The book's main objective is to bring you some inspiration from the real-life stories of global leaders who have toiled, struggled, and succeeded in developing successful careers. To further ground our discussion, I have also included quantitative insights from the latest instance of a Global HR Career Survey, with input from over 1,100 HR leaders from across the world.

During my interviews with global CHROs, I was astounded by the level of support and time each of these 45 leaders personally dedicated to this project. Many of them mentioned how meaningful it was to contribute and give back to a function that has given them so much. As an author and management consultant, I found immense value in talking to these talented executives for my research. They were gracious to generously give their time and provide fantastic insights to contribute to this book. Spending time with each of them and hearing their compelling life stories – filled with challenges and learnings – was a treasured experience for me. Moulding these insights into a practical and actionable career management approach to help our global HR community warmed my soul.

This book is not meant to be a how-to guide on becoming a global Chief HR Officer but certainly provides first-hand perspectives on what it takes to get there, perform at that level, and even grow beyond the role. Readers who do not aspire to get to the #1 role, for instance, those on an expert track, should also find a lot of value in the book's insights as it takes a holistic view of career development.

To be sure, if you are looking for a quick career fix, perhaps because you want to find a new job urgently, this book will be less immediately helpful to you. While it includes practical career management tips and plenty of things you can start doing next Monday, it takes a long-term view of career-building. Our journey together will teach you "how to fish", based on the views and experiences of expert "fisher(wo) men", rather than give you the immediate gratification of the fish you might be craving for. Trust me, your career will be better off for it in the long-run.

One theme that kept coming up in my career discussions during the book's research is that, beyond working hard and being great humans, executives who built great careers somehow got lucky. Discussion after discussion, things like "I was just fortunate", "it happened by accident", "out of the blue", "it was fate", or "I was at the right place, at the right time" – in essence, "I just got lucky" – kept on coming back at pivotal moments of many CHRO careers. In practice, this would come across as

- A seemingly random call from a former colleague who moved to a new organisation and thinks you can help.
- A boss who resigns unexpectedly and you are chosen to replace them, even though you feel clearly under-qualified.
- A personal initiative that you are pushing on your own, which coincidentally happens to become a priority for the global business, turning you into an early expert.

Taken from any single individual's perspective, such events might indeed seem to be coincidental. However, as the old saying goes, luck happens when preparation meets opportunity. When I looked across the varied career paths of these outstanding careers and processed our nearly 100 hours of career conversations together, clear patterns emerged. The large majority of leaders I interviewed displayed four attributes that are foundational to how they approach their career:

1. **AWARENESS**: They are acutely self-aware, monitor their context deliberately, and know their purpose and priorities.
2. **BRAVERY**: They are relentless learners and mindful risk-takers, guided by strong personal convictions and values.
3. **CONNECTIVITY**: They treasure purposeful relationships, big and small, and are committed connectors across cultures and organisations.
4. **DELIVERY**: They are known to think business first, to get things done with intention, and to foster trust.

Throughout this book, we will detail these four foundational attributes and see how they break down into specific career practices that can help you grow your own healthy, successful, and happy career – a Thriving Career. You are welcome to read this book sequentially, or to pick and choose the chapters that look most relevant to where your mind is at. Here is how we will go about it:

- Chapter 1. The curious case of the lucky career. In the initial chapter, we will set the scene for the foundational elements required to build a Thriving Career. We will establish the Thriving Career stack that structures how you should think about short-term vs long-term career development. We will introduce the concept of Career Health, which underpins the broader ideas of career performance and career satisfaction and will articulate how they build on each other. This will provide us with the conceptual framework supporting the concrete application of your own Thriving Career practices.
- Chapter 2. Activating your Awareness. We will reveal how successful career builders develop and evolve a clarity of purpose regarding their professional development. They have a clear and prioritised view of what motivates them, across their work and their lives, and they are acutely conscious of their context and constraints. Developing a high level of self-awareness allows them to make better career decisions more often.
- Chapter 3. Betting on Bravery. We will explore how courageous career builders are always on the lookout for learning opportunities, even when it makes them uncomfortable. They are not afraid of failure and cherish feedback. They are clear about what they stand for and have the courage of their convictions. This brave attitude allows them to grow continuously into a better version of themselves and to seize on challenging new growth opportunities with confidence.
- Chapter 4. Cultivating Connectivity. We will uncover how astute career builders adopt a strategic relationship-building approach. They shun indiscriminate networking and, instead, cultivate a range of meaningful mentors. More broadly, they strive to nurture a positive people ecosystem and develop a deep appreciation for unfamiliar cultures. This intentional approach to relationships increases the chance that meaningful career options will come their way, without having to actively look for them.

Chapter 5. Driving Delivery. We will show that determined career builders have strong business acumen and a relentless focus on making things happen. As a result, they build a reputation for getting things done and are known as colleagues who can be trusted, not only with difficult business problems but also with sensitive personal matters. This commitment to deliver, both for the business and people, is integral to their continued track record of career growth.

Chapter 6. Managing your career flow. In this chapter, we will explore how successful career builders have evolved and applied their Thriving Career practices over time. In their formative years, they strive to maximise learning through challenging assignments. In their development years, they aim to optimise the growth of their capabilities and experiences. In their leadership years, they seek to maximise their impact at-scale. Heading towards their legacy years, they focus increasingly on purpose, joy, and giving back.

Chapter 7. Mastering pivotal HR career moments. We will look at a few concrete examples of pivotal moments that can make or break a career and will especially emphasise topics relevant to HR careers. We will show how, when faced with an unexpected event, you can improve outcomes by deploying your Thriving Career practices. Whether you find yourself pigeon-holed in a narrow role, are offered an unexpected opportunity, or face a career accident, we will show how you can increase your chances of coming out on top.

Chapter 8. Your career (re)starts here. In this final chapter, we will boldly move to action and get very concrete. We will detail how Career Health works in practice and help you self-diagnose the state of your current career. We introduce the role of a career therapist who can help guide you through any issues and arm you with concrete tools to address any long-term career issues. We will touch on the topic of your executive branding and put everything together for you in a comprehensive programme to boost your career prospects.

In conclusion, we will look towards the future and attempt to anticipate any change in the patterns of successful careers for years and decades to come. How confident should we be that what got us here will also get us where we need to go?

As mentioned, you may choose to read this book sequentially or pick the topic(s) you are most curious about. Chapter 1 is probably the best place to start for any reader to understand the framework that underpins much of this book. If you are looking for human-powered inspiration and to learn from the real-life experiences of successful senior executives, Chapters 2–5 will likely get your juices flowing. If you need structure, process, or immediate clarity of what to do next with your career, Chapters 6–8 will likely resonate most with you.

Chapter 7 is very heavily geared towards HR careers and will be most immediately useful to leaders from the function. Non-HR readers may be forgiven for skipping it but should find the rest of the book sufficiently broad to be highly relevant.

My wish is that you use this book as the starting point for a career conversation, first and foremost with yourself. I hope that you will find value in coming back to it, time and again, over many years, each time you find yourself wondering how you should move forward in your career with confidence.

This book is dedicated to any professional who wants to be more intentional in achieving their full career potential and finding happiness along the way. So, if you're ready to accelerate your career and make better decisions about your future, I invite you to join me and 45 amazing global HR leaders on this journey.

Together, we will uncover the secrets to building a Thriving Career.

Meet our Fearless Leaders

Before we get deep into our research, let's get familiar with some of the Chief HR Officers who bravely and selflessly agreed to share their career experiences for the greater good of our global community.

First, how did I arrive at this sample pool? I started simply, and admittedly quite arbitrarily, from the 2,450 Group-level CHROs in my direct LinkedIn network. This random sample was both large and diversified, with 50% of them in the United States, 37% in Europe Middle East & Africa (EMEA), and 13% in the rest of the world, so it felt broad enough as a starting point. With the objective of targeting large multinational companies, I picked out global organisations with a minimum of two billion dollars in annual revenue. This quickly narrowed the sample down to 219 candidates from the initial list. To make the list more exhaustive, I examined the careers of the CHROs of companies in the 2024 Fortune 500 list and added the relevant ones to my target list.

The next step was to study each CHRO career individually and eliminate those who had only ever worked and lived in a single country. Many CHROs, who otherwise had a very high profile, dropped out of the list at that stage, particularly from the United States. This left 101 potential CHRO candidates to interview for this book, and 45 of them were kind enough to agree to participate in my research.[2] I got to spend time with each of them and conduct an in-depth career conversation focusing on the drivers of their most important decisions and pivotal moments of their career.

As a group, these 45 executives have led HR organisations for some of the largest organisations on the planet. They feature well over USD 1 trillion in combined revenues, looking after around 2 million employees globally. With an average professional tenure of 29.6 years, they have an aggregate 1,350 years of professional experience, gaining great career wisdom along the way.

They are a very diverse bunch, split 56% female and 44% male, and feature a broad geographic mix, with 29 currently living in Europe, 9 living in the United States, and 7 living in the Asia-Pacific/Middle

East region. As a group, on average, they have lived and worked in four different countries, across at least two regions of the world, during their career.

Let us get to know a little bit more about each of these leaders, whom we will learn from over the course of this book.

Allison Pinkham

Originally from: the United States   Now lives in: Switzerland
Professional highlights:
- Chief Human Resources Officer – Galderma (2021–Present)
- Chief People Officer, USA – Heineken (2020–2021)
- Vice President, Human Resources and Corporate HR Head Asia Region – Boehringer Ingelheim (2016–2020)

What drives me: I have a limitless drive and belief that I can accomplish anything I set my mind to, regardless of the obstacles encountered. This mindset has been innate since I was a child and showed itself in various ways, whether through being the only girl playing on the baseball all-star team, winning state championships in basketball, soccer, and javelin, or finishing third in a 5K race on a ruptured Achilles. My father instilled in me a strong work ethic, uncompromising values in integrity and ethics, and a growth mindset before that was even a common vernacular. This growth mindset also shows up in my passion for continuous learning, sparked by my transformative study abroad experience, which instilled a love for global perspectives and diverse cultures.

Amanda Rajkumar

Originally from: United Kingdom   Now lives in: United Kingdom

Professional highlights:
- Executive Board Member, Global Human Resources, People and Culture – adidas (2021–2023)
- Chief Human Resources Officer, USA and CIB Americas – BNP Paribas (2018–2021)
- Global Head of Human Resources for Global Markets and Financial Institutions Coverage – BNP Paribas (2014–2018)

What drives me: My work interests are in kind, honest, disruptive change. I love the challenge – "it cannot be done"! I want to make a real difference to the lived experience of employees. Happy employees equate to better performance. This can only be achieved by having a top HR team that demonstrates tangible outcomes to support the company's goals. I am not afraid to take risks as it's the only way to grow. But I believe HR must be the conscience of the firm, holding up the mirror to the C-Suite on the company culture. On a personal level, I love being nourished by the arts and culture, but I also like strength training. I have spent the last few years much more invested in my self-development. I am driven by my values-led purpose, accompanied by a love of continuous self-reflection.

Archana Bhaskar

Originally from: India   Now lives in: India

Professional highlights:
- Chief Human Resources Officer – Dr. Reddy's Laboratories (2017–Present)
- Shell: India, Global HR roles in Shell Downstream business (2007–2017)
- Unilever: India, Regional and Global roles (1993–2007)

What drives me: For me, it has always been about growth, learning, and enjoying my work. As a leader, I am passionate about making a real business impact and empowering my team. I thrive on challenges, whether it's turning around a struggling business or implementing progressive and innovative HR strategies. Personally, I'm driven by strong values and the courage of conviction. Family is my priority, and I have a deep desire to give back and help others. Oh, and let's not forget my love for pushing boundaries, whether professionally or conquering mountains!

Athalie Williams

Originally from: Australia   Now lives in: United Kingdom/Australia
Professional highlights:
- Chief Human Resources Officer – BT (2022–2025)
- Chief People Officer – BHP (2015–2022)
- Workforce strategy and transformation consultant – Accenture (1991–2005)

What drives me: What drives me is the belief that where you start in life shouldn't limit where you end up. As a proud mother to twin daughters adopted from China, I've learned that love, opportunity, and access to education can change everything. I'm relentlessly drawn to solving for inequity – finding ways to open doors wider, especially for those who've never even seen the door. I'm at my best driving transformational change at scale and when my work reaches beyond the walls of the organisation and into the heart of society.

Charles Bendotti

Originally from: Switzerland   Now lives in: Switzerland
Professional highlights:
- Chief People & Culture Officer – Philip Morris International (2017–2023)
- Global Head of HR, Asia – Philip Morris International (2012–2016)
- Global Head of HR – North, Central & South America – Philip Morris International (2008–2012)

What drives me: I'm a vivid learner disguised as a business leader. Restless in stillness, fuelled by progress, and drawn to meaningful change. Whether I'm building companies or climbing mountains, both real and metaphorical, I thrive on challenge, evolution, and real human connection. I believe in shaking up the status-quo, pushing myself (always), helping others shine, and leading with radical honesty wrapped in real care. Today, success isn't just performance – it's purpose, impact, and giving back with heart.

Darrell Ford

Originally from: the United States   Now lives in: the United States
Professional highlights:
- EVP & Chief Human Resources Officer – UPS (2020–Present)
- SVP & Chief Human Resources Officer – DuPont (2018–2020)
- Xerox – EVP & Chief Human Resources Officer (2015–2018)

What drives me: I'm motivated by the chance to grow and make things better for people. I like starting where the action is – on the front lines – so I can really get to know the heart of the business. I'm always looking for new opportunities to contribute in bigger ways. At the same time, I try to instil shared values of curiosity, accountability, and the passion for impact within my team. Those values, combined with the drive to make a meaningful difference, are what keep me energised and committed to helping our people thrive.

Deborah Borg

Originally from: Australia   Now lives in: the United States
Professional highlights:
- Chief People & Culture Officer – International Flavors & Fragrances (2022–Present)
- Chief Human Resources and Communications Officer – Bunge (2015–2022)
- President, USA – The Dow Chemical Company (2014–2015)

What drives me: Growing up in Australia shaped my adventurous spirit, fuelling a love for exploration and fresh perspectives. I thrive on challenges – whether navigating bold new paths or solving intricate jigsaw puzzles. I see the world as a puzzle itself, filled with pieces waiting to fit together. As an entrepreneur, I don't just follow roads; I build them, driven by curiosity, creativity, and a passion for crafting opportunities that empower others to succeed.

Farnaz Ranjbar

Originally from: Iran (German National)   Now lives in: United Kingdom
Professional highlights:
- Group Chief Human Resources Officer – Coats (2022–Present)
- SVP Human Resources Europe – DHL Express (2019–2022)
- Vice President Business HR, Global – DHL Express (2010–2018)

What drives me: I leap at opportunities and figure things out along the way! My passion lies in making a real difference in people's lives. As a leader, it's about creating a positive, inclusive culture where everyone can thrive. As a human being, I'm fuelled by resilience, a can-do attitude, and a deep-seated belief in the power of connection. Honestly, I love what I do and pour my whole heart into it. It's all about passion, energy, and making the most of every single moment.

Frédéric Chardot

Originally from: France   Now lives in: United Arab Emirates
Professional highlights:
- Chief Human Resources Officer – Jumeirah (2024–Present)
- Chief Human Resources Officer – Audemars Piguet (2022–2024)
- Chief Transformation Officer – Moët Hennessy (2021–2022)

What drives me: There's always something to learn from any given situation, from any conversation. Great, good, bad, ugly … it doesn't really matter – just try to get something out of it. No regrets, no excuses, I never look back because you can't change the past, but I strongly believe that you can always improve ... and that with energy and enthusiasm, you can help people and organisations get to their best. And remember, we don't have problems ... we just have situations!

Geoff Lloyd

Originally from: United Kingdom (Wales)

Now lives in: United Kingdom

Professional highlights:
- Chief Human Resources Officer – DS Smith (2024–Present)
- Chief Human Resources Officer – Meggitt (2017–2022)
- Group Human Resource Director – Serco (2008–2017)

What drives me: I feel honoured to have had a career in HR. We are privileged to support our colleagues in delivering their potential and that of the company we are part of. Even when we must take on difficult tasks, we can do so in a way that gets the most positive outcome possible. We work with people during incredibly important times of their lives, and it continually motivates me to help build the best teams I can so we can create bright futures for people and the organisations they are part of.

Helio Fujita

Originally from: Brazil

Now lives in: Belgium

Professional highlights:
- Global People & Organization VP – Mars Petcare (2025–Present)
- Chief Human Resources Officer – Fresenius Kabi (2024–2025)
- SVP HR, Global People Partnering and HR Simplification – Novartis (2021–2023)
- SVP HR, Sandoz International Region – Novartis (2018–2021)

What drives me: For me, it's all about learning and purpose. I'm driven by a deep curiosity to understand how things work and a desire to collaborate, explore, and experiment – all anchored in a strong commitment to contribute to a more just, sustainable, and thriving world. I truly believe HR has a social mission: to create workplaces that can be catalysts for that purpose. My approach to life, leadership, and work is simple, human, real, ethical – and grounded in my mindfulness practice.

Hugo Martinho

Originally from: Portugal   Now lives in: Switzerland
Professional highlights:
- Group Head Human Resources – Schindler Group (2024–Present)
- Human Resources Director Asia Pacific – Schindler Group (2017–2022)
- Managing Director Singapore – Schindler (2011–2014)

What drives me: I'm driven by the desire to learn and grow, constantly pushing boundaries and not being afraid to take a leap of faith. As a leader, my passion lies in empowering people, building strong teams, and fostering a positive culture grounded in our values. Ultimately, as a human being, it's about making a real impact, opening doors for myself and others, cherishing my family, and always looking for that next opportunity to make a difference.

Ingolf Thom

Originally from: Germany   Now lives in: Germany
Professional highlights:
- EVP, Human Resources and Safety – Huhtamaki (2022–Present)
- Chief Human Resources Officer – K+S Group (2018–2021)
- HR leadership roles in Europe, India, Asia, and North America – Dow (2001–2018)

What drives me: What truly drives me is a deep curiosity and a desire to constantly learn and grow, both professionally and personally. Having been born and raised in Eastern Germany, after the wall came down and new horizons opened, I've always been passionate about embracing international experiences and understanding different cultures. I was fortunate to have had the opportunity to live and work in Europe, India, Asia, and North America, which has greatly shaped who I am today. As a leader, I'm driven to build strong teams, nurture talent, and contribute meaningfully to the organisation's success. I find immense satisfaction in navigating complex change and transformation, always eager to tackle challenging tasks and go the extra mile. Ultimately, it's about valuing people, building genuine relationships, supporting others in their growth, and, above all, prioritising my two wonderful children as a single parent.

Janice Deskus

Originally from: the United States   Now lives in: the United States

Professional highlights:
- Chief Human Resources Officer – Staples (2018–2025)
- Group Vice President Human Resources – Medtronic (2015–2018)
- Global Vice President Human Resources – Covidien (2012–2015)

What drives me: I strive to live an interesting life and embrace learning, especially when it feels hard or a little intimidating. One of my longest – and most fascinating – learning journeys has been beekeeping, a passion I've pursued for over a decade. I currently have more than 100,000 bees, and it still amazes me how closely a hive's organisational behaviour mirrors the corporate world. I find real joy and benefits in quietly observing, guiding, and influencing both. For me, leadership is rooted in curiosity, lifelong learning, and making a positive impact – one bee, or one person, at a time.

Jean-Sébastien Blanc

Originally from: France   Now lives in: France
Professional highlights:
- Executive Vice President, Human Resources – Engie (2021–Present)
- Executive Vice President, Human Resources – Plastic Omnium (2012–2021)
- SVP Human Resources Transport Division – Alstom (2010–2012)

What drives me: I have a constant appetite for a good challenge, something that might even frighten me a little. As a leader, I'm passionate about building strong teams and creating a culture where people learn by doing and watching. I truly enjoy seeing talent grow and helping them find their path. As a human, my early life taught me the value of connecting with all sorts of people and understanding their cultures. Now, I find real meaning in the energy transition and seeing the impact we can have.

Jessica Teo

Originally from: Singapore   Now lives in: Switzerland
Professional highlights:
- Chief Human Resources Officer – Louis Dreyfus Company (2019–Present)
- HR Director, Asia – Louis Dreyfus Company (2011–2019)
- Head of Human Resources – Neste Oil (2008–2010)

What drives me: My values and principles in life are shaped by my humble beginning, having been taught since young to be responsible and accountable for myself and for my family. This translates to being responsible for my team, not just in HR but as a senior leader of the company, for the workforce of LDC. The thought of disappointing the team often drives me to work harder and to explore avenues to bring in more results and value for the teams. My competitive nature also pushed me to seek success each time I took on a new challenge or met with an obstacle, which sometimes would land me in trouble. Over the years, I learned to manage my expectations and adjust my pace – instead of winning, I go for win-win solutions.

Johanna Söderström

Originally from: Finland   Now lives in: the United States
Professional highlights:
- Non-Executive Director – Neste (2020–2025)
- Executive Vice President, Chief People Officer – Tyson Foods (2020–2024)

- Senior Vice President, Chief Human Resource Officer – The Dow Company (2014–2019)

What drives me: I spent most of my younger years playing competitive team sports. As the captain of our team, we won three Finnish handball championships in our league. My grandmother taught me about Finnish sisu – to never give up, there is always a way. It translates closely to resilience and grit, and has guided me through life, being it sports, or my professional or personal life. My other "drive" in life has been fast cars and the thrill of speed. Keeping your eyes on the apex makes you focus on what is important in the moment without losing track of the big picture.

John Holding

Originally from: Australia   Now lives in: Australia
Professional highlights:
- Group Executive, People and Performance – Nufarm (2017–Present)
- Global Human Resources Director, Minerals Division – The Weir Group (2013–2016)
- HR VP Global Sourcing Regions & Supply Chain: RB&IS – Avery Dennison (2010–2011)
- HR VP Asia Pacific (and other roles) – Nortel Networks (1999–2008)

What drives me: I have been fortunate to have lived in four countries, which has helped me develop a deep appreciation for diverse perspectives. My curiosity drives me: "stay curious" is a principle I live by. I find purpose in helping others grow, and I'm passionate about developing emerging leaders. These relationships are mutually enriching. I focus on achieving practical, commercially sound outcomes while supporting others to reach their potential. Looking ahead, my goal is to contribute by guiding the next generation of leaders, creating a strong foundation for their success. Senior global roles can be demanding, and I achieve a sense of balance in my life through my love of the natural world, spending time in the garden or working on our hobby farm.

Kerstin Mariella Knapp

Originally from: Austria   Now lives in: Switzerland
Professional highlights:
- Chief People & Culture Officer – Vestas Wind Systems (2020–2024)
- Chief Human Resources Officer – Puma Energy SA (2016–2019)
- Platform HR Leader CASC – Cargill (2011–2014)

What drives me: As a true Sagittarius, I bring boundless optimism and I am a restless explorer of ideas, cultures, and the ever-fascinating world of human potential. Austrian by birth and married to a brilliant Italian Aquarius, my life is a blend of precision and passion. I thrive on curiosity, laughter, and inspiring teams to reach for the stars, all while navigating witty debates at the dinner table about whether pasta or Schnitzel reigns supreme.

Larissa Cerqueira

Originally from: Brazil   Now lives in: the United States
Professional highlights:
- Chief Human Resources Officer – Fluence (2020–Present)
- VP, Global Talent Management, Transportation Technologies – Fortive (2019–2020)
- Global Talent Management and Leadership Development Manager – Henkel (2010–2012)

What drives me: I enjoy "new": new places, new people, and new challenges. I also enjoy "more": more activities, more conversations, and more accomplishments. My strong family values have driven me to always be aware of my choices and my ownership in them. My mother always says, "life is made of choices" … I take that with me everywhere!

Laura Garza

Originally from: Mexico   Now lives in: Singapore
Professional highlights:
- Chief People Officer – Dyson (2021–Present)
- Global Head of Talent – Nissan Motor Corporation (2019–2021)
- Global Head of HR Transformation – Nissan Motor Corporation (2017–2021)

What drives me: Driven by an insatiable curiosity and a thirst for learning, I have always sought new and challenging experiences, from navigating cultural nuances in Japan to leading HR transformations in complex global organisations. As a leader, I am passionate about delivering tangible results and fostering positive change, often embracing the uncomfortable to drive progress. Personally, I am deeply enriched by global connections and diverse cultures, as evidenced by my family life. Ultimately, my journey has been about continuous growth, resilience, and a commitment to making a meaningful impact wherever I go. And if things ever go completely off the rails? Well, at least my autobiography will be a bestseller complete with both successes, dramatic failures and plot twists worthy of Mexican TV soap operas!

Leanne Wood

Originally from: United Kingdom   Now lives in: United Kingdom
Professional highlights:
- Chief Human Resources Officer – Vodafone (2019–Present)
- Chief People, Strategy and Corporate Affairs Officer – Burberry (2015–2019)
- Group Human Resources Director – Diageo (2013–2015)

What drives me: Having left university with no idea at all about a future career, I've spent the last 30 years seeking to answer that question – and learning a huge amount about people and organisations along the way. The chances that I've had to live and work outside my home country have given me a deep appreciation and love for the diversity of people and cultures. I'm passionate about building teams and businesses where everyone can contribute and thrive.

Lucien Alziari

Originally from: United Kingdom   Now lives in: the United States
Professional highlights:
- EVP & Chief Human Resources Officer – Prudential Financial (2017–2025)
- EVP & Chief Human Resources Officer – A.P. Moller-Maersk (2012–2017)
- CHRO and SVP, Human Resources and Corporate Responsibility – Avon (2004–2012)

What drives me: As CHROs, we do noble work, and I want to make a meaningful impact on organisations of significance. The through-line of my career has been making HR more of a business leadership function, developing world-class HR leaders and truly contributing to business success. I'm an acquired taste – sometimes tough and not always easy to work for – but genuinely committed to helping people grow. I love being part of the big conversations about the future of work and the role of HR, but my greatest professional satisfaction comes from seeing people I've worked with succeed in really significant CHRO roles. Having said all that, the most important thing is to be a good dad and spouse – nothing else matters if we lose sight of that.

Mario Ceccon

Originally from: Argentina   Now lives in: France
Professional highlights:
- EVP, Head of Human Resources – Geodis (2017–Present)
- VP Human Resources Asia Pacific – Air Liquide (2013–2017)
- VP Human Resources, Engineering & Construction R&D – Air Liquide (2008–2013)

What drives me: What has consistently driven me is a fundamental desire to engage with the world and learn from diverse experiences. As a leader, I am passionate about creating meaningful impact through HR, even amidst instability and challenges. My approach centres on resilience and continuous learning, embracing difficulties as opportunities for growth. I am motivated by a sense of purpose and the courage to take calculated risks, even when faced with uncertainty.

Mayuko Seto

Originally from: Japan   Now lives in: Japan
Professional highlights:
- Chief Human Resources Officer – Ricoh (2020–2024)
- VP Human Resources, Japan Business Unit, Europe & Canada Business Unit – Takeda (2016–2020)
- Executive Officer & VP Human Resources, MetLife (2012–2015)

What drives me: As a child, I was brought up with strong religious teachings, which I later chose to reject. That experience instilled in me core values that came to shape who I am. I developed a deep belief in being honest with myself, in working autonomously, and in embracing challenges to drive change. After I stopped working for titles (like CHRO) or external validation, I found that I could contribute and lead with far greater autonomy and authenticity than ever before.

Mieke Van de Capelle

Originally from: Belgium   Now lives in: Switzerland
Professional highlights:
- Chief Human Resources Officer – dsm-firmenich (2023–Present)
- Chief Human Resources Officer – Firmenich (2016–2023)
- Chief Human Resources Officer – Perfetti Van Melle (2012–2016)

What drives me: There's a sort of innate drive on leaving things better than I found them. Nothing shouldn't be open for discussion and debate on how things can be improved for people, whether it's in an organisational setup or in the private space. Nothing is static either, and that somehow always brings surprises and opportunities I like to say yes to.

Monique Carter

Originally from: Ireland   Now lives in: United Kingdom
Professional highlights:
- Chief People & Organisation Officer – Anglo American (2023–Present)
- EVP People & Organisation – Novo Nordisk (2019–2023)
- Group HR Director – GKN (2016–2018)

What drives me: I am guided by a deep sense of independence and a desire to take control of my life and career. It irritates me when I hear others complaining about things they could change if they took responsibility! I am drawn to challenging roles where I can leverage my abilities to make a significant impact and drive performance. I love to learn new things, which is probably why I have worked across so many different sectors. Trusted, strong, respectful relationships, with the CEO and Board, are critical for my success. I get a lot of satisfaction doing things that others think are not possible and have not been done before. I am not interested in a company where the role is steady state, I would find it difficult to get out of bed each day for a caretaker role.

Muzzamil Khider

Originally from: Sudan Now lives in: the United States
Professional highlights:
- Chief People and Culture Officer – Baker Hughes (2024–Present)
- SVP & Chief People Officer, Enterprise HR – Baker Hughes (2023–2024)
- SVP & Chief People Officer, Oilfield Services & Equipment – Baker Hughes (2022–2023)

What drives me: I am passionate about creating environments where individuals can thrive and contribute. My career has been shaped by a belief in hard work and trusting the process, with a constant willingness to embrace new challenges and learn along the way. Family support has been my bedrock, enabling me to navigate diverse cultures and experiences. While HR has been my core, I remain open to broader opportunities where I can continue to grow and make an impact.

Myriam Beatove Moreale

Originally from: Spain Now lives in: Between Belgium, The Netherlands, and Spain
Professional highlights:
- Chief Human Resources Officer and Member of the Executive Board – Randstad (2022–Present)
- Non-Executive Director Aliaxis SA & Chair of the Sustainability Committee (2022–Present)
- SVP & Chief Human Resources Officer and Member of the Executive Team – Cargill (2020–2022)

What drives me: I grew up in a multicultural family of artists, philosophers, and psychologists: an environment that nurtured both analytical thinking and emotional depth. That foundation sparked a lifelong passion for learning and a deep curiosity about how people grow and thrive. I believe the most effective leaders have a clear vision, a systematic approach to achieving it, and the courage to act. The motto I stand for – dream more, learn more, achieve more, and become more – guides how I lead, inspire teams, and stay anchored in purpose.

Natalie Bickford

Originally from: United Kingdom   Now working in: France
Professional highlights:
- Chief People Officer – Sanofi (2020–Present)
- Group HR Director – Merlin Entertainments (2016–2020)
- SVP HR, Global Corporate Services – Sodexo (2015–2016)

What drives me: I am driven by the desire to make a significant impact and leave a positive legacy in every endeavour. I always view myself as a business leader first, deeply understanding commercial imperatives. I find immense satisfaction in tackling new challenges and continuously learning across diverse industries. Personally, while my career has been a central focus, my family remains a cornerstone, and I value the importance of creating meaningful change wherever I am.

Philip Read

Originally from: United Kingdom   Now lives in: United Kingdom
Professional highlights:
- EVP Human Resources and Transformation, Tetra Pak and CHRO Tetra Laval Group (2021–Present)
- SVP Human Resources, Tetra Pak and CHRO Tetra Laval Group (2014–2021)
- VP Human Resources, Packaging Solutions – Tetra Pak (2011–2014)

What drives me: As an HR leader, my passion is to try to contribute to creating working lives that are fulfilling for the employee and create value for the employer. My job is, together with my team, to create a relationship between employee and employer that is continuously being balanced to achieve this. As a child growing up in a small village in Scotland, I was deeply curious about the many different cultures of the world and consider myself extremely lucky to have been exposed to living and working in many countries; these experiences have deeply shaped my perspectives and enriched my life and that of my family.

Prerana Issar

Originally from: India   Now lives in: United Kingdom
Professional highlights:
- Chief People Officer and Head of Corporate Affairs – Sainsbury's (2023–Present)
- Chief People Officer – NHS England (2019–2023)
- Director, Public-Private Partnerships – United Nations World Food Programme (2017–2019)

What drives me: I have met tens of thousands of people across more than 50 countries. In all those interactions, one thing stood out: we are connected by our shared humanity. We all want the same things, no matter our colour, income level, or nationality: safety, a life of meaning, a sense of belonging, and our kids having a better life than ours. In my life and in my work, in small and not so small ways, I try to honour this truth every day. And create some joy on this journey as well!

Ranjay Radhakrishnan

Originally from: India   Now lives in: United Kingdom
Professional highlights:
- Chief Human Resources Officer – Reckitt (2020–Present)
- Chief Human Resources Officer – InterContinental Hotels Group (2016–2020)
- EVP Global HR (Categories & Market Clusters) – Unilever (2015–2016)

What drives me: I have thrived in the Human Resources profession for the last three decades doing several roles across many countries and industries – thanks to my family! I enjoy creating lasting business impact while bringing people to centre stage. I am energised by challenges and actively seek opportunities outside my comfort zone, prioritising learning and diverse experiences. Personally, my family is paramount, and I strive for a balance across my various life roles. My focus is towards building a portfolio of joy, encompassing personal fulfilment alongside professional contributions.

Raymond Co

Originally from: Philippines   Now lives in: Hong Kong
Professional highlights:
- Chief People and Culture Officer – Jardine Matheson (2023–Present)

- Senior Vice President – Human Resources, Americas and Global Learning – InterContinental Hotels Group (2018–2023)
- Vice President, Human Resources, Greater China – InterContinental Hotels Group (2013–2018)

What drives me: I tried to live a purpose-driven and principle-centred life. I am also driven by a desire to leave a legacy by building a strong HR function and developing my team members, so I am constantly thinking about leaving a good organisation for my successor to build on. If my successor is more successful than me, I have done my job. My passion lies in fostering growth and making tangible impact on people's careers. I get the biggest joy watching my team members succeed and reach greater heights in their career. As a human being, I am deeply motivated by genuine connections with others, and I aspire to make a positive impact on people's lives. I am a businessperson first, HR person second and I focus on driving "repeat-business" with my customers. You can only experience this if you consistently meet or exceed their NEEDS. In addition, I am driven by continuous learning and constantly trying to increase my self-awareness.

Rob France

Originally from: the United States   Now lives in: the United States
Professional highlights:
- EVP & Chief Human Resources Officer – Great Dane (2025–Present)
- SVP & Chief Human Resources Officer – Corning (2019–2023)
- SVP Human Resources, Corning Optical Communications – Corning (2016–2019)

What drives me: I am part of a family that stays in motion – taking in ballgames, hiking new ridgelines, and spinning dawn rides from Japan's Alps to Croatia's coast. Retired from ultramarathons and triathlons, I chase adventure on two wheels (with the occasional park detour), discovering fresh roads with my kazoku. When the bikes rest,

I hit the local pub with my acoustic duo, Woodsedge, stripping Neil Young, U2, Pearl Jam – and the occasional Woody Guthrie – down to their roots. That's what keeps my life moving.

Roberto Di Bernardini

Originally from: Italy   Now lives in: United Kingdom
Professional highlights:
- Chief Human Resources Officer – Danone (2021–2024)
- Chief Human Resources Officer – Banco Santander (2016–2020)
- Chief Human Resources Officer – Global JnJ Consumer (2013–2015)

What drives me: Since January 2025, I have divided my time into three parts: for my soul; to give back; and to offer my expertise to others. The first part is for me, my hobbies, my family, and friends. It feeds my soul assisting my beloved when they need me. I also travel a lot, sail boats, and I am currently ramping up my cycling mileage significantly. For the second part, I spend time with people who need it, coaching talents, or helping connect friends. The last part is dedicated to companies or individuals who need my expertise as a consultant. Everything I do gives me pleasure. For me, retiring is not an end. It is a fantastic new beginning.

Stephanie Werner-Dietz

Originally from: Germany   Now works in: Luxembourg

Professional highlights:
- EVP, Head of Human Resources – Arcelor Mittal (2022–Present)
- Chief People Officer – Nokia (2020–2022)
- VP, Global HR Center of Expertise – Nokia (2018–2020)

What drives me: I am driven by challenging work, adventure, and the chance to make a real impact. I love being around people, learning from them, growing with them, and doing work that matters. This has been a constant theme in my career. Along the way, curiosity has led me to explore many international opportunities where I've found a real passion for adapting to new cultures and working abroad. HR is my perfect environment because I get to blend these passions with purpose. Ultimately, I believe in continuous learning and pushing beyond my comfort zone to grow both professionally and as a human being.

Tamsin Vine

Originally from: United Kingdom   Now lives in: United Kingdom
Professional highlights:
- Chief People Officer – Tate & Lyle (2022–Present)
- VP HR Corporate Functions, VP OD & Talent – Tate & Lyle (2021–2021)
- Group SVP People Development – Sodexo (2016–2021)

What drives me: I passionately believe that we are all able to do amazing things with the right challenge and support. This is as true for my children as for colleagues I've worked with. Personally, my career and interests have been shaped by amazing people around me who have believed in my capability long before it was a seed of ambition – that is as true of my relentless running as of my joy of taking on new challenges.

Tanuj Kapilashrami

Originally from: India   Now lives in: United Kingdom
Professional highlights:
- Chief Strategy & Talent Officer – Standard Chartered (2024–Present)
- Chief Human Resources Officer – Standard Chartered (2019–2024)
- Global Head, Talent, Learning & Culture and Global Head HR, CCIB – Standard Chartered (2017–2018)

What drives me: I'm a purpose-driven leader who is passionate about creating inclusive, human-centred workplaces. My work blends strategy with empathy, and I believe companies thrive when people feel valued and engaged. I'm curious by nature, eager to learn, and committed to empowering others. With global experience in banking and a deep belief in equity, I lead with authenticity and vision – championing culture, well-being, and leadership that makes a lasting impact.

Tatsuo Kinoshita

Originally from: Japan   Now lives in: Japan
Professional highlights:
- Executive Officer and Group Chief Human Resources Officer – Panasonic Holdings Corporation (2024–Present)

- Chief Human Resources Officer – Mercari (2018–2024)
- APAC Senior HR Business Partner & APAC Org. & Talent Development Director – GE (2012–2018)

What drives me: I've always been fascinated by how understanding people and applying business principles can lead to win-win outcomes for both individuals and organisations. My journey has been about embracing challenges, from budget backpacking to transforming cultures at GE, Mercari, and now Panasonic. I'm motivated by the opportunity to drive impactful transformations, learn continuously, and ultimately contribute to a better society. It's about connecting vision to action and always striving to be bold.

Thomas Stassen

Originally from: Netherlands   Now lives in: Netherlands
Professional highlights:
- Chief Human Resources Officer – Perfetti Van Melle (2016–Present)
- SVP Human Resources – Alstom Power (2010–2016)
- Chief Officer Human Resources – Prudential Corporation Asia (2007–2010)

What drives me: I thrive on the combination of intellectual curiosity, pursuing new adventures, and, ultimately, helping others grow and organisations succeed. Therefore, I create an environment where diverse people work together based on trust, transparency, and a good sense of humour. Laughing brings people together! Over the years, I have learned that being effective in HR is about understanding business, people, but above all, keeping it simple.

Tripti Jha

Originally from: India   Now lives in: Switzerland
Professional highlights:
- Chief People Officer – Sandoz (2023–Present)
- Chief Talent & Transformation Officer – Novartis (2022–2023)
- Chief Talent & People Solutions Officer – Novartis (2020–2021)
- SVP HR, People Solutions – Novartis (2019–2020)

What drives me: I am passionate about helping people connect with their purpose and creating meaningful change, whether it's through large-scale business transformations or culture. Leadership is not a popularity contest and the ability to make good decisions comes from learning from the bad ones. Be a learner and not a knower. I cannot focus on too many things, and I want to stay super focused on what matters most and having the courage to learn from failures. I fundamentally believe that if you haven't failed, you haven't tried hard enough.

Usha Kakaria-Cayaux

Originally from: Canada Now lives in: United Kingdom
Professional highlights:
- Chief Human Resources Officer – ofi (olam food ingredients) (2022–Present)
- Diverse HR roles across Estee Lauder Companies, Heineken, and Nike (2004–2022)
- Kakaria Marketing Services (1997–2004)

What drives me: I believe the best learning happens on the edge of discomfort. I have lived and worked in different countries, feeling at home everywhere and nowhere, which is why I always connect quickly with people. I enjoy understanding what matters to them and helping to unlock their superpower to drive value for themselves and the business. Guided by my North Star, I am never afraid to speak truth to power. I believe it is more important to be respected than to be liked, which is not always popular but delivers the greatest impact and self-fulfilment.

Yolanda Talamo

Originally from: Venezuela   Now lives in: Netherlands
Professional highlights:
- Chief People Officer – Heineken (2021–Present)
- SVP HR Americas – Heineken (2016–2020)
- SVP HR, Latin America – SAB Miller (2012–2016)

What drives me: I am driven by a big passion for people and business and always balancing "dare and care" in everything I do: challenging the status-quo, pushing for growth and strong results and, at the same time, caring and respecting those around me. I am inspired by a deep sense of purpose and passion for learning, which fuels continuous growth and development in me and others. I appreciate cultural differences, diversity of minds and backgrounds and creating an environment where everyone can thrive. I love to create a meaningful difference in both the personal and professional lives of the people around me.

Leading in-depth career interviews with each of these leaders was fascinating. Beyond the clear common themes that emerged on their career success factors, which we will explore throughout this book, it is useful to point out what did *not* statistically define them.

Their upbringing did not seem to be a driver of their professional future. While many of them were raised in stable, middle-class, urban families, it is worth noting that there were quite a few exceptions, including

- One CHRO grew up playing pick-up football with drug dealers from Brazilian favelas
- One CHRO grew up studying in refugee shelters during an active war in the Middle East
- One CHRO grew up during the Troubles in Belfast
- Not one, but two CHROs grew up in a religious cult, until they consciously decided to break away from it as young adults

The educational path of this group was broad, and their career start was equally varied. While 60% started immediately in HR as their first job, 13% started in consulting, and 9% started either in legal or in operations.

Their level of initial intention towards the HR function was mixed. Some of them identified immediately the Human Resource function as their long-term professional path, while many others went into it reluctantly, often led by circumstances.

Similarly, their level of professional ambition was mixed. A few leaders decided from the start of their career that they would aim to become #1, while most others were quite happy to go with the flow, usually until they became a direct report to a Group CHRO, which then triggered them to think, "why not me?"

As we can see from these few data points, a cosy family upbringing, a natural passion for the HR domain, or a relentless career drive were generally NOT drivers of career success. So, what did make a meaningful, statistical difference in what allowed these leaders to build a Thriving Career? Let's find the answers together.

NOTES

1 Throughout this book, I will use the generic acronym of CHRO to mean any global, Group-level head of HR role, reporting to a Group-level Chief Executive Officer. Depending on geography and/or industry, equivalent titles would include Chief Human Resources Officer, Chief People Officer, Chief People & Culture Officer, EVP Human Resources or Group HR Director. It specifically refers to the single most senior HR leader in any organisation.

2 Keen observers might notice that only 44 of them are named in this book, as one CHRO elected to remain anonymous at his company's request. Insights from his career are still included in the book's research.

The curious case of the lucky career One

Being in the right place, at the right time, was a big part of my career.

Raymond Co

MEET ALICE AND ZOE

We start our journey with the story of Alice and Zoe, real people with real careers (but not their real names). Alice and Zoe are now in their early 50s and started their HR career together on the same day, straight out of university, 30 years ago. They met in their first week at work during the graduate management programme induction of a retail company in Europe. They both started in similar roles as junior HR executives servicing different business areas. Alice had studied International Relations, and Zoe had studied Psychology in their respective local university; other than that, their backgrounds were very similar. They bonded immediately at work and have remained friends ever since.

Over the next 30 years, Alice's career developed reasonably well, and she is now a regional HR director for a mid-sized consumer goods company. Here are a few key highlights of her trajectory

- After rotating through various positions in her initial company, Alice dedicated a decade to HR generalist roles in a local firm, followed by a few years as a regional divisional HR director at a prominent global technology corporation.
- Two decades into her career, Alice moved to a CHRO role for a small private equity-backed company. However, the P.E. owner divested the business three years later, eliminating her position.
- Finding herself unemployed, Alice faced difficulties securing new employment. Eventually, she compromised and returned to a former employer in a position comparable to the one she had held three years earlier.

DOI: 10.4324/9781003669005-1

- After a couple of opportunistic company changes, aiming mostly at increasing her compensation, she now finds that her career advancement is limited unless she relocates to her current company headquarters (HQ) in the United States – a move she is not prepared to make despite being single and mobile.

Over the same period, Zoe's career has followed a different, and much more global, path, having lived and worked across four countries on two continents.

- Zoe departed from her first organisation after three years and spent a decade moving between generalist and specialist positions across retail and hospitality companies. She then moved to a renowned industrial products firm that promised the international career she was craving.
- Two years later, Zoe's employer was acquired by a major competitor, and she was picked to spearhead their integration efforts in Asia. Having successfully delivered on this, she returned to HQ and received successive promotions to global divisional HR positions.
- When her career reached the 20-year mark, Zoe sensed she had hit a ceiling in her company. Knowing that patience wasn't her forte, she took control of her career and carefully picked a #2 role in a publicly listed company with a possible path to the CHRO role. Events unfolded according to plan, and Zoe became Group CHRO within two years.
- Three years later, Zoe opted to go international again for another high profile CHRO position, where she remained for a couple of years until her family wanted to get back to her home country. Through connections, she secured a prestigious CHRO role back home for a large multinational organisation.

By all accounts, both Alice and Zoe have been very successful HR leaders with careers that many professionals would aspire to. However, despite coming from a very similar background and starting at the same time, in the same company, and in identical roles, Zoe's career has clearly been more successful – something that both Alice and Zoe will admit. Zoe is now a three-time CHRO, including in her current role at a Fortune 500 company. Alice, on the other hand, is regularly speaking to recruiters trying to propel her career beyond regional roles after a series of ill-timed moves.

Was Zoe simply luckier? Was she the right woman at the right place and time? Repeatedly? This is what this book will explore and explain.

LUCK – THE SECRET INGREDIENT OF SUCCESSFUL CAREERS?

When interviewing 45 global Chief HR Officers about their career experience for this book's research, I was surprised how often the concept of "luck" came up. Many CHROs volunteered that, at some point in their career, they benefitted from some form of chance, fate, coincidence, happy accident, and otherwise fortuitous events. Simply put, it often sounded to them like plain, dumb luck. In all fairness, there was one instance of a CHRO sitting in a plane next to a total stranger starting a conversation that eventually led to her being hired into a new organisation. However, waiting for a random conversation to change your life is not a sound career strategy. You might as well wait to be struck by lightning, which I am happy to say none of our CHROs reported.

Listening to their stories, I could absolutely understand why many executives would feel they had some good luck in their career. It might have been a friend unexpectedly asking for their help on a difficult, high-profile project or a former colleague calling out of the blue with a great opportunity to join a new company. It also featured some lucky near misses, such as a new role not taken that turned out to be a dead-end or declining an offer for a big role in a shiny start-up that ended up busting out.

Each of these events, looked at individually, can feel like luck. However, when observed across dozens of successful careers, a clear pattern starts to emerge. These "lucky" events usually featured several of the following elements:

- Someone who knows the executive's strengths and cares enough to present them with an opportunity.
- That executive has a clear understanding of who they are, what they stand for, and what motivates them.
- The executive is making a thoughtful assessment of the context of the opportunity and its potential risk.
- The executive is making a strategic go/no-go decision, balancing short-term gains, long-term career benefits, and personal priorities.

Armed with these initial insights, the key question became – how can you create a pattern for your own career such that more of those "lucky" breaks happen to you? How might you position yourself at the intersection of preparation and opportunity so that you're ready to answer when fortune knocks? Thriving Career builders don't wait for random luck to find them; they create conditions where favourable circumstances are more likely to emerge.

DO NOT LET YOUR CAREER HAPPEN TO YOU

Having been a keen observer of executive careers for the past 20 years, I am often struck by the apparent lack of care and attention that executives, who are otherwise very intelligent and dedicated, give to their career development. It feels akin to being asleep at the wheel in a stable relationship and taking your spouse for granted. You come home every night, have a meal together, chit-chat casually about the small things – carefully avoiding the "big, difficult questions" – and go to bed satisfied that another day has passed without an incident. Until the day comes when everything catches up with you all at once, and reality hits you in the face. At that point, it is probably too late to hope for a great outcome. You then think of your friends who seem to be in a tremendous relationship, always happy and enjoying each other's company. How has their relationship seemingly gone from strength to strength, while yours has festered to the point of implosion?

Perhaps this was too dramatic of a metaphor, but you get my point. Building your version of a successful career takes great care, attention, and not shying away from the difficult questions such as:

- What motivates me and brings me energy? How can I get more of these things at work?
- How ambitious am I, and how realistic is my ambition? What is holding me back from realising this ambition?
- When people see me at work, what do they see? What do I stand for, and what is my executive brand?
- Which part of my life am I prepared to compromise on to grow my career? What will I not sacrifice?

These can be tough questions, but they must be faced head-on. Taking charge of your own career development will require a deep and honest look at yourself. It will involve asking uncomfortable questions about who you are and what will satisfy your needs. Your reward for finding those answers will be to establish a strong platform to shape your professional success. Setting clear expectations and taking charge of your career will also bring an additional benefit: an increased sense of control and overall satisfaction.

THINKING THROUGH YOUR CAREER STACK

The greatest mistake I see some executives make when thinking through their career is to skim the surface by asking, "how successful am I?". This is a narrow question that often points to superficial answers such as their latest performance rating, a recent bonus received, or an upcoming promotion. In short, these executives focus on measuring their current career performance.

To be sure, if your career is successful at that moment, it is a good thing, and you should celebrate it. However, I would suggest an expanded view on what a good career should look and feel like – it should be one that *you are happy with*.

Will a successful career necessarily equate to a happy career? We all know people for whom this is not the case. Having worked as a management consultant earlier in my career, I have seen plenty of seniors working 12+ hours days, six days a week, being regularly promoted, making a lot of money, and feeling rather miserable about it, always wondering when the best time is to quit. On the contrary, we probably also all know people who retired early, made prudent investments, travel economy, and spend plenty of quality time with family and friends. Who is most successful? Who is happiest?

While career performance is an important step in your professional journey, I would argue that the ultimate objective should be career satisfaction, and the missing link is expectations (Figure 1.1). At its most basic level, this idea is very intuitive: if you achieve as much, or as little, as you expected in your career, you will feel like you got what

Figure 1.1 Great expectations: thinking beyond career performance

you aimed for and get a relative sense of fairness (the more spiritual among us will see it as karma). In short, you will not be disappointed with yourself. Figure 1.2 presents a simple way to think about this.

In an ideal scenario, when high career expectations are matched by high achievements, you will be a fulfilled professional. At the opposite end, if you see limited career success but had low expectations, you are likely to see this as a fair outcome. However, if you fail to live up to high career expectations, it will likely lead to frustration. Perhaps counterintuitively, the opposite is also a problem. Achieving unexpected success may give you undue stress due to new expectations that you are not necessarily willing or able to handle.[1] This is commonly known as imposter syndrome.

Now let's dig deeper into the analysis and explore what career performance means in practice. While each of us gets to define what success means to them, let me offer five broad drivers of career performance that can help us frame the concept in a simple and actionable way.

1 **Reaping rewards**. At its most basic, we can evaluate our success based on financial elements. This includes the money we get to put in the bank, as well as the ancillary benefits of a high-flying executive career: lavish expatriate packages, business class flights, club memberships, and the long-term incentives that we may stock up.
2 **Making a difference**. This is the impact we make on the world through our work. For some, this might equate to reaching business

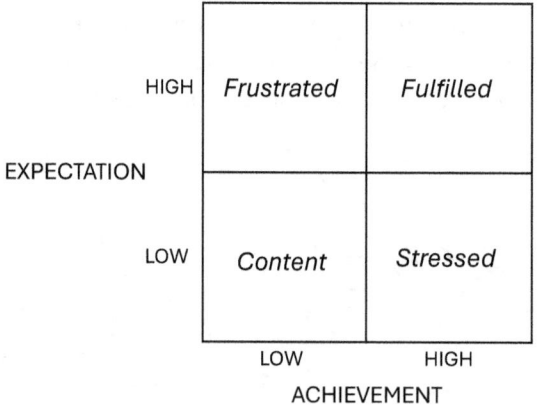

Figure 1.2 Managing the expectation – achievement gap

targets; for others, it will involve the amount of change they bring about, such as stakeholder and community impact. Each of us will have a very personal way of assessing this.

3 **Developing meaningful relationships**. We are all social animals. A sense of affiliation[2] and belonging is a key need that often drives us professionally. Our ability to develop and maintain meaningful business and personal relationships throughout our career can be a measure of our success.

4 **Achieving personal balance**. Careers do not happen in a vacuum. They exist in this complex multiverse called life. They involve constant trade-offs between what is required from us at work and what we want to achieve outside of it. Striking a balance that is right for you will be a key part of your success.

5 **Self-actualising**. Are you able to achieve what you believe to be your full potential? For some people, it might mean a job title or reaching a certain level of responsibility. For others, it might be about fulfilling their need to run their own business or to express their creativity. Again, each of us will have a personal way of assessing this.

Feel free to add to this list if you are missing a critical element, and don't let others tell you what is most important. You get to define what matters most to you. Once you have a list that you are happy with, I find it good practice to prioritise it and make a cold-blooded assessment of how well you are currently doing on each dimension against your expectations. Any small gap between your expectation and reality may be a watch-out. Any major gap should be reviewed and addressed proactively.

I recently conducted this exercise with a friend, who found it very useful as she faced a major career (and life) decision. She was a global VP for a large asset management firm in New York. She is in her late 40s and has been offered her first Group CHRO role for a small professional services organisation. The company has a great culture, but the role would need her to relocate to Europe, which would involve moving to a long-distance relationship with her boyfriend who would likely remain in the United States. In addition, the offer came with a nearly 30% pay cut (after negotiation). Would you take that deal? Together, we listed and prioritised her drivers of career performance and force-ranked the different aspects of the new offer vs her expectations. The exercise gave her much clarity on the trade-offs – practical and mental – she had to make. Eventually, she concluded that, at this stage of her life, financial benefits were not essential, and she decided to take the offer and move to Europe.

MUSINGS – AND HARD DATA – ON CAREER SATISFACTION

As part of my work advising HR leaders globally, I conduct career surveys of HR professionals, with a focus on career satisfaction. I always find the results enlightening (and often quite entertaining). Here are some of the results from the 2025 Global HR Career Survey, across 1,168 respondents from every part of the world (Europe (30% of respondents), Asia-Pacific (36%), North America (15%), and the rest of the world (19%)). It might give you some food for thought as you consider what drives your own career satisfaction.

The good news is that, on the aggregate, HR professionals are globally fairly satisfied with their careers, with 74% of respondents declaring they are satisfied with how their career has progressed.[3] However, this hides some significant disparities when analysed through various segments of the HR population.

Your career stage will greatly impact your career satisfaction. Leaders with less than 15 years of tenure have a satisfaction level 10% lower than average, while leaders with tenure of 30+ years have a career satisfaction level 8% higher than average. This strong correlation between tenure and career satisfaction should give you comfort that the best is (likely) yet to come – no matter how far along you are in your career.

Spending some career time outside of the HR function will not negatively impact your career satisfaction, unless you spend more than 20% of your time outside of HR. The survey clearly shows a steep step change (−10%) in career satisfaction for leaders who spend more than one-fifth of their career time outside of HR. So, while it can be a great idea to venture out of HR for one assignment, there can be too much of a good thing. We will discuss this further in Chapter 7.

Developing a global HR career is strongly correlated with career satisfaction. Going from living in one single region of the world to spanning two (+4%), three (+7%), or even four (+13%) different regions throughout your career will steadily increase your career satisfaction. Never hesitate to get that international experience. It will help develop your cultural agility and pay off nicely in the long-run.

Finally, HR executives who are clearer about their long-term career objectives are more likely to be satisfied with their career. Survey results show that executives who are clear about their career objectives[4] show a significantly higher career satisfaction level (80% satisfied) compared to executives who do not have such clarity (56% satisfied). As we will see later in this book, developing a career North Star will not only help you make better career decisions faster but also give you a sense of peace that you are always moving in the right direction.

CAREER HEALTH – THE FOUNDATION THAT MAKES CAREERS THRIVE

I contend in this book that long-term career satisfaction is the ultimate objective we should strive for. However, if career performance is what determines how well we are doing today, how can we be sure that this performance will be sustained, even improved, over the long-run? What do we need to focus on today to make sure we play the long game? The missing element, the foundation of your full career stack and the focus of most of this book's research, is Career Health (Figure 1.3).

If you want to preview your career's future, but lack a crystal ball, you must distinguish between performance and health. As suggested earlier, career performance is a lagging indicator that tells you how successful you are currently. The performance horizon is generally measured in months and bound by the annual performance appraisal cycle or your next job rotation. If you receive good feedback from your boss, a pay raise or a promotion, you can be confident that things are good. For now.

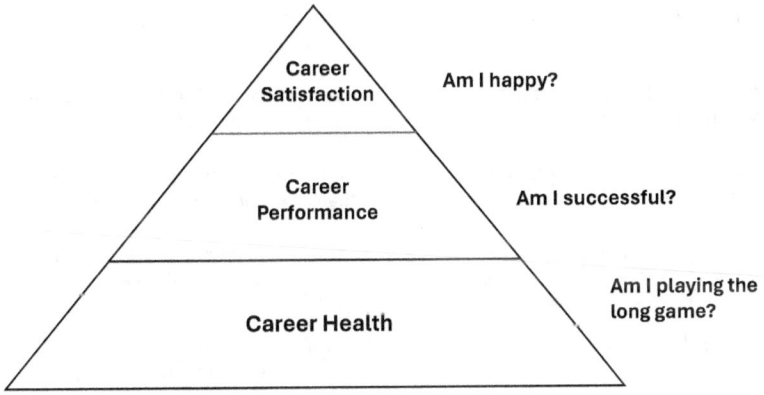

Figure 1.3 Building your career stack

Career Health, on the other hand, is the leading indicator you need to keep an eye on so that your career performs for the years to come. It is your career's insurance policy against any accident such as being on the wrong side of a merger or facing a global economic downturn.

Throughout this book, we will get to the details of the elements of Career Health, but first let us take a practical look at the subtle but powerful differences between performance and health. Figure 1.4 illustrates some of the symptoms of what good performance and good health will feel like for your career. See if you can spot the contrast.

To be sure, you need to aim for both performance *and* health. Career performance without health will be unsustainable and Career Health without performance may not get you where you want fast enough. The key to balancing the two is to manage your career with purposeful intention. This idea goes well beyond "taking charge of your own career" as many management books and social media influencers have rehashed over the last decade. To make this concrete, let us distinguish three different levels of career management – transactional, functional, and intentional.

At the most transactional level, executives go through their career by moving from job to job. At each juncture, they evaluate the potential of a role based on the short-term value they would get from it. Often, people who operate at this level focus on job titles, compensation level, the scope of responsibility, and similar short-term metrics. There is nothing inherently wrong with this if the objective is to maximise

Signs of Good Career Performance	Signs of Good Career Health
• You are well-compensated	• You feel *fairly* compensated for your seniority level
• You are rated high on your annual performance appraisal	• You are a *trusted* advisor to some senior people in your organization
• Your colleagues are comfortable sharing their problems you	• Senior executives feel they can discuss their *strategic* issues with you
• Each of your career moves gave you increasing scope and responsibility	• Each of your career moves helped you get you closer to your ultimate *objective*
• You regularly get calls from recruiters	• You have a strong set of relationships across diverse organizations

Figure 1.4 Distinguishing between career performance and health

immediate gains and progression. However, in my experience, such people eventually hit the wall in their career. Opportunities will stop coming their way, and they will find it progressively harder to progress as the years go by. These executives are often left confused about what changed, typically blaming a weak job market, without realising they simply brought it upon themselves through years of transactional career choices.

At the next functional level, executives go through their careers by looking at each new role as an opportunity to make a difference. They typically focus on the problem to solve or the business to build. It is an inside-out view. They see each career transition as an opportunity to leave their mark and pick roles based on their perceived fit to address that challenge. Managing your career at this level is perfectly fine, and many people do it very successfully, provided their employer recognises and rewards their achievements. It is particularly well-suited to expert and consultant tracks and can fit people with personal constraints that may limit their professional options, such as trailing spouses or people who want fractional careers. However, it is still not optimal if your aim is to maximise your long-term career potential.

At the intentional level,[5] executives look at their career as a succession of growth opportunities separated by moments of strategic decision. Beyond merely looking at the impact they might have in a new role, they foresee the stretch they would get and the learning they would gain from it. It is an outside-in view. As Tripti Jha summed up beautifully during our discussion, "Go for the experience, not the title, as titles change with time, but experiences help you grow". The most successful leaders operate at this intentional level most of the time.

This is where playing the "long game" takes its full meaning. Rather than focusing on the immediate outcome, it is most important to master the process. One analogy would be trying to lose weight. Sure, you can go for surgery or take slimming pills, but these fix the symptoms, not the underlying problem. Playing the long game means building your general fitness, improving your nutrition, and introducing habits into your life that will foster a sustainable shift to address the root cause of your issues.

Managing your career at an intentional level means that you need to reflect deeply about yourself and invest in understanding the context of any new opportunity you are presented with. It also means pragmatically assessing whether it would give you a step up in terms of capabilities, confidence, or reputation. It can happen when you are offered a promotion, asked to take a new role, or looking to change employer, but it can also happen in more subtle ways. I still remember being in my first job as a young propulsion engineer in Rolls-Royce when my manager called me into his office and told me that he had been invited to an engineering conference a couple of weeks later to present a new technology developed by our department. He tells me he'd love to go but has been asked to a meeting at HQ on that day, and he would like me to go and represent the company instead of him. Being the young (and stupid) person that I was, I immediately responded that I was not interested in wasting time attending such fancy schmooze events. I would much rather stay at my desk and work on our cool new technology, thank you very much. Nearly 30 years later, I still remember his blank look and stunned two-second silence, after which he smiled and said, "That's ok, I understand. I will ask someone else".

When such things happen to you, please be smarter than me. It is as important to recognise and respond to "micro" growth opportunities as it is to the big ones, as they accumulate and compound over time. Blindly passing them on might also hurt your career in ways that will only become apparent later.

If you are interested in the outcome of my Rolls-Royce story, about one year later, my boss had to decide for my personal development plan whether I belonged to the Management track, which would lead towards senior executive roles in the company, or the Technology track, which would lead towards technical expert roles. No prize for guessing that, to my indignation, I was forcefully pushed towards the Technology track. The only way for me to get out of that situation was to leave the company to pursue an MBA and reorient my career.

In the face of this apparent complexity, despair not. We will see through the course of this book that developing a few foundational attitudes and applying some pragmatic practices throughout your career will

1 Increase the likelihood that you will come across more attractive opportunities more frequently.
2 Help you assess the true potential of each opportunity you encounter and how well they would fit you.
3 Improve your chances of making better strategic career decisions repeatedly.

This is how you can become intentionally lucky and build a healthy, successful, and happy career. A Thriving Career.

BECOME A THRIVING CAREER BUILDER

It was a real privilege for me to spend time listening to, and learning from, the insightful stories of some of the most senior and successful HR leaders on the planet, as they cumulated over 300+ career-years in Group CHRO positions among them.

One of the most striking features of my in-depth career conversations with these leaders was how consistently some themes and actions kept coming back through their experiences. They displayed, unprompted, four distinctive attitudes that helped them set the foundations for a successful career: **Awareness** (82% of them), **Bravery** (87%), **Connectivity** (76%), and **Delivery** (82%).

It should be highlighted that they did not consistently display all of those, all the time, so there is, thankfully, no need to aim for super-human performance. However, it will be important, as much as possible, to fire-on-all-cylinders to increase your chances of long-term success. As a case in point, 20 of the 45 CHROs I interviewed gave evidence of displaying all four foundational attitudes across their careers. Seventeen of them displayed at least three of these attitudes, and the remaining eight displayed at least two. None of them displayed fewer than two.

These four foundational attitudes, in turn, translated into 12 practical career practices, as detailed in Figure 1.5. Applying these practices led them to consistently and confidently access and assess the right career opportunities and create their own luck. It also allowed them to perform in each role in a way that would maximise their chance of generating new and better career options in the future. Along the way, they developed new capabilities, established strong reputations, and grew in confidence.

During my conversations, it was also striking that these leaders often did not consciously apply these practices for career management purposes. They just did it because it felt natural to them. Whether consciously or subconsciously, applying most of these practices, most of the time, has a compounding effect that creates and sustains the foundation for strong Career Health and, over the long-run, a Thriving Career.

Thriving Career builders show a high level of self-awareness and actively monitor their context, including any pressures from their

Figure 1.5 Deploying your Thriving Career practices

personal life. They understand what motivates them and make career decisions that best fit their needs and desires while being lucid about the internal and external constraints that might hold them back.

Thriving Career builders are brave, relentless learners and mindful risk-takers. They are not afraid to follow a challenging career path if it brings them meaningful development. The risk of failure does not deter them if it is balanced with a clear learning opportunity. They hold strong views and are confident in taking a stand when they feel the need to uphold their values.

Thriving Career builders are culturally agile and stay actively connected to people who matter most to them. They treasure meaningful relationships and naturally develop mentors across the organisations they work in, and beyond. They shun generic professional networking in favour of purpose-driven relationships that often last for life.

Thriving Career builders are relentless in seeking to deliver results, much as a business owner would. They see themselves as business leaders first and people leaders second. They focus on outcomes rather than processes or policies and build a reputation for getting the job done. While doing so, they build trust and respect with superiors and peers alike.

Putting all these elements together gives us a picture of the full stack of the Thriving Career that you should be working on (Figure 1.6).

1. Throughout your journey, play the long game by building a foundation of Career Health with intention.
2. Along the way, enjoy the benefits of great career performance with successes and rewards you can be proud of.
3. Over the long-run, drive towards career satisfaction and be confident that you will be able to look back over your professional life with a deep sense of happiness and fulfilment.

Do you recall Alice and Zoe, whom we met at the beginning of this chapter? Was Zoe simply luckier than Alice? If we go beyond the surface and apply a Thriving Career lens, the drivers of Zoe's relative success become fairly obvious.

Alice had a good career; however, she made several mistakes. She did not assess properly the risks of taking an early career CHRO role for a small private equity-backed company and was left in a lurch after the investors exited. Following this, she settled for moving back to a role she had held before, which provided her with no new learning or growth. Once her career progression restarted, she felt she had to catch up financially and chose mostly to prioritise compensation in picking her new roles. She had a good career. But not a thriving one.

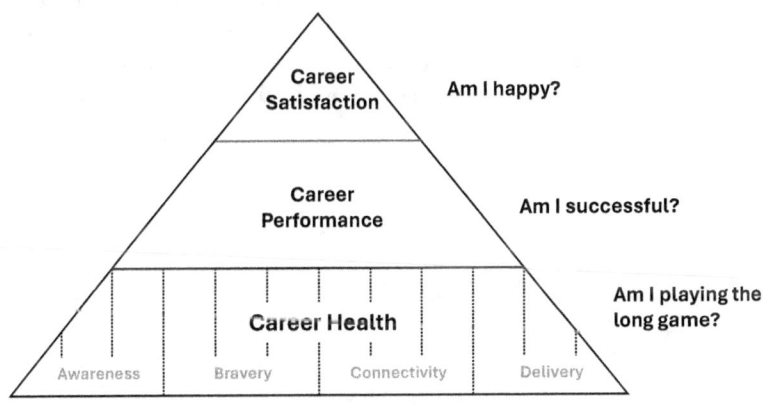

Figure 1.6 The Thriving Career full stack

In contrast, early in her career, Zoe jumped at opportunities that came her way to grow her career internationally. She performed well in her roles and built a reputation for being a no-nonsense HR person who gets things done. As a result, when her company got acquired, she was seen as a talent and given greater opportunities. Zoe's career path was certainly not smooth, but she took it in her stride. When she found that her progression slowed, she was aware that she needed to take charge, so she decided to proactively make a move. She was offered a #2 role with a path to CHRO. She did a lot of due diligence to ensure this was a risk worth taking, and it turns out she made the right bet. Her career thrived, and she is now in her third successive global CHRO position.

That's it for the theory. We will now leave anonymous Alice and Zoe behind and get personal. We will dig into the specifics of the foundational attitudes and career practices that drive Career Health, leaning heavily on our CHRO's life-tested experience. Over the next four chapters, we will also start to discuss practical ways you can start applying these insights to build your own Thriving Career.

NOTES

1 Examples are commonly found in highly specialized professions, such as sales and trading, where top individual performers are sometimes promoted to management positions, only to realize this requires a very different skillset and mindset from what had made them successful, which can end up in a career tailspin.
2 See McLelland's Theory of Needs for more on this.
3 Respondents who agree to the statement "I am very satisfied with the way my HR career has progressed so far".
4 Respondents who agree to the statement "I have a clear view of what I want to achieve in my career going forward".
5 For more on the mechanics of intentionality, a great read is Intention: The Surprising Psychology of High Performers, by Sekoul Krastev, Dan Pilat and Mike Ross (2023).

Activating your Awareness

Two

> Each time I made a career move, it was intentional. It was to get me closer to my goal.
>
> Jessica Teo

Good decisions require reliable situational information. This principle applies to everything around us, yet we often seem to pay much more attention to the big decisions of our personal lives than of our careers. When accepting to join a new organisation or selecting a new internal role, are you putting as much time, effort, and soul-searching into it as you would into getting engaged or buying a new house? Few of us would. Thriving Career builders do.

Making the right career decisions involves having a clear idea of what you want to achieve over the long-run, a thoughtful understanding of what drives you as an executive and human being, and a deep appreciation for the context in which you operate professionally and personally. Underpinning all these elements is a foundational level of Awareness of yourself and your surroundings.

Eighty-two percent of the leaders interviewed for this book's research displayed unprompted career practices related to Awareness:

- Clarify your purpose and objectives
- Know your motives
- Establish your priorities.

From this point on, and for the next four chapters, we are going to rely heavily on the life lessons earned and learned by the CHROs interviewed for this book. If you wish to know more about each of them, their career track and what motivates each of them, refer any time to our earlier Meet our Fearless Leaders section.

Let's look at Larissa Cerqueira's example who applied her strong Awareness attitude to resolve a thorny mid-career issue. Larissa is

DOI: 10.4324/9781003669005-2

a Brazilian lady with two school-aged kids and a husband[1] working in the military and at the U.N., which can make it challenging to build a global career. However, Larissa is very intentional about how she manages her career, and, as a family, they have regular and open two-way conversations about what they want to achieve.

At a particularly sensitive moment in the mid-part of her career, Larissa recalled having to make a gut-wrenching decision.

> Early in my career, I took the opportunity of an expatriate assignment in Germany with Henkel, which was an amazing experience. When my family and I returned from Germany to Brazil in 2012, my husband and I made a pact that we would go international again within the next four years. By 2016, I had transitioned to Danaher, leading Latin America HR for one of their operating companies. As our self-imposed four-year deadline to leave Brazil loomed, I felt a strong urge to explore new horizons. I told my boss, 'Look, my job here is complete, and I have my successor ready. I think I can contribute more, and I would like to discuss opportunities for relocating abroad.' They offered me a role in the US, but it felt like a lateral move.

At that moment, Larissa faced a serious dilemma and found her answer thanks to her family.

> My husband and I discussed it extensively. We wanted our kids to grow up in the U.S., but the role they offered wasn't particularly exciting. It was a talent planning role, something I had already done at Henkel several years before. It felt like a step backward in my career. Additionally, the compensation was modest and on a local package. I remember feeling quite torn; my ego was bruised. My husband, however, provided the clarity I needed. He said, 'Why do you care? They are offering exactly what the family wants. It will get us a foot in the door in the U.S., and then we'll make things happen ourselves. That's our family philosophy – all we need is a chance, and we'll take it from there.' He was right, and that's exactly what happened. We moved from Brazil to the U.S., and nine months later, another opportunity arose within the company. It was a much bigger role, and I seized it. Everything worked out well; we just had to take that leap of faith.

I found Larissa's story to be very inspirational. She believes in what she calls the internal locus of control and is outspoken about it. She lives by the idea that everything starts and ends with you and your choices. This is a mindset that several of the most successful CHROs share. Let's explore how others have displayed a high level of Awareness in building their career. It will give us examples of practical ways you can apply those practices for yourself and lay the groundwork for making the best decisions for your career.

AWARENESS PRACTICE #1 – CLARIFY YOUR PURPOSE AND OBJECTIVES

Having a clear understanding of your professional and personal purpose will guide you throughout any major career decision you need to make. This will not be set in stone and might shift over the years. In fact, you should anticipate some changes as you develop as an HR leader and as a whole person. Mayuko Seto experienced this first-hand when she was approached to be an internal candidate for a potential first CHRO role. She shared,

> At the start of my career, I was ambitious and set my sights on becoming a CHRO. Having entered HR through a mid-career change, I felt a strong drive to catch up and prove myself. In one company, I was told I was being considered as an internal candidate for the Group CHRO role. It was a competitive process, and under normal circumstances, I would have been eager to fight for it, but I knew I wasn't ready. I also started questioning whether becoming a CHRO – something I had worked so hard toward – was truly what I wanted. Eventually, someone else was appointed to the role, and I was given a new assignment. It was a challenging one for many reasons. I struggled and did not perform well, not just with the work itself, but because I had lost sight of what I was striving for. I felt isolated and unsure of myself, and, in hindsight, it was the first major setback in my HR career.

While she had this profound experience, Mayuko did not let it bring her down. She continued

> Sometime later, I was offered the CHRO role at Ricoh. This time, I didn't hesitate. I couldn't say with confidence I was ready, nor did I have a renewed ambition to become a CHRO – in fact, I had stopped

defining my career in terms of titles – but I felt I couldn't let a second chance slip away. Maybe now I had the resilience and clarity I lacked before. I've learned it's okay to admit when you're not ready. You may feel disappointed in yourself, even lose confidence, but when the time is right, opportunities will come again and the struggles you've endured will give you the strength to rise to them.

Mayuko displayed a high level of self-awareness through this experience, which she built over the years. This should give anyone hope that, with mindfulness and self-care, we can develop that clarity and purpose when it comes to our career.

Your purpose will shape what you aim to achieve professionally and how far you want to go. Think of yourself as a one-person enterprise. As the owner of this small business, you need to know your mission, vision, and what you stand for as a professional. Some might call it ambition, but that is a narrow view. Successful career builders treat it as their North Star. It is a general sense of where you are headed professionally or at least where you are *not* prepared to go. As Usha Kakaria-Cayaux put it,

> As long as I can remember, I have always set a direction for myself – a North Star. I don't need a detailed plan, but my North Star guides me so I can tie every career decision back to it. It's not a job title; it is an articulation of what I want to do. I am very curious, so I want to keep learning. I am ambitious, so I want to stretch myself. I also want to use my position to have impact that expands beyond my work. Have a North Star, and it'll be easy to say yes or no when opportunities arise because you'll know if they align with your values and what matters to you. It's like turning on the GPS. You can take the scenic route, the direct route, or the toll-free route, as long as you know your ultimate destination.

If you are not entirely clear on where you want your career to go, it may help to pause and evaluate your Why. Much like Simon Sinek suggests in a few of his books,[2] you might find it beneficial to distil your purpose into a one-line purpose statement. Frédéric Chardot has experienced this and puts it well. "Some people think about their legacy, but not me. I just want to make an impact and be useful, helping people and organizations get to their best".

 **Helio takes a step back to explore his purpose**

After almost 10 years in Novartis, and over 20 years into my career, I realised I needed a break to think. I'd been constantly moving countries and jobs, hopping from one challenge to the next without pause, and I wanted some time to breathe. That's when my break started – not from burnout but from a genuine desire to create space for reflection. I wanted the opportunity to step back, to experience being unemployed by choice, and to decide what I would do next thoughtfully. Would I return to corporate life? Would I launch my own start-up? Would I transition into consulting?

I deliberately went into exploration mode, but initially, I just focused on reclaiming simple joys: reconnecting with people I love, taking long walks with my dog, being fully present with my family, and deepening my meditation practice. I absolutely loved it. I can't emphasise enough how important it is to create space to reflect outside all the pressures and expectations of work. This distance helped me to focus on what truly matters in my life – not what others think should matter. My self-awareness expanded dramatically during that period. I found tremendous value in meeting people who think completely differently from me, volunteering with young start-ups working on innovations I never imagined existed and collaborating with academics on emerging ideas – all simply to help and create a positive impact in society.

There were certainly ups and downs during that time. I declined several senior roles without any guarantee that I would find something better or even anything at all. It was an emotional roller coaster at times, but I remained committed to staying centred and taking time for deep reflection. The uncertainty was uncomfortable but necessary for genuine growth. Looking back, it was a period of massive learning and transformation, both personally and professionally. In the end, I felt incredibly fortunate. It was an extraordinary year of discovery. I eventually returned to work fully recharged, with much greater clarity about my purpose, my priorities and how to approach my HR practice.

Once you have defined your purpose, do you have a solid grasp of your overall career objectives? As mentioned earlier, this is akin to the mission (purpose – your Why) and vision (objective – your What) a company might have. While your purpose will be long-lasting, your objective(s) will be more concrete and specific. For instance, how critical is it for you to get promoted to the top of your function or business? How curious are you about experiencing different cultures and ways of living? How attractive is it for you to be your own boss? Answering such questions, even directionally, will help shape the type of endpoint you may set for your career.

Yolanda Talamo exemplified this and shared,

> I never had a career plan, it's only more like a direction, or an ambition, but not the concrete step by step plan. You need to be flexible to adapt when unexpected, but great, opportunities are put in front of you and grab them.

Keeping that flexibility, rather than working out a step-by-step ten-year career plan, will let you adapt to changing circumstances and still allow you to move professionally in the right direction.

Once you have explored your purpose and your objectives, giving you some directional clarity, you should think about the contexts in which you might thrive. At a minimum, you should be able to quickly identify contexts that are not likely to be right for you. Think of context as the different types of ownership structures, organisational cultures, decision-making norms, business challenges, or industry structures that characterise a business. Which combination is more likely to suit you?

Someone might instinctively know that a non-profit organisation isn't suitable for them or that a private equity-backed environment isn't a fit. For instance, I am sometimes surprised by private-sector executives who tell me excitedly that they have signed up to join a government organisation. I would challenge them to ensure they have thought about the trade-off. Are they prepared to adjust to a totally different culture? I would often be told they understand my concern, but "this one is different". Well, maybe. But they usually leave to return to the private sector after a couple of years.

Geoff Lloyd, who is never shy about speaking his mind, put it more colourfully than I ever could.

You have got to know yourself, especially as you become more senior, because there's a connection between who you are, the values you hold, what you aspire to deliver, and what an organization will offer you. Not knowing yourself or not investing time in understanding what's important to you will lead to poor career decisions. People can easily get caught up in the moment and take a job they shouldn't. To be clear, I'm not saying you must always be a good person who wants to do good things. You could be an absolute jerk wanting to make a lot of money. In that case, go find a business where you can be a jerk and get rich. It's fine; it just means you're aligned. The alignment between who you are, what your objectives are, and the context you're operating in, will give you balance.

We will return to this idea of balancing priorities before this chapter is over. For now, once you have a directional picture of what guides you, you should get deeper and explore the more specific drivers of your motivation.

AWARENESS PRACTICE #2 – KNOW YOUR MOTIVES

Understanding what truly drives you is a key practice for you to make more intentional career decisions. The alternative will often spell trouble. Several CHROs candidly shared stories and hard-earned lessons of picking the wrong job for the wrong motives. Often, they did this because of a sexy job title or an attractive compensation package without keeping in mind what truly motivated them and made them thrive.

For example, Rob France candidly shared a lesson he learned early on as a young executive.

> After my first few years at PepsiCo, I got an offer to join a smaller independent food producer, and I left for financial reasons and a job title. It was so dumb, just plain stupid. In my defence, when you grow up without much, like I did as a kid, money matters, and you want to prove something. During the interview, they make you feel like the best-looking guy in the room; they sell you on how they want to grow, etc., and big titles make you feel good, so why not? However, I quickly learned that it was too small, and the culture was not right for me. They looked at labour purely as a cost and some old-school behaviours did not fit my values. I ended up leaving after two years

A smiling stranger helps Roberto find his purpose

Many years ago, I was vacationing on a Caribbean island with my family, and one morning, while walking through our resort to the beach, I met a lady. She cheerfully greeted me, "Good morning, mister". She looked genuinely happy, and I said, "Good morning to you, and forgive me for asking, but who are you?" The young lady replied with a warm smile, "My name is Esther, and I am here to make sure that you feel at home". As you might have guessed, Esther was the cleaning lady.

Engaging in conversation with Esther, I learned that she woke up at 5 a.m. every day and walked five kilometres from her home to the hotel, rain or shine, without complaint. Most importantly, she wasn't merely thinking about going to clean rooms and toilets – she had completely reinvented her job's purpose. She saw herself as going to help people feel at home every day, and this profound reframing brought that genuine smile to her face.

While it may have been incidental to her, that true revelation struck me deeply. I realised how fundamental it is to give meaning to what you do, to mentally separate yourself from the mundane transactions and concentrate instead on the potential outcome of your work – what you can do for others. That day, I realised I wasn't just managing processes or leading HR functions. I was helping people become better, more effective leaders. I was helping people develop to their full potential. I was helping my organisation be more effective and have a more meaningful impact on society.

I got this profound lesson, for free, from Esther, and it completely transformed my outlook and life. From that day on, I have tried to identify a meaningful purpose for everything I do, professionally and personally. You can approach this by dedicating tremendous energy to your professional life or seeking a balance between professional achievements and personal fulfilment. I believe finding the balance that works specifically for you matters most – one that brings meaning and satisfaction across all aspects of your life.

and learned my lesson. Fortunately, along the way, you make great connections with people, especially if you're a decent human being, which I like to think I am. You make good friends, and you get phone calls. That's how Corning happened for me, and I loved it so much that I spent the next 23 years there.

What a near-miss for Rob. If he had not quickly recognised that he had made the wrong decision and persisted in that small food company, he would likely have missed out on the amazing career and life experience he subsequently had.

Geoff Lloyd had an equally sobering experience. While he was already senior at the time, he still received an eye-opening lesson about cultural fit.

> There was one role I took where the culture simply didn't work for me. I wasn't true to my values and my own sense of self. It was not a pleasant experience, and I learned the hard way. When I made the decision to join, I got caught up with my ego. In that company, I was treated like I had become some sort of superior being, but I'm just a normal person who happens to have some talents and experience in HR. I enjoy getting things done and don't like politics – that company was a completely different animal. In hindsight, I should have chosen another role that would have been a better fit for me, but my ego, and no one else, took me in the wrong direction.

One leader who made intentional decisions throughout his career is Philip Read, who shared

> Several times in my career, I have traded compensation for something else, either for a more interesting challenge or personal reasons. Short-term, it hurt a little bit, but long-term I benefited greatly. I feel it made me a better candidate for next-level roles because it gave me richer experience compared to my peers. For instance, when I moved to Dow in the U.S., I joined a division with around 7,000 people, and my new job was as part of the HR team. However, on my second day on the job, my boss left unexpectedly. I was then offered to take on her role 'primus inter pares', which meant that I did not get compensated for the role. I still signed up for it and learned many valuable things

from that experience. Later in my career, when I left Novartis to join Tetra Pak, I was made an attractive offer to stay with the company. I was convinced however that the move to Tetra Pak was the right move for me, and for my family, at the time.

Don't let your ego and your wallet take you in the wrong direction when deciding on a new role. At the same time, you must keep on monitoring your environment. It may not be you who is changing but your context. It is important to keep a proactive eye on what is happening with the business and the organisation, as Janice Deskus did when she got a new boss at Medtronic. She shared,

> My boss Bryan left the company to become a CEO. Six months after he left, I remember thinking, I can't do this anymore. Bryan had been the architect of chaos and change. He liked to shake things up constantly and believed that's how you progress. It was a crazy way to work, and I was always pulling my hair out, but it was really fun. I remember calling Bryan, and I said, 'This is your fault; you did this to me. I am addicted to the adrenaline, the change, and the transformation'. Now, it had all gone quiet. That's when I knew I would have to make a move, even though I loved the company.

In this instance, Janice demonstrated probably the highest level of Awareness: the ability to make a tough decision, which she did not have to make, simply because she had recognised a new pattern in her context. Not much had changed around her, yet everything had changed for her.

Even if you are very clear about what drives you, you should still expect awkward glances when you make decisions that others may not understand. You will know they are right for you, but only *you know you*. This happened to Archana Bhaskar when she left a high-profile global HR role in Singapore to return to India. She shared,

> I never planned anything for my career. I look at any new opportunity and ask myself, am I going to learn? Is this something I will enjoy? Will I make a difference? Titles and money don't matter. I left a company once when many people asked, what's wrong with you?! Why are you leaving when you are on a good track? However, my choice was to be back in India. My husband works in the social impact space and lots of exciting things are happening in the

economy, society, government and industry. There's a different buzz about this country because there's so much growth, with so many young people and so many new businesses. Both my husband and I wanted to be back, and Dr Reddy's – with its great purpose, values and ambition to reach patients globally – was the right company for me.

Together with a high level of Awareness, Archana possesses a strong internal compass. She knows where she stands, and she does not get swayed by how others may judge her. Eight years on, she still knows she made the right decision.

Getting a good handle on what motivates you is important and will set you up for the next and most critical step: prioritisation to find the right balance.

AWARENESS PRACTICE #3 – ESTABLISH YOUR PRIORITIES

Once you have identified your motives, you must prioritise them to deploy these insights into your career decisions. To avoid surprises, it is useful to be open with others on your criteria when looking for any new role, internally or externally. For example, after Johanna Söderström concluded her first CHRO role at Dow, she became very selective about new roles and shared that openly with recruiters.

> I shared with head-hunters that I would only be interested if something really special became available, and I outlined my three criteria. First, I wanted to ensure great chemistry in my CEO relationship. I had experienced it once in my career, and wanted it replicated. I knew that the chemistry is a must for best possible performance. I won't compromise on it. Second, I wanted to be able to deliver true transformative work. I don't want to be a CHRO who is tasked with just running operational HR. There will be many others more suitable than me for that. Third, I wanted my family to be happy with the location. I asked the search companies to respect these three criteria so I would not disappoint anyone.

Getting an explicit sense of your priorities is particularly important for female executives, who often must balance high expectations across work and home. In fact, several female CHROs I interviewed scoffed at the idea that you can "have it all" and stressed that it is all about making conscious, often difficult, choices.

Mieke learns she can't have it all

About ten years into my career, I moved from Europe to the United States with Sara Lee, together with my husband and two young kids. It had been a big international move for us. Suddenly, the company announced a major restructuring initiative, as we would carve out part of the business. The CHRO called me and asked whether I would mind working out of the Netherlands, where I just came from, for a while during the transaction. Since it was supposed to be only for a short while, I agreed. I started commuting weekly to Europe, with my family still in Chicago ... which ended up lasting 15 months. There were many moments when I cried in airplanes, thinking about my young kids. Why the hell was I doing this?

On the other hand, it was such a privilege to work on this large transaction. I was learning a tremendous amount about how companies restructure and how they transform. I was working with the best external consulting brains and our corporate strategy team. It was super interesting, and I felt I was learning on steroids. The impact was also amazing; we were accompanying thousands of people through the very difficult process of being sold out of the company. I felt it was worth the trade-off we made as a family.

Many of us get to our roles because we have guts, and we say yes to challenges, but most importantly, you need to have a massively good support network. Otherwise, it's just impossible. Whoever tells you that you can have it all is lying. It's not true. You can't have a great and satisfying career and all the happiness of raising a family and seeing your friends whenever you want and having time for hobbies at fixed dates. That just is not possible; at least it wasn't for me. You must make conscious choices. To be clear, I wasn't a victim. My husband and I made conscious choices.

Tamsin Vine is one female CHRO who expressed the view that it is not possible to have it all.

> I love working, I can't sit still, but with two kids, no full-time childcare and a husband who works full-time, the juggle is very real at times. There are moments when I think 'am I missing out on moments with my children? Are there different choices I could make? Is it all worthwhile?' I think I'll always keep asking those questions simply not to lose sight of them. I don't believe that 'having it all' is real. We have the privilege of difficult choices and compromise when we shape our careers, especially as parents. I think we are now in a place where we can be far more authentic about the choices that we make. You make choices that work for you, based on what's important to you. What are your boundary conditions? It's a constant dance of questioning yourself and whether you need to recalibrate. You just can't have it all without conscious sacrifice or compromise.

Thriving Career builders understand that making tough choices is a part of life, and some things will have to give. It helps to keep an eye on the long-term picture. I often see young executives highly motivated by financial rewards, which is understandable when they are looking to start a family. However, it is important to look at your full career earning potential. A quick buck on changing employer early on might feel good now but spoil your trajectory and prevent you from getting the bigger jobs later.

One helpful way to prioritise is to think through the different roles you have in your life and how you balance them. This idea is particularly dear to Ranjay Radhakrishnan, who promotes role–life balance, a concept he came across when doing some personal development work at Unilever.

> I went through a Leading with Purpose programme in Unilever during which something unexpected happened. This was a programme to define my purpose and create my professional development plan. However, I ended up working on it in a unique way. I made a development plan for myself as a holistic person, not just in my role as an SVP HR. I have many roles in life – being a professional is just one role. I have roles as a father, a son, a husband etc., all of which need to be fulfilled. Naturally I have aspirations for each of these roles

Lucien is deliberate about his "trade-up" leadership style

There are two types of leaders. The first are trade-down leaders. They are well-intentioned – they see themselves as working side-by-side with their people, helping them to solve their issues. However, they are actually taking over the first half of their direct reports' job. It leaves their direct reports with no choice other than to do the same to their direct reports. As a result, gravity pulls everyone down in the organisation and nobody grows. With trade-up leaders, direct reports do the first half of their bosses' jobs – in that way, everyone learns and grows. When the time comes for succession decisions, you've already seen people doing half of the role and the risk is lessened. However, you can only be a trade-up leader if you have a great team – there's nothing you can do to overcome having average people.

I haven't been in the office on a weekend for 30 years. I'll take the call if somebody calls me on a weekend, but it needs to be important. I want to be a good executive, but I also want to be a good husband and dad, and I think I have managed that by maintaining this discipline. Having a life outside of work has made me a better leader.

I'm very selective about where I spend my time. I tell people they will be remembered for doing three things in their role – therefore, think deeply about what you want those three things to be. Choose them carefully and then spend 80% of your time on them over a multi-year period. That is what I've tried to do in each role. Prioritisation also means making deliberate choices about what not to focus on, and I am comfortable with doing that. I make sure that these areas are in the hands of excellent people and I trust them. They only need to give me the briefest of updates unless something unusual happens.

Most of the time as a C-Suite leader, you're familiar with what's happening – you've seen it and done it before, and you have great teams to handle things. In reality, you earn your compensation on a few critical decisions, perhaps on as few as 10 days a year. On those 10 days, you really, really earn it. Those ten days a year make the difference. Make sure you are ready for them.

and these are interdependent. So, I visualised and planned for the entire me. For instance, as a father I wanted to give more stability to my children to finish their education in one location, so I decided not to be internationally mobile until I saw this phase through. This had implications for my role as a professional, but I was happy with the choices and the balance. Our biggest challenge is balancing our various roles we play in life. It's not work-life balance, I call it role-life balance.

One potential pitfall of having an unprioritised list of motives is that you might be tempted to improve too many things at once. This is risky, and I would advise addressing things only incrementally. Amanda Rajkumar experienced this when she moved to adidas as an Executive Board member responsible for People and Culture. It was a new role in a new industry with two new cultures (country and organisation) all at once. She felt

> You can't say no to adidas, it's such a great brand, so I took the opportunity readily as it elevated my career and, during covid, it was a way to get back from the U.S. to Europe. However, I did my entire interview process virtually, because of the pandemic. I should have done much more due diligence. I never visited the adidas campus and living previously in big cities like London and New York, I had a lot to adapt to. I also feel I could have done more research on the culture. Being on the Executive Board meant my role was strategic and far more advisory – a big change. No Excel pivot tables anymore! I had got used to being independent and autonomous in my execution, but in adidas, I had a small army to support me, which was new, and different and took some time to accept, unbelievably! The readjustment had to be quick going, from extremely lean HR teams in banking, to a large one with ample resources. It enabled a change of output but also, importantly, to upskill myself for strategic Board content and company decisions. This was a huge transition for me because, historically, I had been very hands-on. The adaptation and focus to coaching and strategic advisory with my Board members, and other senior leaders, was the biggest change. And, like all change, it was tough, but my experience, knowledge and capacity grew hugely and positively.

When advising executives on their career, I refer to this as your "four degrees of freedom" – role, industry, company, and country – and recommend changing only one at a time, or two at the very maximum, if you wish to mitigate your career risk. A wise HR friend of mine advised that if you are going to move within the same company, changing two degrees of freedom at once might stretch you a lot, but it can also provide the greatest learning opportunity.

The foundational attitude of Awareness is complex, very personal and hangs on multiple interdependencies. It is also an organic and dynamic attitude that will evolve as you grow as a leader and human being. Getting a good handle on it will be fundamental to steer your career effectively.

ARNAUD'S TAKE

My personal experience with activating Awareness, started with an MBTI[3] profile during my early years as an engineer, who painted me as ISTJ. I took it as gospel. However, I also grew increasingly frustrated with my role as an engineer, something I was allegedly good at but did not enjoy because of its high process orientation. One MBA later, I joined McKinsey & Company and, as a new consultant, I got to take the MBTI again. To my surprise, the results showed me to be **INTJ**. I scoffed at the idea, having convinced myself several years prior that I had a preference for S-Sensing (detail/process-orientated) rather than N-Intuition (pattern recognition). Thankfully, McKinsey gave us access to a coach, who helped me figure out that, indeed, I preferred Intuition – in fact very clearly.

That's when I first realised two critical things that would change my root cause perspective:

1 Understanding myself was perhaps not as easy as I thought and would require me to do some regular soul-searching.
2 When I did get to understand what drove me, I could become much better at putting myself in situations that would play to my strengths, or at least at avoiding situations that did not suit my natural style.

Being in strategy consulting was certainly much more fitting than being an engineer, but I was still missing one big piece. I did not know what my professional purpose should be.

Throughout my years as a management consultant, I found that I liked the intellectual challenge, but my work on large-scale organisational transformation with hard-to-define results left me quite indifferent. Moving to become a leadership advisor with a big-5 global executive search firm felt much more meaningful, and I found my "Why" along the way – *to help people think through the pattern in their lives in a more insightful way*.

However, I also realised that my professional context was not ideally suited to my motives. Through the help of a coach, I clarified that I was highly motivated by a high sense of autonomy and an ability to drive measurable results, and that I had no appetite for management responsibilities or political environments (and really no skill at dealing with those). This heightened Awareness led me eventually to join a smaller, much more entrepreneurial firm, which ticked pretty much all my motive boxes. These insights also led, eventually, to my ambition to write this book.

I dare say that, while I will leave it to others to judge whether my career has been successful, I feel it has been very satisfying, largely because of the Awareness I developed along the years.[4]

TOP TEN THRIVE-STARTERS TO ACTIVATE NEW AWARENESS HABITS

Here is a summary of the top Awareness habits that you can start building into your professional routine to lay the foundations for a more sustainable path

1. Search your soul and identify the North Star that will guide you through difficult career decisions.
2. Set your ambition but be ready to adjust it – balance boldness with realism.
3. Define and pursue the professional contexts that are most likely to favour you.
4. Monitor your current context actively – it might be changing faster than you realise.
5. Don't let your ego and your wallet lead you to the wrong career decisions.
6. When considering a new role, don't change too many degrees of freedom at once.
7. List out and prioritise the motives that truly get your professional juices flowing.

8 Don't let others dictate what is most important to you – you know yourself best.
9 Communicate clearly and proactively to others what are your must-have, or red lines.
10 If you think you can have it all, think harder.

NOTES

1 According to Larissa, he is "the world's most wonderful husband". Fun fact, many of the female CHRO interviewed for this book seem to have the world's best husband. Let's shape up gentlemen, there is some fierce competition for that job title!
2 See *Start With Why* (2009) by Simon Sinek and *Finding Your Why* (2017) by Simon Sinek et al.
3 Myers-Briggs Type Indicator.
4 However, please do not get too excited for me. While I believe I score high on the Awareness dimension, I clearly lack in at least one other Thriving Career practice, and possibly more.

Betting on Bravery
Three

> I pride myself on being someone who can get thrown into new situations and learn quickly. That's been my whole career.
>
> Allison Pinkham

Besides a high level of Awareness, building a Thriving Career requires actively seeking out new experiences to learn, grow, develop new capabilities, and gain confidence. This process, while intuitive, will require for you to proactively and consistently step out of your comfort zone. It requires Bravery and a strong learning mindset.

Some environments are purposefully designed for this. The top management consultancies, for example, are renowned for up-or-out cultures. Young consultants move relentlessly from project to project and are constantly under pressure to take on more responsibility. They are also expected to act swiftly on the feedback they constantly receive. Perhaps it is no coincidence that several of the leaders in our project started their career as management consultants, learning early to thrive in such demanding environments. When looking across CHRO careers, 87% of the leaders interviewed for this book's research demonstrated, unprompted, one or more of the career practices related to Bravery:

- Enjoy being comfortably uncomfortable
- Seek to learn from failures and feedback
- Have the courage of your convictions.

Through the interviews for this book, I was privileged to hear many enlightening and entertaining stories relating to Bravery, but one that stuck deeply with me is that of Jean-Sébastien Blanc's early career in a Peugeot factory in France. He recalled,

> When I went for my first job interview as a young HR job applicant, they asked me to come to the factory. We pushed the door,

DOI: 10.4324/9781003669005-3

and I was immediately assaulted by the heat, and the noise. It was both overwhelming and frightening. My rational brain then took over, and I realized that because it was frightening, it was attractive. It became a pattern in my career. Every time I've looked at something, and I thought it would be challenging, that I may not be capable enough, or would be afraid to fail, I would have to try it. I ended up joining Peugeot. A few years later, I was having coffee with colleagues when I heard about a new HR position helping to launch the end-to-end production of a new car model. For a factory, it is a hell of an event, and it takes a lot as HR from a social and human standpoint. I told my friends that sounded like the job from hell, even for someone very seasoned. Good luck to the person who gets it.

Jean-Sébastien thought that was the end of it … but not quite!

Guess what? That Friday, a boss three levels above me calls me in his office. He says, Jean-Sébastien, I want you to take that job. I was shocked. I uttered, thanks, I appreciate the trust but I'm not sure about it. Please give me a few days to think about it. He said, of course, take all the time you need, but you start on Monday. I took the weekend to think hard about it. If those senior people thought of me for this frightening challenge maybe I had a blind spot. I decided to play the game, and I started at 8 am that Monday morning. It was indeed a big project with a lot of challenges, but one year later, the new Peugeot 406 was successfully launched in time, cost, quality, and without any social unrest.

Things that make you grow will be painful, and I can relate to this as a long-distance endurance athlete. I have learned over the years that, if you train hard enough, you become essentially permanently mildly injured. The key to performance and sustained growth is to continue training through these mild injuries without tipping over into irrecoverable harm – somewhere between the comfort zone and the damage zone. Jean-Sébastien's learning journey as an HR executive, and also more fundamentally as a human being who develops an understanding of what drives him, illustrates well what distinguishes Thriving Career builders from the masses.

Let us peel the onion further and explore the three specific career practices that turn leaders who stand out in Bravery into Thriving Career builders.

BRAVERY PRACTICE #1 – ENJOY BEING COMFORTABLY UNCOMFORTABLE

In our increasingly complex world, there will be plenty of assignments that push you outside of your comfort zone, challenge you to develop new capabilities and help you grow as a leader. Brave career builders actively seek out such challenging assignments and embrace being comfortably uncomfortable.

Many of the CHROs I interviewed highlighted their willingness to "Say Yes" to challenging projects as foundational to their leadership and career development. They also highlighted that, with good learning agility, you can develop an ability to handle those tough situations. Frédéric Chardot put it well when he shared,

> We never put talented people in really difficult situations because we want them to be successful, but that is the wrong thinking. People with potential should get in the worst possible jobs because that's how they're going to learn and develop a thick skin.

Frédéric lived through this himself and described how he grew to be a stronger leader by working for a bad boss.

> I learned a lot from a tough assignment for a very difficult leader in the U.S. After four years under that boss, I knew you could do anything to me, and I would be OK. Later in my career, I worked for a visionary but very emotional leader. We had a weird relationship where we often argued and disagreed. He would always push back on me 'Forget it Frédéric, this is not a battle you will win!' My secret weapon was always to respond, 'You know what, I disagree with you, but you're the boss. You decide.' Then, I would leave the room to let him think about it. And, not always, but a fair share of the time, he would come back later and say, 'Well, I've been giving it some thought; maybe we could try your thing.' I had learned so much from my bad boss in the U.S. that it made my life easier for the rest of my career. What doesn't kill you makes you stronger, right?

Ranjay is always chasing butterflies

I used to have a quote printed and stuck on my table for many years that read: "Opportunity lies outside the comfort zone". I did it to remind myself that I should not get too comfortable and always keep learning. I should take up assignments outside my comfort zone, ones which make me nervous, even a bit scared. The prospect of taking on the assignment had to give me butterflies in the stomach, with productive adrenaline pumping through. Whenever I followed this mantra, it worked out well.

All instances when I was cajoled into taking up roles which I knew I could do (i.e., in my comfort zone) I did not ultimately enjoy it, as the learning curve was not steep enough. I was once offered a country HR role by a very senior HR leader – it was a big country functional lead role and a promotion to a VP-level job. I was due for a promotion, so it did make sense. However, I had done single-country operations before and knew I could do that job. It did not make me nervous, so I said no. I still remember his words, "If you want a VP-level promotion, this is the only job I have. You will have to wait for the next one and I cannot promise you when that would be". I had a lump in my throat as I said, "It is OK, I will wait". One year passed and I got a great multi-country assignment, which was one of the most enriching experiences for me. I did the right thing.

As a counterexample, a few years later, I was "influenced" to choose a promotion with a long title and in a key location working and networking with some very senior leaders bringing me into the limelight. In hindsight I did not learn enough and could have done better. People will argue my career went very well after that; however, I was not getting the best out of myself in that job. I had a long and fancy job title (meaning no clear boundaries of the role), and the job gave me some profile, but I could have been challenged and developed more.

Taking on challenging assignments will help you develop many new capabilities that will help you become a more effective leader as you grow your career. Challenging assignments

- Often present problems with no simple solution and require innovative thinking, quick decision-making, and the ability to handle ambiguity and uncertainty.
- May require you to work with teams and stakeholders over whom you do not have direct authority, and you will need to lead through influence and develop skills, such as persuasion, negotiation, and conflict resolution.
- Will teach you to manage risk effectively, make informed decisions with partial information, and adjust your strategy as circumstances evolve.

Developing these capabilities and delivering against the odds will enhance your emotional resilience and your confidence. It will also help establish your personal reputation as a reliable problem solver, which will serve you throughout your career – and give you entertaining stories to share with your grandchildren and nerdy book writers who are keen to learn about your career.

Making an uncomfortable move can take more subtle forms than big, hairy assignments. It can simply mean surrounding yourself with great minds who will challenge you daily. Several CHROs highlighted that they purposedly hired people in their team who were smarter than them. They did not see this as a threat but as an opportunity to learn. Charles Bendotti, for instance, shared,

> I always took a number two next to me who was much more knowledgeable than I was. When I moved to a new role, I also made a point not to bring them along and I got someone new because I always wanted to learn more. I needed more brains than one.

Taking risks can also mean having the courage to take a break from your career when circumstances require it, to balance your priorities. Prerana Issar experienced this and described her proactive mindset about such moves:

> In the early part of my career, I was full of confidence. If things didn't work out, I was sure I could get something else. Later, as you get

Tanuj takes a painful risk that pays off

After a successful stint in India at HSBC, I got a call from the Group HR director saying I needed to come and work in the Group headquarters. She gave me two options. I could become the HR Head for a large business division, or I could become the Group Head of Learning and Development (L&D). When I picked the latter, she was shocked. In banking, the HR Head of a business unit is typically the "sexy job". That was THE job in HSBC then, and the role our CHRO did before she got promoted to the top role. However, I had thought a lot about it, and while it was the bigger and sexier job on paper, I had been an HRBP for three years already and I would be deploying a very similar skill set in a business I knew well. On the other hand, the L&D role was a pure transformation job, with 15+ learning management systems to be integrated into one. We had to think very strategically about how the skills agenda linked to growth. I knew I would enjoy it less, but I saw it as a big investment for my career.

In hindsight it was absolutely the best decision, but I must say, I did not enjoy that job initially. I was sitting in Head Office and frankly, you don't interact with the business as much. However, it was a very big tech and content transformation role that set me up well with everything I've done later, including the end-to-end bank transformation I'm currently looking after. The learning was phenomenal, even though there were days I thought, why am I doing this to myself? I had to remind myself that I took the job because I knew it was outside of my comfort zone, and it was an investment I needed to make to fill a gap.

older, obviously, more constraints will come to you. For example, when my husband left his job to pursue an MBA at INSEAD in Europe, I left Unilever India to join him (we have always taken turns with being 'lead career'). Unilever were great and offered me a sabbatical. However, I thought a sabbatical would feel like there was a safety net, and I wouldn't allow myself to truly think about my options, so I simply resigned. People told me, my God, you have such a good job and a one-year-old child; it's so risky, why are you doing this? Some people were envious and said they wished they could do it. I said you can do it too. The constraints about what is possible are in our mind.

Prerana and her family had an amazing time in Fontainebleau. Eventually, through former colleagues and having left with a good reputation, she rejoined Unilever in the United Kingdom 18 months later.

While many stories of challenging assignments have a happy ending, taking a career risk may not always pay off, which should be expected. The key is to take any failure as life's feedback and a learning opportunity.

BRAVERY PRACTICE #2 – SEEK TO LEARN FROM FEEDBACK AND FAILURES

Few of us have the perspective to introspect in real-time or the luxury of going on reflection-orientated retreats. Yet, learning is a fundamental growth mindset, and nearly every CHRO I spoke with highlighted that it has been a driving force in their development and careers. Brave career builders must develop a knack for being mindfully present and processing learning just-in-time, including when receiving feedback. They thrive on that feedback and receive it as a gift that helps them grow further.

Lucien Alziari recalls a particularly memorable time in his early days at PepsiCo when he was asked for breakfast by the chief HR officer of the international division and got a serious beating.

> He was at least six grades up from me in the organization, so it was like meeting a demi-god. He was very, very direct. I felt like I was in a scene from the movie Goodfellas. He told me, 'Lucien, you're talented, but you try to do everything yourself, you don't access the resources around you, and people don't know what you're working on.

If you continue this way, you are going to fail'. He pulled no punches to make sure I really got the message. It was a tough experience. However, as I reflected on it later, I came to see it in a different light: he didn't have to meet me but chose to invest the time. He clearly thought the only way to get through to me was to be brutally honest, and he was probably right! Well, I got the message – I adapted my approach and ended up having a good career with the company.
At that time, PepsiCo was a school of tough love and this extreme version of it was not one I ever wanted to experience again.
I'm sure If you ask people who have worked for me over the years, they'll probably mention tough love – hopefully not as extreme as I experienced, but it was the school I grew up in.

It is interesting to note that while this tough and direct feedback not only had a profound impact on Lucien but also shaped his own coaching style for decades to come. What goes around comes around.

When you receive feedback, it is important to take a step back and decide which elements will help you grow and which may just be counterproductive. Usha Kakaria-Cayaux put it well when she shared, "You need to learn how to take feedback, know which parts will help you and which parts you can discard. But to do this, you've got to be grounded in who you are; you need to know yourself". The synergy between Bravery and Awareness will give you that growth.

Taking risks in your career will occasionally lead to failures, and that is OK. Many CHROs openly shared setback stories and how they were able to learn and move on to greater things. Raymond Co probably summarised it best by sharing, "I screwed up a lot in my early career, but I think my contributions were way ahead of my screw-ups" and showing us that it is critical to keep a positive momentum. Farnaz Ranjbar was equally direct and open about the flipside of having a relentless, risk-taking attitude. She learned from an early childhood that the most important thing is to keep your spirits up through disappointments, draw your lessons and move on. She confided,

> I never regretted anything I have done in my life. If I do something, I go full-hearted into it, I take the consequences, and I learn from them. Whether you succeed or fail, it's about what you learn and you learn the most when you fail. One thing I learned from my early years

Usha needs to learn Chinese

In one of my first jobs, I remember being called to the big boss' office, and he told me, "I hope you know you don't always have to be the smartest person in the room, right?"

I must have given him a funny look because he continued, "Even if you ARE the smartest person in the room. With more senior leaders, sometimes you must recognise wisdom and not prove yourself by being the fastest to respond. Even if you know the answer, wait". In my mind, I thought, oh geez, office politics and needing to conform, that is why I never wanted to work for a big company. Upon reflection, I realised his point was about listening, seeking to understand before you speak, so I agreed I would work on this. He pushed me to commit "what will you do differently?" My response, "I'm not going to be the first to speak". "How are you going to make sure you do that?", he asked. I told him I was going to count to 10 backward. He looked at me and added, "In Chinese". When I said I don't speak Chinese, he told me that's precisely the point!

From that experience, I learned that you need to constantly monitor your environment, calibrate, and be intentional. I know I am a high-energy person, I'm highly motivated, and I drive for outcomes stemming from my upbringing and playing competitive sport. Context matters. If you are in an unfamiliar environment, or people don't know you, you can come across as intimidating or arrogant. If a senior leader, or anyone, thinks that, then it is your responsibility to change it.

I am many things, but I have never felt superior. I am certainly confident and self-aware, which I think you need to be successful, and I always took feedback to heart, probably too much in the beginning. I was tough on myself. I would go back and write it down, think about it, and analyse it, even if I didn't like it and it felt hurtful or a personal attack. I asked myself; how can anyone think that about me? What am I going to do? When I realised it was not personal and I did not need to change who I am, I decided to help people understand me and my story.

in Iran during an 8-year war, when I spent many a night in shelters studying in candlelight, was that if you wake up in the morning and you're alive then that is already a miracle! That's how I deal with the challenges I face at work and in life in general. Face challenges headfirst and be positive about it. It could always be worse.

This highlights that the key is not just to be taking career risks but to do that in a mindful way and with a positive spirit.

To constructively manage any personal setback, one great tip shared by Leanne Wood is to separate the situation from the person. A failure does not mean you are not good; it may just mean this was not the right challenge for you. As she put it

> I don't have regrets for my career because the most difficult experiences are the ones where I learned the most. I know that is a cliché, but it helped me build my resilience and gave me an appreciation for what some people may go through. I learned that you could have somebody great, but things still don't go right. It doesn't mean they are not good. Nobody's ever as good as people rave about, and nobody's ever as bad as people say. Failure and learning go hand in hand.

Keeping this wise perspective, not only for yourself but when evaluating colleagues, can be a tremendous asset to increase your willingness and ability to take on unfamiliar challenges.

This ability to keep things in perspective and to remain forward-looking when things don't go your way is crucial. It is particularly important for HR professionals, who often must balance the conflicting priorities of a complex role with multiple stakeholders.

BRAVERY PRACTICE #3 – HAVE THE COURAGE OF YOUR CONVICTIONS

HR leaders often live in a professional grey zone, performing a juggling act requiring a backbone of strong values. To be clear, this is not a moral or legal grey area, but the need to manage the constructive tension between what the business needs and the people want.

On one hand, HR leaders need to defend the company's interest and implement consistent policies and processes, which sometimes involves making tough decisions such as leading redundancy programmes. On the other hand, they must champion employees' needs, advocate for them, and create a positive and inspirational culture. In most instances, HR leaders must do these two things concurrently, which is a demanding balancing act. Ranjay Radhakrishnan used flowery language and smiled when he shared that

> HR is for cacti, not orchids. One of the things I love about HR is that you need real strength of character to sustainably succeed in this profession. You are tested everyday as you manage paradoxes, juggle facts you know with feelings you have, and constantly being sought to provide a nuanced point of view on delicate matters. It is difficult to succeed in a function where everyone thinks they know what to do, but nobody wants to do what the function does.

He validates the popular saying that HR is one of the hardest jobs that looks easy.

Geoff Lloyd also put it well when he described this as the Yin & Yang of HR, which is a balance he looks for in people.

> You have got to be courageous, and you have got to be empathetic. You must be courageous because you must do things other people don't want to do. You must speak truth to power, sometimes to people several layers higher than you. You often also deal with people who are in a bad situation, so you must be courageous. However, too much courage can turn you into a bully, where you are pushing people around and not listening. Therefore, you need the other side, which is empathy. You must be able to put yourself in the shoes of others. When someone loses their job, that's someone's daughter or son, husband or wife, father or mother. If I forget that, I can't do my job properly. When I see people who don't understand this, I don't want them in my team or business. I don't care how good they are at everything else; I want them gone. That is the balance HR people must strike. You must appreciate people, and you must have courage. Personally, I am probably not as empathetic as I should be sometimes, so I like to have people around who can remind me of that.

Once again, we see Awareness popping its beautiful head to make Bravery most effective.

Good HR leaders do not give up in the face of adversity, and they are not afraid to draw the line when their values may be compromised. They are thoughtful in determining when it is OK to "let it slide" and when it is necessary to take a stand, often using personal values as a guiding light. Part of this may be driven by your personal style. Mario Ceccon summarised it as, "I am brave, but I prefer to avoid conflicts if possible. I have no problem in taking very strong decisions that may have big consequences, but I will do it the softest way possible to keep things human". His experience is illustrative of some of the moral conflicts HR leaders must strive to address and still be able to sleep at night.

Philip Read shared a concrete example of walking that tightrope between the company's and the employee's interests and how this shaped the view of his role as an HR leader.

> At one point in my career, I had to lead a significant downsizing of a large manufacturing operation. The downsizing was unfortunately necessary, and the only way to achieve this in the time needed, was for myself and each of my team, to have exit discussions with 32 people per day, 15 minutes each, for many weeks. Some of the stories I heard in those weeks were devastating – what the impact would be on them, on their family, what they thought the company had promised them. It taught me that one of the most important things we do as leaders is to be very careful with promises, explicit or implied. For example, I never tell people that our company is 'like a family', because you don't line up your family and fire them. What I tell them is that a company is an economic entity; it is an economic entity with a purpose, a place where you can make great friends, where you are hopefully engaged. But never forget the economic reality that underlies it all.

Avoiding over-promising and learning to keep other leaders from enthusiastically committing to things they are not prepared to live up to will help build your reputation as a centred leader who will stand up for what they believe in.

When it comes to strong convictions, it is worth pointing out that several female CHROs highlighted they would resent any career advancement based on gender. They would rather not be promoted than be promoted on diversity grounds. One female CHRO, among several others, put it very clearly.

> When I got selected for an internal promotion to global CHRO, I asked my Chair if it was because I wore a skirt, and our company did not

Archana won't take no for an answer

After a few years in my career working for a local consulting firm in India, I wanted to do hands-on work in a company. I had worked on a project for a reputed multinational and wrote to the India CHRO. I got to speak to him, and he was happy for me to be considered to join, so he passed my application on to the recruitment head. From there, I didn't hear anything. I kept calling and calling until one day, he finally answered. I reminded him of the background, and his response was: "you know, it's OK for our CHRO to say you could join, but you're a woman. You will get married; you will have children, then you'll say you don't want to move out of Mumbai. Our jobs are all over India, so I am sorry, but I don't think this will work". I felt very offended. Not giving up, I wrote a nice letter to the CHRO saying that I have great regard for the organisation, and I would still love to join, but I find it very difficult to accept that I will not even be considered for the opportunity because I am a woman. I am perfectly fine if you tell me I'm not suitable or I don't have the capability, but I will not accept this answer. Sure enough, the day the CHRO received the letter, I got a call from the recruitment head ... and everything went smoothly after that!

I realised quite early in my career that I have much courage and conviction. I will stand up and speak out; I'm not concerned about hierarchy. I think it's one of the things that really helped me in my career. You need to come from a place of deep conviction because a lot of the CEOs and heads of business don't really understand or care about the HR stuff, they care about the business outcomes, so if you have conviction, it's much easier to make things happen. Good leaders can always be persuaded by data, facts, and best practices, but it must start with personal conviction.

have any female leaders at that level. She said, 'no, it's because you are very sensitive to human perspectives, and we are short of this skill within the executive team. I agreed with my Chair that I think many ladies would prefer to be appointed through meritocracy, not because we wear skirts. She and I are aligned on ideas like this. I personally don't believe in hard targets for gender diversity.

In a reverse, but equally telling, example, Mayuko Seto had a similar experience that led her to resign from a company.

In the middle of my career, I worked in Japan for a non-Japanese company. One day, they offered me to take on a job at HQ overseas. I know my performance was rated highly by my local CEO and the regional HR head, and they wanted to help advance my career, however I saw that people at HQ wanted me mostly for diversity reasons. I felt disappointed because I liked and respected the local leaders, but I did not share the values of HQ. I realized this was not a company where I would like to build my career further. Instead of taking the promotion, I turned in my resignation.

This shows the dark underbelly of some diversity initiatives which, while well-intended, can end up alienating people. Brave career-builders will look beyond these and stand for what they believe is the right thing to do.

By extension, it might run contrary to the widespread wisdom that "managing politics" is the way to get ahead. Leaders will gain respect within their organisation, and beyond, by showing Bravery and standing up for what they believe in. Laura Garza experienced this when she joined a U.S. company with strong internal networks that she struggled to break into. She shared,

I never tried to position myself to gain influence. I just wanted to deliver something valuable. I listened and I tried to cater what they need, in a very customer-oriented way, so people got to know I did not have a political agenda.

Speak truth to power, in a respectful way, and your reputation and confidence will grow tremendously. A strong values backbone and a reputation for integrity will strengthen your relationships, allowing you to turn that Bravery into a great career-building asset.

ARNAUD'S TAKE

As a guide through this dimension, it might help to describe what Bravery is *not*. I routinely have candidates tell me that they "not interested in a role that is business-as-usual" or that they "love challenges", want to "drive some change" or "make a big impact". To be clear, these are not signs of Bravery. Everyone says this. Congratulations, you are simply a normal person. Case in point: I never had a candidate who told me they "like things that are routine" or that they "prefer to avoid challenges", "dislike change" or would rather "not rock the boat". It simply does not happen because (1) people are generally not like this and (2) even if they were, they would not admit it.

If you want to stand out on Bravery, in your current company or when trying to impress a recruiter, you need to get concrete with practical examples of challenges you have tackled which, not only you thought were brave, but others did as well. For example, did you raise your hand for an assignment that everyone else declined? Did you agree to work for a boss who had a terrible reputation? Did you persist on a project that everyone else thought was impossible to complete? In short, if your Bravery benchmark is simply based on your own perception, you might be missing something.[1]

One final thought on Bravery is that the optimum time to build it will be the first part of your career. This is when you stand to gain the most from new experiences and when a failure may be more quickly forgotten. It may also be a time when it is easier to adjust to changing circumstances, professionally and personally. I was reminded of this during my time at McKinsey, which has a deeply engrained feedback culture. As I had decided to leave the Firm, a Senior Partner gave me some advice for my next role and said

> In McKinsey we work very hard to help you 'close your gaps'. We measure performance closely and we give you incessant feedback, whether you like it or not. We just want to see if you will survive, but, actually, your objective should be to thrive. To do that, you should instead aim to 'play to your strengths'. This is how people are most successful over the long run.

I never forgot that advice and, as my own career developed, I have tried to always keep it in mind. Put yourself in circumstances where your strengths will shine, particularly in your early to mid-career, and your Bravery will be handsomely rewarded.

TOP TEN THRIVE-STARTERS TO BET ON NEW BRAVERY HABITS

Here is a summary of some Bravery habits to keep in mind as you start to play the career long game more strategically:

1. Seek out challenging assignments that everyone else is shunning, and enjoy proving them wrong.
2. Surround yourself with people who are smarter than you, and get out of their way.
3. When a clear growth opportunity is presented to you, just say yes and figure out the rest later.
4. Keep in mind that roles outside your comfort zone are an investment in your future.
5. Fail often so you know where the limits are.
6. Remember that the longer a job title, the less the role is likely to have actual impact.
7. Take feedback like a pro, but discard it if it is not helping you grow.
8. When it comes to your values, adapt but never abdicate.
9. Always speak truth to power and keep your bosses honest.
10. Never accept a job given to you because you are a diverse candidate.

NOTE

1. For more on this, feel free to look up the cognitive bias known as the Dunning-Kruger effect.

Cultivating Connectivity

Four

> The incidental mentor is incredibly valuable, in any career.
>
> Tamsin Vine

Many people instinctively know that networking will be important for their careers but often don't have a clear view about how to go about it beyond "more is better than less". In fact, the opposite is true. The Thriving Career building approach is getting people to care to help you, not simply getting them to know you. Connectivity, not networking, is what will make a difference for you. Quality, not quantity.

I got to experience this many years ago in my first few weeks as a new executive search consultant. Eager to network with industry leaders as quickly as possible, I asked my boss to sponsor me to attend an industry conference for a few days. She strongly discouraged me, declaring those events a waste of time (unless you are a featured speaker). I persisted, as young people do, so she let me go. I spent three days there, met as many people as I could, collected hundreds of business cards, sent dozens of thoughtful follow-up emails, and met many of those people again over the following weeks. Absolutely nothing useful came out of it. The following year, that conference came up once more, and my boss asked me whether I wanted to go. I sheepishly told her thanks, but no thanks. I had decided that, from then on, I would always go for quality, not quantity.

Connective CHROs consistently confirmed that the quality of a few targeted relationships, more than the breadth of their network, was a big driver of their career success. Seventy-six percent of the leaders interviewed for this book's research showed, unprompted, career practices related to Connectivity:

- Appreciate unfamiliar cultures
- Cultivate meaningful mentors
- Nurture a positive people ecosystem

DOI: 10.4324/9781003669005-4

One theme that came across repeatedly in my CHRO conversations is that building strong internal relationships is much more important for career-building than external networking. In today's age of flexible working, video meetings, and social media frenzy, let us not forget that nothing replaces the human element in creating true Connectivity.

Hugo Martinho experienced this during his career at Schindler, eventually reaching the top HR role. He explained

> One of the best things we can do to our careers is to get under the leadership of very impactful people. I had that chance early on in Portugal, and it continued through my career. For example, I briefly encountered a Schindler colleague in an IMD[1] training, and I immediately felt he was a special leader. I thought that he could make a difference, and I could learn from him, so I tried to get close to him. Later, I worked for him for six years, directly reporting to him. Over the years, he made it all the way to the executive committee, and eventually, he became Group CEO and then Chairman of the company. You should have an instinct about where to bet, and this was certainly a good bet for me. It changed my career and my life. Of course, you must perform but you also need to have these door openers, people who are willing to give you a chance, the benefit of the doubt. It is critical to have a strong internal network if you want to progress within a company. This is why social connectivity is so important. That may be an issue for the younger generations, and the not-so-young, spending so much time on our phones and social media without truly interacting. The power of physical and emotional connectivity makes a huge difference. You can smell someone a bit, assess if this person will make a difference, if they are special. You should also assess if it is someone you would like to work with, someone who will respect you, who will teach you. That can only come through close interactions.

If you ever meet Hugo, you will know that he is a warm leader who meaningfully practices what he preaches. Let us explore what we can learn from leaders like him about how to practice great Connectivity to enrich our careers.

CONNECTIVITY PRACTICE #1 – APPRECIATE UNFAMILIAR CULTURES

Good career builders are able and eager to build bridges across cultures. As I have personally lived and worked in six countries across three continents, I know that getting experience in cross-cultural environments will set the stage for many more career opportunities globally.

Developing cross-cultural agility will improve your leadership profile, and Ingolf Thom recalls living through this. He shared,

> It makes a big difference when you work and live in a new place where everything is different from where you were born and raised. You must make sense of life and figure out ways for how to succeed and be happy there. It shaped me as a professional, but I also found it enormously rewarding personally. The idea of living and leading in India, the Far East, or the Midwest can be uncomfortable for some people, and that's OK – not everybody needs to have that kind of life, but I found it gave me many life-changing experiences. During my career, at times I've seen colleagues taking what felt like the easier of two offered opportunities. My experience has taught me, however, that if you want to grow, you better take the tough job.

I would argue that leaders who have never lived and worked outside of their home country have a major blind spot. Worse, they are likely to develop an undue level of confidence from a fly-in-fly-out approach. They may develop a warm feeling that they have seen and understood other countries by spending a few days there, mostly secluded in business meetings, fancy dinners, and the occasional local outing for the obligatory LinkedIn selfie. Darrell Ford, an American CHRO, also realised this halfway through his career:

> I was working for Honeywell, and I had global HR responsibility, but I had never lived outside the U.S. I was asking myself, am I really a global leader if I've always done it from Phoenix or Morristown, New Jersey? For me, the answer was no.

Darrell joined Shell U.S. with an explicit understanding that his next move would be abroad. After a successful assignment stateside, he moved to London, leading Shell Retail, then Lubricants HR globally for his first international role. Fast forward to today: he has added four global CHRO roles and a non-executive director role to his already impressive career – made possible in part by gaining that international experience.

Mindful HR leaders will welcome the opportunity to spend time not just living in a different country but immersing themselves in

Rob gets a passport, and much more

Before I went to work for Corning, I had never been outside the United States, and did not even have a passport. As a kid, we didn't grow up with much money. There were no European summer vacations and fancy skiing in wonderful places. In my first three years with Corning, I did get to China once for a few days to integrate a small acquisition. Hence, I got my first passport, but that was the extent of my international experience at that time. After three years of tough restructuring work, my boss told me, "I know you came here because you wanted to be a part of a growth story and you wanted to do something exciting, so we would like you to move to Asia and help start a new global LCD glass business there for us. We have no one there with your level of experience, will you go?" As I mentioned, the extent of my Asia experience was a three-day jetlagged trip to Shanghai a couple of years prior, and now they asked me to choose between Tokyo and Taipei to move my family to! I remember asking a colleague who knew Asia, which one I should choose. He told me I should go to Japan, so I trusted his opinion. My wife and I packed our bags and our three young kids – we added a fourth a year later – and moved to Tokyo.

We ended up staying in Asia for 12 years, and we loved it. While I was there, I started to learn Japanese to better understand the culture, and to this day, I still do a couple of hours of Japanese every Sunday. Along the way, I also got posted in Taiwan and picked up some Mandarin. Once I returned to the United States after 12 years, I found it easy to pick up Spanish since we have operations in Mexico, and our Mexican employees are such warm and wonderful people, so I studied Spanish too.

I've always been a curious person. If you ask my mother, she will say I was always tearing something apart, getting into places I probably shouldn't. I was a curious kid, and I am a curious adult. When we took the assignment in Asia with Corning, we decided as a family that it would be about more than the job. We wanted the whole experience of being in a different culture and learning about different people. You let it influence you, and at the same time, you influence it. For me, language was a big part of that. It also keeps you humble because you make many mistakes, but it's all a part of the experience of growing as a person.

the culture to drive their own learning. One leader who learned that getting an early international experience can have a profound impact is Allison Pinkham. She is one of the very few American CHROs of a European company. She shared,

> Moving to Switzerland during my university studies was a complete game changer for me. It was the first time I had lived outside the U.S. and made me realize how my perception of 'reality' was based on only one view of how the world worked. My mind was like a sponge while living abroad. I was blown away by how different societies, governments, and cultures worked.

Living in this new reality, Allison underwent an unexpected change in root perspective.

> I realized that what I thought was 'normal' in the U.S. was only a U.S. view and that normal is simply a perception we have based on our experiences and how societies work. I knew different countries lived and operated differently, however living it and embracing different views of cultural norms, and ways of looking at life, was truly eye-opening. Living abroad made me feel alive because every sense of sight, taste, sound was activated each day through different foods, language, social norms, government protocols, education systems, and even architecture. It created an open mindset in me beyond anything I had before – quite simply because I didn't have the experience. I experienced so much growth and learning during that time that I kept wanting to put myself more into those opportunities.

Allison greatly benefitted from having that experience early in her life, and that is a clear pattern: the earlier you can go live abroad, the more open-minded you will become.

The CHROs I spoke with often aimed to get fully immersed in local cultures when taking on an international assignment. Rather than staying within an expat circle, they would most often want to live like locals, to understand them better. Helio Fujita is a great example of this attitude, sharing,

> In our first expatriation, when my family moved from Brazil to Belgium, we decided to try to live like Belgians. We did not want to reproduce our life back home by getting into the Brazilian community,

Kerstin learns to love another culture

A few years into my career, I got an offer to join OMV in Austria, and I thought I was going to work from the headquarters in Vienna, so I was very excited. However, the hiring manager said I must go to Romania. My initial reaction was, I really don't want to go there. I then reflected and asked myself why wouldn't I go? I realised I was prejudiced against going to Romania, but I didn't even know the country; I had never been there. I thought, let's try not to be biased, explore it, and see how it goes. One of my bosses would be a Hungarian with a tough reputation. People warned me on the way to the interview. If your interview lasts five minutes, it's not good but if he gives you 10 minutes, well done. I thought they must be kidding, so I went in there and spent 10 minutes with him. I asked him what his expectations of me would be, if I joined. He said, "Kerstin, I want you to die for me every day". When you're young, you don't take it so seriously, I just found it funny. Later, I realised what he meant. He meant relentless dedication to the job, and he was a role model himself in that. I also met my future team, who were lovely, like all Romanians. So, I thought, let's try!

I moved to Romania, and what followed were the two and a half toughest years of my professional life. It was overwhelming and extremely hard work. Thank God I had no other commitments at that time; nobody required me to focus on anything other than my work. The first year was extremely tough and brought me to my personal limits, but you learn to deal with it while you keep going. The second year got better and by the third year I felt settled and had made friends. When the company asked me to go back to Austria for a promotion, I really did not want to leave Romania from an emotional perspective, but I loved the company, and they needed me at HQ, so I accepted a return to Austria.

which would have been very easy. We applied this attitude each time we moved, trying to see through the lens of the local people as much as we could. From that first international assignment in Belgium, I learned that you need to have cultural sensitivity, and if you treat human beings as human beings, things will work out. There are certain things like respect, honesty, and some basic human needs that are the same no matter what culture you operate in. It might appear differently with different rituals, but the essence is the same.

Once again, this intentionally open-minded attitude is often a function of how early in your life you move abroad. So don't delay going after that first international assignment.

Another way to think about cultural agility is simply to work with companies that have different cultural contexts. For example, working in a large publicly listed multinational can be very different from working in a family-led business or a nimble start-up. Each of those environments will require you to adapt and flex your cultural muscle.

After spending their career in large public multinationals, one CHRO experienced working in a private equity-led business and had quite a lot to adapt to. They explained

> I have only worked for one private equity firm, so I only have one experience in that world, but I have spoken to many of my CHRO peers in the private equity world. They are usually amazed when I tell them about the things I have been able to influence and get approval for with our owner when it comes to the organization and the people. There are a few reasons I was able to get the support I have – I built credibility and only asked for things that could advance the broader turnaround goals. I was also able to self-fund much of what I needed. I realized that our PE owner is one of the gentler and kinder private equity firms but, to be very clear, they are neither gentle nor kind. It's the 'best house in the worst neighbourhood' if I can put it that way.

Exposing yourself to varied cultural contexts as early as possible in your career will help shape your attitude towards different ways of thinking, which will broaden your horizons. This, in turn, will help drive your ability to create much deeper personal relationships, which will serve you well as you build your career.

CONNECTIVITY PRACTICE #2 – CULTIVATE MEANINGFUL MENTORS

No one succeeds alone, and many CHROs highlighted the key role mentors played in helping build their careers. They are individuals whom you feel close enough to be very open with and who, in turn, care enough about you to give you their unvarnished opinion. John Holding,♦ who benefitted from mentorship and still makes a point to mentor younger leaders, put it very well when he explained,

> There is real value in finding a sponsor or a mentor; someone who's able to provide you with guidance over a long period. Get on the coattails of somebody early on and use them as much as you can. If you can do that with two or three people in senior roles, that's a good way to get set up. Connect with people who are invested in your growth and development and hang on to them, ask them lots of questions, and build a relationship with them. Aim to have both HR mentors and business mentors because the senior HR person is going to help you build your functional expertise, but the business leader is best placed to be your advocate and help you land the job you want.

In that description, John touches on a few critical points that will distinguish someone who can help you get over the next hurdle from someone who can help you over an entire career. When evaluating potential mentors, you should look beyond how senior they are and assess whether they have a career path that you'd wish to emulate, experiences that you'd like to learn from, and, of course, whether you might have personal chemistry. You should also be clear about whether you are looking for that special type of stakeholder, the Sponsor, who is someone who may give you direct access to opportunities, as John alluded to. We will talk more about the Sponsor role in Chapter 8.

For maximum effectiveness, it is best to have multiple mentors. A few CHROs mentioned being very closely associated with a single internal mentor/sponsor, which worked out great for a while but left our leaders quite isolated once that senior person left the organisation. Instead, Ranjay Radhakrishnan highlighted the useful practice of creating a wisdom council that you can tap into for help and advice:

> When you start your career you are not too wise, but you are soon required to make wise decisions. One thing that helped me was to outsource wisdom (i.e., rely on external sources of wisdom). I have

Usha builds her personal Board of Directors

I believe in creating your own Board of Directors (BoD). Someone coined this term for me way back and I loved the idea. I have people on my BoD who have been there for over 10 years, and some are my go-to mentors. They are all different and I intentionally picked people who will be super honest with me and give me a different perspective, as having only one mentor can become too lopsided offering limited perspective. One is a very well-connected former CHRO I got to know when I interviewed for a job in his team. I did not work for him, but we stayed in contact. He offers a different perspective, feedback, and things to think about. Others include my best friend and former colleagues from across HR, supply chain and general management, some still working, others retired. The other person who has been a fantastic mentor throughout my career is my dad. He has always been really interested in what I am working on, he is a fantastic listener, and despite being his daughter, he can be objective and always asks me the difficult questions.

Your personal BoD needs to have people who have seen you evolve, are familiar with what you want to achieve, and know your challenges. Find people who will be in your corner and still push you. When you go to them with choices, such as "I got this job offer; what should I do?", they should advise you on where the option might take you, not on the decision itself. I call on these different people depending on where my mind chatters. Sometimes, I want to bounce an idea off them or gain an outside perspective as I'm sitting entrenched in my day job, but sometimes, I just want to talk because I know they're going to inspire me. It is so important to have people you get energy from and I know some people will charge my battery. When things get hard, you may not discuss all your sorrows because you are a professional, or it might be confidential, but you know if you just have a 30-minute conversation with them, you will hang up and feel energised. I am grateful to have those people in my life and in turn I strive to pay this forward to others.

always had a 'wisdom council' – a network of advisors who guided me. My father who himself had a corporate career was my first natural advisor. There was nothing formal about this; it first started unconsciously, and I then consciously cultivated it over time. I have constantly renewed my wisdom council, as I evolved and changed. For example, when I started to work in the hotel industry, I had a high potential finance manager reverse mentor me about understanding financial metrics peculiar to that industry. In my current role I have a Gen Z reverse mentor. I found that my council of advisors go beyond professional aspects into personal aspects (e.g., nutrition, physical well-being, even spiritual matters). I had the great benefit in having a cherished wisdom council not just for shaping my professional development but for life.

When it comes to Connectivity, depth will always be better than breadth. Cultivating meaningful mentors rarely happens through broad networking but through shared experience. Geoff Lloyd gave us a great reminder on this, highlighting that

Networking is a waste of time. Going to cocktail parties and spending 10 minutes with someone will get you nowhere. It's a free drink but a wasted hour of your life. You need to find people who will be advocates for you, people you've worked with.

As an introvert, I absolutely relate to this and dread cocktail parties, networking sessions, and industry conferences. They feel awkward to me and, most importantly, they are largely useless as career-building interventions. Don't think of collecting business cards, think of collecting professional soulmates. Muzzamil Khider held similar views and reflected that official mentorship programmes did not quite work for him. "I never had a formal mentor but, when I think back, I had lots of mentors. I was very curious and always went to people to ask for advice and ask on how they manage".

As a parting thought on this topic, it might be useful to point out that very few of the CHROs I interviewed mentioned having a head-hunter friend as making a meaningful difference to their career. To be sure, it is perfectly fine to include head-hunters in your reach-out efforts when you are actively looking for a new role, but your relationship with them will always be transactional by nature. As an HR leader, you will probably never be much more to them than a potential future fee-generating client.[2]

Most CHROs highlighted that, instead, personal relationships had the biggest impact on their career. For example, Tatsuo Kinoshita pointed out that he has many head-hunter contacts, but nothing much ever came out of it. He confided,

> I would use them in my HR job and sometimes they would call me for external roles but, when I look back, every job I found was through personal contacts, friends, and ex-colleagues. I sense that, because my friends understand me well, they can be more creative in thinking of wider possibilities for my career. They understand my interests and my experience better than a recruiter can. For instance, I got my current job as CHRO of Panasonic after an ex-colleague sent me a Facebook message asking out of the blue if I would be open to a new role.

Frédéric Chardot drove it home by pointing out that he does not often get called by head-hunters

> because I'm not spending much time with them. I don't know if it is right or wrong; if I had spent more time with recruiters, maybe I would have got a big HR role earlier, but that is not me. I'm just focused on getting my job done and learning new things.

Focusing on quality versus quantity and depth versus breadth will be key to developing meaningful mentors. However, beyond this close set of personal advisors, Thriving Career builders also think about developing purposeful relationships throughout the entire ecosystem they operate in.

CONNECTIVITY PRACTICE #3 – NURTURE A POSITIVE PEOPLE ECOSYSTEM

Savvy executives know well that making your boss happy is not enough to get ahead. On the contrary, as we discussed earlier, they have no issue speaking truth to power and working across the organisation to create connections. Thriving Career builders do not think of career management as a vertical exercise but as an ecosystem of relationships, both within and outside of their organisation, to be created and nurtured. This approach, compounded over years of practice, creates a foundational asset for any career.

After an illustrious HR career of nearly 40 years and three separate CHRO roles in the United States and Europe, Lucien Alziari reflected on this with the wisdom of great experience:

> I recently counted over 25 CHROs of big public companies that have worked for me over the years. It is clear they are in their job because of who they are, but it is still nice to see because my passion has always been to develop world-class HR people. In each of my CHRO roles the HR team was very different by the time we finished. Over time, you develop a playbook on how to do that, and it creates such a positive cycle. You are surrounding yourself with great people, watching them grow and succeed, it's fantastic. I locked in on this as my purpose in life early on – to help show people the way. It has been my through-line, but I have never mistaken that for a popularity contest or being the world's most liked person. I will just help people get much better than they are, even if sometimes that means showing some tough love. And if they're not going to be good enough where they are currently, let me help find them a place where they can be an A-player rather than the C-player.

One of the simplest and most direct ways you can start developing a network of meaningful relationships is to work actively on your own succession in a way that will make people feel valued. Athalie Williams shared that is something she is most proud of, after she spent over 15 years in BHP, including seven as Group CHRO.

> One of my proudest moments as CHRO was to be able to give my CEO three internal successors to choose from for my role. He chose one of them and the other two are now in CHRO roles in other organizations. I loved seeing people who worked with me go on and do amazing things.

The beauty of that approach is that you don't need to wait to be a CHRO. You can do this in each of your roles, throughout your career, and it has a compounding effect.

Developing your own people ecosystem should start today. It is built around a personal philosophy, like Lucien described earlier,

Raymond works five senses to build followership

Over the years, I realised I have a natural affinity for working with people, which started early on in university, leading large student organisations. I can naturally remember things about people, even years later. If you told me things about your mother 10 years ago, I would still remember them today. I am also blessed with being down to earth, and I treat everyone, from front-line people to senior leaders, very similarly with a lot of respect. That helps build many bonds.

Over the years, I have built good followership because I am very loyal to people. However, I am also very tough with them. I'm a very direct guy who will never beat around the bush. It's not about being nice; it's about being kind, and there's a difference. I'm very direct with my people because I care about them. As a result, I built deep relationships with most of my direct reports. However, I don't take care of my people hoping they will be loyal to me. If you give yourself wholeheartedly, they know you have the best intentions and will always watch out for them. They will reciprocate in a very sincere way.

Learning to manage people well is hard. Early in my career as a manager, two people left P&G because of me. I promised myself that this would never happen again. I will be a reason why people stay in the company, not why they quit. Our job is to make it emotionally difficult for people to think about leaving the company. To make people want to stay, I discovered I need to work on "five senses" with people: the sense of purpose, growth, achievement, belonging, and security. If I keep working on that, people will find it hard to leave the company.

but it is also made of very intentional habits to create and maintain relationships despite the busyness of business. Jean-Sébastien Blanc describes it as having an unlimited coffee budget for connections who need help:

> Former colleagues or people I know, often ask me to meet and help, especially when they are in transition. I am always happy to do that. I put myself in your shoes if you are looking for a job, or you have a problem or you want to develop your business. Thirty minutes in my life costs nothing; it's just 30 minutes. I was blessed by life, and I believe I must give back to people.

Thomas Stassen has been equally proactive throughout his career.

> I have always been disciplined in keeping in touch with critical people whom I thought could be helpful in my career. It could be former colleagues, executives in my industry, vendors, or recruiters. I would send a small Christmas message with a short report on how the family was doing. When I was traveling, I tried to meet up for coffee. There may not be an agenda; we just update each other on what is happening. I knew a 30-year career is a long time, and I might need advice or help. It turned out to be very useful over the years.

One aspect of maintaining a positive people ecosystem is the trail you leave behind when you depart organisations. This goes beyond avoiding burning bridges or ensuring you have designated a successor to fill your role. It needs to leave both the organisation and you in a positive place.

Carefully managing your transitions is a key part of long-term career success. Deborah Borg clearly highlighted this as part of her leaving Dow especially as, by that point, she had moved from HR to running a large regional business.

> When I left Dow after almost seven years to join Bunge as CHRO, I was mindful about my resignation. The way you leave a company matters a lot. I built some credibility and reputation there for so many years, and I didn't want any animosity on my way out. I also didn't want anyone to feel like anything was wrong with the organization. I was conscious that we all cast a big shadow in senior leadership

Tamsin's boss makes a shocking prediction

I made some accidental career moves at the beginning of my career, driven by the desire to learn and embrace new challenges. I became more thoughtful as I got older. Many of these opportunities came about because I was in the right place at the right time. I found that a lot of career evolution happens almost organically through relationships, opportunities you've identified or capability you have demonstrated.

After the first seven years of my career at Sodexo, on paper, I was very much on a specialist track with a focus on Talent Management. I was really enjoying what I was doing but felt I should move to a generalist pathway, or it might shut some doors for me and limit future development opportunities. I talked openly to my boss, and we explored it. I asked to explore a business partnering role to develop my commercial awareness. Everyone was supportive, which was great. However, at that time in Sodexo, I didn't feel I had the technical expertise required to take on one of their HRBP roles. One of my mentors introduced me to the CHRO at Vodafone, and I was offered an HR business partner role there which was more commercially aligned, so I decided to make the move.

The Sodexo team was amazing because they knew exactly why I was leaving, so this wasn't a shock. We had talked about it, and they understood my motivation for making a change. On my last day, I remember my boss saying to me, "You will be coming back. You're going to leave, have your first child, and then you will come back". I laughed and didn't think much of it. It turned out she was right; this is exactly what happened! I was back in Sodexo a few years, and one child, later. There was something about the company and the heartbeat of people and the values that I held very dear, and I still do today.

roles. How you act on your way out matters; how people talk about you on the way out also matters. I was very gracious, and Dow was very gracious as well.

As we have seen, building Connectivity goes well beyond what is commonly considered networking. It relies on developing a set of meaningful personal relationships, often in unfamiliar cultural environments, to create a thriving, long-term people ecosystem. This requires open-mindedness and a great deal of intentional practice.

ARNAUD'S TAKE

In my experience, people often make building professional relationships a somewhat self-serving, opportunistic endeavour. It will involve cocktail parties (for the extroverts) or coffee one-on-ones (for the introverts) with strangers with whom they have little in common. It does not have to be this way. People often overlook that they probably already have all the relationships they need at their fingertips.

If you think hard enough, you may only be a couple of degrees of separation away from anyone who matters. When was the last time you had a thorough look through your LinkedIn connections to see who *they* are connected to and might be relevant to you? Have you ever mapped the former leaders of companies you have worked with who might be CEO or Board member today? Or the alumni of universities you attended, to see where they are now? You may not know them personally, but having a common point of reference, however slim, will make them more likely to answer your call and want to be helpful.

Possibly the most important piece of advice I can share is that you should not wait to make new connections until you need them. This is a cardinal sin that makes it awkward for you, and obvious for the other party, that you are trying to build a one-sided, transactional relationship. Creating connections for the purpose of career-building should be an intentional habit that you dedicate time to on a regular basis. If you wait until you have an obvious need, you are already behind the curve. Invest in creating those connections when you genuinely have no need for them, so you will not have to feign being casual about it when you do. It is one of those instances when focusing on the process, with no immediate objective in mind, will be more important than obsessing about the outcome.

The issue, of course, is that we are all busy, and when things are good with our career, we feel they will be good forever. The people

I know who are most successful at this block specific time in their calendar for making new connections or might give a mandate to their executive assistant to make it happen. Whatever works for you, you need to make it a habit. Start today and thank me later (over coffee – I am an introvert).

TOP TEN THRIVE-STARTERS TO CREATE NEW CONNECTIVITY HABITS

Here is a recap of the top Connectivity habits that have served successful leaders well and that you can start implementing on Monday to increase your chance of long-term career success:

1 If you want to grow, take the tough job on the other side of the world.
2 It is never too late – or too early – to immerse yourself in a new and different culture.
3 Spend your time and energy on people who will care about you and be truly invested in your growth.
4 Never rely on one single mentor or sponsor; spread your bets.
5 To build a meaningful network, focus on depth rather than breadth.
6 To make mentoring sustainable, personal chemistry trumps process.
7 Don't wait to connect with others when you have an issue – do it when you have no agenda.
8 Don't take care of your people so they are loyal to you – do it because you care.
9 Make yourself available for others who may need your help, and it will pay off. What goes around comes around.
10 Manage your exits gracefully; your decisions cast a long shadow.

NOTES

1 Institute for Management Development.
2 Retired head-hunters might be a better bet, and they might enjoy joining your "wisdom council" for a free lunch, or just for the fun of it.

Driving Delivery

Five

> The best way to get a new job that is amazing is to do an amazing job in the one you are in now
>
> Prerana Issar

You are a good HR leader with a good HR career, so the most important professional attribute to develop your career further is being great at HR, right?

Wrong.

The best CHROs view themselves as business leaders, before they are HR leaders. This view was shared not only by CHROs who had started their career outside of HR but also by HR lifers. Sure, having functional expertise is important, but that is table stakes. It is just expected. Being the best at HR will not make you stand out in a field stacked with strong functional leaders. The attribute that is in high demand, and rare supply, within the broad HR community is strong business acumen.

When looking across our set of interviews, 82% of the CHROs interviewed for this book's research demonstrated, unprompted, one or more career practices related to Delivery:

- Behave as an owner
- Build a reputation for getting things done
- Act as a trusted advisor

Johanna Söderström, who has had a long and varied HR career, knows this well.

> Whenever I start a new job, either with more traditional or more forward-thinking business leaders, I don't talk about HR specifically. I talk about strategy, growth and value creation. Then I interpret what they shared about the company, competition and customers back to

employee-related strategies. When I bring my input, I try to package it using business vocabulary and financial returns. That is often better understood than HR terms and usually is not questioned or argued with. For example, some people might say 'employees get paid, so that should be enough motivation for them'. I would push back by saying 'well, what do you tell your customers? They get your product, so they should just be happy. Do you stop there?' Similarly, when you speak to a finance person, you must be able to put the concepts you want to promote in financial terms. Talk about metrics and the return on investment. What's the economics of a good/bad hire? What is the price tag of retention? What is the cost of regrettable losses at different levels in the organization? You should have all the data, but you need to be able to simplify so that your audience understands, then be able to deep dive as need be.

Having been an executive recruiter for longer than I care to remember, with most of my clients and many of candidates being HR leaders, I can say it is obvious who the HR leaders with the strongest business acumen are. In interviews, or at the water cooler, they start conversations by talking about products, markets, and customers. They have their financial numbers top of mind. They have a sense for the next quarter's financial performance. They worry about outcomes much more than process and obsess about performance management.

Let us explore in more detail how HR leaders can excel at driving Delivery, both with business and with people, and build a stand-out reputation for it.

DELIVERY PRACTICE #1 – BEHAVE AS AN OWNER

The large majority of CHROs I interviewed highlighted that having a strong business mindset and focusing on delivering business results were key to their success. To do this, you should think of your business or function much as an owner or shareholder would. While this is easy to say, the key is to do it genuinely and consistently. The best measure will be how your business colleagues speak of you and your contributions.

First, you need an affinity for financial numbers and data that goes beyond employee engagement scores or turnover rates. You need to be able and willing to deep dive into understanding the value drivers of your business. Learn to read and understand a P&L and a balance sheet and ask the tough financial questions. As Tatsuo Kinoshita put it, "everyone in HR should have a foundation in financial literacy", which he was lucky to get in his early years in a GE leadership rotation programme. Others have gotten this knowledge through an early career in consulting or pursuing an MBA, but many have gathered it on the job by simply being relentless in asking business questions.

There is a great debate of "nature versus nurture" on business acumen. Personally, I believe it can be developed in anyone. Of course, your early career experiences or education can greatly shape it, but it is an ability you can grow by being curious and intellectually rigorous. Simply do not let anything pass you if you don't fully understand it. The "it will surely become clear later" mindset is a curse that must be fought.

On this idea, Usha Kakaria-Cayaux shared a revealing anecdote.

> People have told me, you are not like HR, you are more like a business leader (funny – I thought they were the same). The fact that I am both curious and observant helps me a lot. For example, I was on a regional business review. At the end of the meeting, I approached my finance colleague and said, 'Great presentation but I can't seem to make the numbers work.' He looked at me clearly surprised that this question had come from HR. I asked, 'please can we review slide six together as I'm not getting to the same Profit Before Tax number.' He was surprised and quietly reviewed it. You're right,' he jokingly said, 'it seems you are the only one paying attention, thank you!' I told him it was not my intent to correct him, but I couldn't get the numbers to work for myself and wanted to be certain I understood the regional targets so HR could partner to drive outcomes. While it turns out it was an oversight, we had a great discussion about financials and the role of HR to partner to unlock value. It reinforced the importance of paying attention, asking questions and translating value drivers of the business into human capital investments.

Usha displayed a behaviour that is perhaps too rare in HR people – a genuine curiosity about the business and a learning mindset, mixed with the ability and courage to ask insightful questions.

Learn to spot business problems before they arise, and you will gain great credibility with your business colleagues. In fact, the best HR leaders should be seen as a natural stand-in when their business head is

Raymond inadvertently switches careers

Growing up as a Filipino Chinese, children usually must help in the business after doing their homework. My parents had a trading business, and my uncle had a construction business, so I worked in those businesses every summer from the age of 10. I never had a summer off until I was 22. I didn't know it at the time, but it was basically child labour! However, as a result, I knew everything about how to run a small business. I knew all about accounting, inventory, and cash flow by the time I graduated.

When P&G offered me my first job in trading and procurement, I took it thinking I would just do it for three years before starting my own business. After my first couple of years, my boss came to me and said, "Raymond, you're moving to HR and you're going to help us set up a new learning function". Of course, my first reaction was to ask what I did wrong. I asked him why he was not happy with me? He exclaimed, "No, no, Raymond, this is not a job I would give to anybody. We want to create a world-class learning function and make it strategic. That is why I am giving you this job. We're going to invest in you. You're going to be trained in the United States, learn from the best, and bring it back to us in P&G Philippines". I remember I went home that night, and I told my parents, "Mom, Dad, can you loan me money? I need to start my own trading firm right now". Guess what, I never did, and it turned into a 28-year HR career. However, throughout those years, I never thought of myself as an HR person, even up to now. I think of myself as a businessperson who is doing HR work. Because of all those years in the family business, my mind thinks commercially first, financially first.

travelling or busy, on par with the CFO. You will know you display the right behaviours when non-HR projects naturally come your way. For instance, Helio Fujita recalled when he had just joined Solvay in Brazil.

> As I started, I was doing my due diligence, talking to people, basically leading my own onboarding. I quickly realized the business numbers were not matching the story I had heard from the CEO during the interview process. I had been told about an ambitious growth agenda, a doubling of market share, etc. However, once I arrived, people said we were seriously losing share and joking about who would be here to turn off the lights at the end. It was a whole different story. I returned to the CEO to share this and asked for his strategic plan because I could not do my HR job without a clear strategy. He gave it to me, but I investigated the numbers, talked with market intelligence, and realised it relied on the wrong product mix and M&A strategy assumptions. When I told this to the CEO, he said he had not figured these things out yet... and asked me to develop his business strategy! I told him I had never done anything like this, but his argument was, 'It looks like you are already doing it, so just carry on.' That turned out to be an amazing experience: leading the development of the business strategy from one side while leading the people agenda from the other. It was a key moment in my career, and that experience shaped how I operated from that moment onwards.

Behaving like an owner is to counter the traditional way, some would say the cynical way, HR is seen mostly as a haven of empathy, where crafting the perfect onboarding experience or ensuring there is always enough artisanal coffee in the breakroom are seen as the highest callings. While those things certainly have their place (especially the coffee!), it is your duty as a "business leader who happens to lead HR" to ensure that HR's value is directly tied to the business's overall success. Farnaz Ranjbar put it very clearly when she shared,

> As business leaders who happen to lead HR, it our responsibility to ensure that HR is not siloed but fully integrated into the broader business landscape. It must operate as a vital part of the organization, with its values clearly linked to driving overall business success. It's essential not to speak to the business in terms they don't really care about. HR should focus on initiatives that are meaningful and have

a tangible impact on the bottom line. One of the common missteps we make in HR is using consultancy jargon – language that resonates with HR professionals but holds little relevance for the business. We sometimes speak in abstractions or undertake initiatives that were never requested. In my view, that's the biggest mistake we can make.

Stephanie Werner-Dietz echoed this, saying,

> HR always needs to be an enabler who is very close to the business. No business leader will listen to you if you only focus on things like policies and processes. I learned always to bring solutions. It's important how you bring those solutions too. If you tell a business leader they cannot do something, that could be the end of your career. Try to think like a business leader. Put yourself in their shoes, understand their issues and come up with solutions. Personally, I spend as much time as possible with business colleagues.

As an HR leader, it is your duty to drive this business mindset into the rest of your HR teams. Always start with the business end in mind: what will your HR initiatives deliver for the business? How will you quantify their impact? How will you decide which people initiatives to start or stop to improve financial results? Jessica Teo shared her tactics for challenging her teams when she got to lead HR at Louis Dreyfus Company.

> HR was very administrative, which was driving me crazy. To challenge my team, I told them that there are three important things. First, you cannot tell me 'This is how it was done in the past.' If you do that, you'll be fined five dollars, and when the piggy bank is full, we will buy a meal for the team. Second, for everything you do, ask yourself, is this really your role as an HR person? If not, then don't do it. Finally, you need to know how the business perceives your value. If you can't articulate that, you bring no value.

Think of it this way: a fantastic HR strategy in a failing company is like having the world's comfiest life raft on a sinking ship. It might feel nice, but ultimately, we're all going down together. That's why acting like an owner is not just a nice-to-have for HR professionals; it's the bedrock upon which a Thriving Career is built. So, embrace

John drives his teams to drive the business

As an HR professional, commercial acumen is a critical attribute. Developing this early in one's career is important to help understand the drivers of profit, the products or services that generate the revenue, and, importantly, the EBIT or the profit. Knowing this and being able to convey it adds enormous value to your credibility as a support function. It doesn't matter whether you're in finance, legal, HR, or IT; you should talk to a P&L owner in commercial terms about how you can contribute value.

I've worked in predominantly industrial companies. They make tangible products, so you're working with left-brain thinkers like engineers, scientists, and finance people who don't necessarily respond well to intangibles or the latest fad. They want to see a business case with an ROI, know that you are using credible research to support your case, with risk and reward that you can quantify. I find that's how you get much more leverage and influence with your colleagues.

To understand the capability of HR people I work with, I just ask "What's happening in your business?" I don't try to trap them, but if they only talk about people, they miss the point. When I ask what's going on in your business or region, I want to know if we are selling product and making money. First, are we on budget? If we're under budget, what are you and your local leaders doing about it? Once that is settled, we can discuss people because the state of the people is less relevant if the business is failing. If the business is not succeeding and we're talking about investing more money in people, there may be a disconnect.

the spreadsheets, delve into the data, and become the business-savvy HR hero your organisation needs. Your career and the company's bottom-line will thank you for it.

DELIVERY PRACTICE #2 – BUILD A REPUTATION FOR GETTING THINGS DONE

Human Resources professionals are too often seen as the office counsellors, the birthday cake organisers, and the keepers of the employee handbook. While this can certainly get you through the day and possibly sleepwalk through an entire career, you'll need something more potent to get ahead. For your career to thrive, you will need to be seen as someone who *Gets Sh*t Done* (pardon my French). It will make people want to give you more opportunities to progress.

By showing that you can get things done, you get allocated to more important projects, where you get exposed to higher levels of management. When you deliver on those, your reputation grows, and you keep getting bigger opportunities to shine. This creates a virtuous cycle, and that pattern was evident in the career of most of the CHROs I spoke with. Laura Garza summed it up very well in saying "I'm always passionate about getting things done. People who work around me know I'm going to deliver. Whatever it is, I'm going to make sure it gets done". She has built and sustained that reputation throughout her career up to her current CHRO role.

This creates a positive momentum, which often starts early in your career. As your reputation grows, so will your opportunities. Kerstin Knapp experienced this and is thankful for it. She pointed out,

> Things happened for me because people saw me in action, liked me, and recommended me. For the first 10 years of my career, every job I got was based on a recommendation. I was invited to apply through a recommendation of friends or people I worked with who say, 'Hey, Kerstin's good, you should give her a chance'.

Geoff Lloyd had a similar experience.

> Early in my career with Nortel, I really did not like my work, as it was a large organization and management was not great. One day, someone told me, 'Geoff, people here get fired when they wait for things to happen. The way people do well is by getting on and doing

Johanna wins over the Works Councils

Early in my career, Dow gave me a real challenge. They sent me to Germany for my first international assignment. East and West Germany were coming together, and people did not really talk to each other or work together across old borders. My boss said, "They don't want to be in the same boat at all, and if they are, they're just going to fight, so we think you should be there and see how you can help". I thought, let me give it a try.

My goodness, I felt so alone. I was young, a foreigner, a woman, and I did not speak German. They did not really talk to me and, if they did, they mostly spoke in German, understandably. The first six months were tough, but my grandma had taught me about "sisu" – a Finnish virtue about how you never give up and how you must always find a way. It became one of my traits early on in life. Resilience is in my DNA. At times I felt ready to jump on the train back home, but somehow all the challenges I was facing made me try harder.

As weird as it sounds, the first group to accept me in Germany were the Works Councils – not my HR people or the local Dow leadership, although everyone was nice. Why? My take is that since I was not able to speak German fluently at the time, I was always very direct and chose simple ways of presenting things. I guess they thought I was overly transparent and honest with them, and they really appreciated it. OK, maybe they felt a little sorry for me as well, but they knew I just wanted to get things done right.

My values guide me and are as strong as they get. I will not waver, and I know where I must draw the line. If I feel something isn't right, I will put it on the table. If that's not accepted, I will try another way and try again. It's not about being blue-eyed or naïve; I have realised that I must be able to look at myself in the mirror and know what I did was right. This approach and authenticity helped me a lot in Germany. As a result, my reputation grew. Management felt they "could give all the hard cases to Johanna, because she got the Works Councils to buy in".

things.' I thought, well, I'll just deliver things and see what happens. Suddenly, my career turned around. I started being given more work and delivering. Then I got lucky as I had one boss who gave me more and more responsibility. In meetings, he always asked, 'Geoff, what do you think?' He would give me the limelight, so people got to know me. Both the Canadians and the Americans started to trust me, so they kept on promoting me and, at 30, I became the youngest Vice President in the business.

Opportunities to build a reputation for Delivery will come throughout your career, and you should learn to spot and seize them. Muzzamil Khider experienced this as a leader when GE Oil & Gas and Baker Hughes merged.

I came from the GE side, and I was picked to lead that project, which led me to give quarterly updates to the GE CEO and the Board of directors. It was a big deal for them. When they picked me to lead it, I asked Why me? They said, 'We want you because we want someone who can challenge the status quo'. I took it as a positive sign because they did not see me as the typical GE-raised HR person, who may tend to look at everything in a GE way. It was a great experience to learn more about mergers and acquisitions, how two companies that were very different – the people, the culture, the systems, the practices, policies – can be brought together. This gave me good visibility and, as a result, two months after the merger, I moved into a new role leading HR for the global oil field services and equipment business. That was a huge step for me as it had around 35,000 employees, operating in over 100 countries.

To achieve this level of internal recognition, consistency is key, and you should think of it as developing your executive brand. What do you stand for within your organisation, not just with your teams and boss, but with more senior leaders and the business? Larissa Cerqueira knows that nothing happens without hard work and a conscious effort at storytelling.

My career advice for people is: if you don't like your job, and you want the next one, then do your current job really well, then you will get more opportunities. You also need to recognize that being good at your job is often not enough. You need visibility. People must know who you are and have an impression of you, fair or unfair. When you go to meetings, you might prefer drinking coffee in the corner, but you must meet people and tell your story.

Amanda Rajkumar opined and summed it up well by sharing, "My driving mission as an HR professional is to be clear on the tangible outcomes of our work. If they're not well known, we must make them visible. Marketing of our HR work is important".

One of my senior HR friends advises that it can be hard to get visibility when you work for a leader who, themselves, seeks to be in the spotlight. To counter this, you should respectfully request to present work you have delivered or look for opportunities to share your lessons learnt. This friend spent his career in a very large European multinational and feels there is still too much early talent hidden in organisations, often partly because they are too shy to want to show their qualities. We will expand more on this when we discuss executive branding later on.

As a parting thought on this practice, it is worth highlighting that "getting things done" can be understood in many ways, and HR leaders have a wide range of deliverables that all need to get done. However, when it comes to building your reputation as an HR practitioner, there will be activities that will just be points-of-parity, i.e., they will simply be expected and will likely not make you stand out. Others will be points-of-difference, i.e., if you can be truly outstanding at it, they will leave a lasting impression on your stakeholders (see Figure 5.1). Which ones will you want to be remembered for?

What people will remember you for?

Sample points-of-parity	***Sample points-of-difference***
• Knowing the most about {*insert HR topic*}	• Getting deals done with unions
• Organizing memorable team retreats	• Sussing out poor performers and turning them around (or getting them out)
• Making people feel good and appreciated	• Digitalizing and modernizing people practices
• Designing the best policies and processes	• Coaching a struggling business leader

Figure 5.1 Determine how you will truly differentiate in your Delivery

While being an average HR professional might be enough to keep you employed, cultivating an outstanding reputation is the fuel that will power your career. We will come back to this – and expand on it – in our executive branding section in Chapter 8. When it comes to Delivery; however, it is not only about getting known for solving business issues. Thriving Career builders also know how to build trust with their stakeholders and maintain those relationships for life.

DELIVERY PRACTICE #3 – ACT AS A TRUSTED ADVISOR

As an HR leader, you need to be close to your business head and be their conduit to the organisation's pulse. You also need to hold up the mirror to them and give them unvarnished, real-time feedback on how they are doing when it comes to connecting with the organisation. Great business leaders will truly value this from their HR head.

In an ideal world, you and your CEO will have a natural and personal connection, a feeling that you can be complementary. Athalie Williams experienced this when one of her bosses changed at BHP.

> The company brought in a new operational leader to head up the area that I was in. He sat me down early and said, 'Look, I know nothing about this HR thing, but I know the business. You seem to know a lot about HR but don't know the business. Together, we can do this'. And we really did. I learned a lot from a couple of operational leaders I was lucky to work closely with.

In this case, Athalie was fortunate to have a boss who was so self-aware and open-minded.

Similarly, John Holding enjoys a trust-based relationship with his CEO, which benefits the entire organisation.

> I've enjoyed my role so much because my philosophy is aligned with that of our CEO on the role of HR and how our practices will be deployed. I enjoy that he and I are in lockstep on this, and he tells me regularly how much he values the role of HR. The CHRO role is different from every other executive team member. You become a confidant to some degree, the sounding board, sometimes the agony aunt. There's a whole range of roles that a CHRO plays with the CEO, but most importantly, the trusted advisor is critical. It helps enormously to have an aligned philosophical mindset as I find it very important for the CEO and CHRO to be aligned.

Getting to this level of alignment is hard but will be critical for your success.

When you are not getting the alignment you need from the business, the burden falls on the HR leader to find a way to make things work and build a high level of trust. Gaining trust is a slow but critical process. Janice Deskus shared that this important objective breaks down to simple things, often driven by asking thoughtful, caring questions.

> The things to remember with leaders, especially top leaders, is they don't have a lot of people to talk to. If they come to trust you and see you as somebody there to help them succeed, you become a trusted advisor in many aspects of their lives. I like to have that advisor role, that confidant role of someone to talk to about their feelings. I like to be the person to whom, behind closed doors at six o'clock, after everybody's gone home, they can say what they're really thinking and feeling. One of the questions I ask most leaders, whatever job they're in, is When you leave here, what do you want your legacy to be? What do you want your reputation to be? Let's think about that today, and let's build towards that together until the day you leave. When I ask that question, I find that it breaks down a lot of walls. Because it's still mostly men in business leadership roles, I think there is an advantage to being a female. The male competitiveness breaks down, and it's a little less intimidating.

Ultimately, your success in HR is largely defined by your leader's success, so it becomes your responsibility to equip them to succeed. Sometimes, this means passing on difficult messages. Usha Kakaria-Cayaux, never one to hold back from sharing what she thinks, is not afraid to speak her truth.

> To work with a CEO or senior leader takes courage, and you need to be willing to speak up. You must be confident to look them in the eye and tell them the truth because many of their direct reports will not. HR has a special role in doing that. The CHRO needs to be candid with the CEO and other C-Suite leaders and say, 'I'm going to tell you what you don't want to hear.' I remember early in my career a senior executive did one of his first presentations, and he asked me how I felt it went afterwards. I told him it was okay. He looked at me sideways, 'What do you mean only okay?' I then gave him honest feedback on

Lucien learns how to pick his CEOs

In my first CHRO role, I joined Avon because Andrea Jung was the CEO and, over time, I also grew to love the company. Working for Andrea was a special experience. She made me a partner at a very deep level. We didn't socialise outside the company, but in a business setting I felt I could finish her sentences. Some other CEOs didn't know exactly what to ask for from HR but knew that they should expect more. You make the bet that they're smart and pragmatic and, once they've experienced what a difference a great HR team can make for their business, they'll never settle for anything less. Those are the leaders you want to work with.

In contrast, I was once asked to interview to be the CHRO for one of the biggest banks in the world. It was a huge job. Honestly, I wasn't ready for it, and I couldn't understand why I was a candidate, but hey, you never know if you don't try. I learned a lot from that experience. I met 15 senior leaders, and the last stage in the hiring process was a meeting with the CEO. He told me, "Lucien, this CHRO role is critical. In fact, this job is so important for me that you and I will meet once a month for 45 minutes, and I will let you share all your ideas with me". He meant well, but it was clearly never going to work. I didn't get the job, but I did not regret it – within four months, 12 of the 16 people I met were gone, including the CEO.

things that, in my opinion, could have gone better. He looked at me like he didn't know whether to promote or fire me. I felt I had to be sincere because I wanted him to be fantastic for the sake of all of us. Speaking truth to power strengthens trust hugely. It comes from a place that I, and the whole company, need and want our CEO with their Leadership Team to be successful because, ultimately, they work for the people (and not vice versa) and it's my job to help.

This obviously also means that if the HR leader feels they are not being supported, or the conditions for success are not there, it is their responsibility to bring it up.

Over time, a successful business/HR relationship might, and probably should, evolve into a close personal one. However, it is also important to keep a distance so as not to be seen by the rest of the leadership team as potentially biased. Your peers need to feel secure confiding in you, without any fear that the information will leak out to their boss. Maintaining that fine balance between being a close confidant and an impartial advisor is a strong pillar of trust.

As an HR leader, intentionally driving Delivery both for the business and for people will allow you to gain respect across the organisation and maintain solid and broad relationships throughout your career. Remember that your peer today could well be your boss tomorrow.

ARNAUD'S TAKE

Having interviewed thousands of senior leaders over the past 20 years, I can safely say that the "signs of Delivery" – or lack thereof – are usually clear and obvious. It often comes down to the language people use in describing their work. It shows

1. How clear the leader is about what creates real value for the business.
2. How articulate they are about the relationship between their activities and actual financial results.
3. How good they are at putting themselves in the shoes of their audience when bringing their points across.

This was brought home to me early on in my career as an executive search consultant when I was approached by a former McKinsey

Monique makes a CEO friend for life

As CHRO, it is critical that you have a good relationship with the CEO and other ex-co members. Personally, I need to like, respect, and trust them. Your business leader needs to be someone who cares about you, and you need to care about them. When you've got that relationship, you can challenge each other.

When I worked for the CEO of Novo Nordisk, my first year was difficult. I was a foreigner in Denmark, and it felt like there was tissue rejection to me as they had never had an EVP for People and Organisation before me. I had been brought in to drive much change; however, the organisation felt they were successful, so why change? One year into the EVP role, I told the CEO, "This is hard. You brought me in to drive culture change, but when it comes to the crunch, I feel it's me against everyone". I told him, "If you're not up for this, that's fine. I'll be on my way, and you can get somebody else to do this for you since everyone in Denmark would love to work for the company. You will be better off than having me frustrated. However, if you do want this, we must work differently because I cannot be the one always pushing everything alone. You must also say you want it, or it won't happen". We had a very frank conversation, and he said, "Actually, I never worked with a strong HR partner, I don't really know how to do this, you have to help me".

From that moment, it was super easy. We would speak all the time, talk about how he was feeling, and we made things happen. Ultimately, it was really difficult for me to leave Novo Nordisk because I was leaving him, and we had a great working relationship. He's a good person as well as a great CEO. My advice to others is that when you go for interviews, you must also be interviewing them. You need to find out about people and decide whether you respect them. Are you going to be able to work together and be effective? And if you've got any question marks about that, be very cautious.

colleague who was looking for a job outside of consulting and hoping to transition to a corporate environment. When I asked him what he had delivered as a consultant, he described his achievements as "having delivered significant impact for large-scale multinational clients by driving deep operational improvement initiatives that created lasting bottom-line impact and ingrained new change management capabilities at the front line of the organization". Now, read this sentence again. If you have no idea what it means, don't worry, you are a normal human being. I looked at him, equally bewildered and amused, thinking, "Oh boy, this is going to take some work". The worst part was that, because I am also an ex-McKinsey consultant… I kind of understood what he meant! But I knew that no other interviewer with a sane mind would ever make any sense of that description, so we got to work on simplifying this.

The language you use is critical to your ability to convince people of your achievements. As the saying goes, "what is well conceived is clearly stated". Use fewer words and make them matter. Most importantly, you need to understand what your audience will see as a true impact. In my experience interviewing HR leaders, it is relatively rare to see them getting spontaneously energised and detailed about business. Many get excited about some change management initiative they have delivered, or the great team they built. Those are certainly worthy achievements, and if you are talking to another HR leader you might just get away with it. However, they are only means to an end. The outstanding HR professionals who stand out in Delivery talk about their business, how it is doing, and how they were able to help move the needle on the P&L through the initiatives they led or the leaders they coached.

TOP TEN THRIVE-STARTERS TO DRIVE NEW DELIVERY HABITS

Here is a list of proven Delivery habits that you can act on immediately to build the foundations of your Thriving Career

1 Develop your financial literacy. Learn to read a P&L so you can ask the tough questions.
2 Develop an instinctive knack for quantifying the impact of all your initiatives to the business bottom-line.
3 Be curious and intellectually rigorous. Do not accept anything from the business you don't fully understand.

4 Think like your CEO – what should they be most worried about? This is what you need to work on.
5 No business leader will listen to you if you talk about policies or processes. Talk solutions.
6 When in doubt, challenge the status-quo.
7 Get things done and make sure the right people know about it. Seek people out and tell your story.
8 Keep in mind that it takes a long time to build trust, and very little to lose it.
9 Tell people respectfully what they don't want to hear, but need to know, to gain their trust.
10 Be very close to your boss so they have complete trust in you, but not so close that your peers feel they can't talk to you any more.

Managing your career flow

Six

> When I look back on my career, I feel I got to live the dream.
>
> Philip Read

As we have now explored the four foundational attitudes of Thriving Careers – **Awareness**, **Bravery**, **Connectivity**, and **Delivery** – you might wonder if and how these principles evolve throughout your professional journey. The truth is that career management isn't static; while the fundamentals remain the same, it's a dynamic process that requires a different focus at different stages of your life.

When you're starting out, the stakes might seem straightforward: land that first role, make an impression and climb the ladder from there. But for seasoned executives nearing retirement, the calculations change dramatically as it becomes about legacy, knowledge transfer, and finding meaning. The problem is that most career advice treats these vastly different scenarios with the same generic prescriptions.

I recall speaking with a leader who, at 58, was struggling with this exact dilemma. "I've spent over thirty years building my expertise and network", he told me. "But now I'm being pushed toward the exit when I still have so much to contribute". His frustration was palpable as the career tactics that had served him well for decades suddenly seemed insufficient for this new phase. Conversely, I've spoken with young HR professionals who approach their careers with rigid five-year plans, only to find themselves paralysed when unexpected opportunities arise that don't fit their predetermined views.

So how do you adapt the Thriving Career principles we discussed to your specific life stage? How do you build a career strategy that remains flexible enough to evolve as you do? These questions become increasingly critical as careers grow longer and less linear than ever before.

When looking across the careers of our 45 CHROs, they have an average tenure of 30 years. Over that time, on average, they changed companies only four times. It means they stayed in each of their companies, on average, for six years. That is some solid staying power. It points to picking each company change smartly and carefully. You should do the same.

These days, it is not uncommon to see executives who have changed companies two or three times by the time they reach the age of 30. Think of the damage they are doing to their CV. If you change companies every two years, you are implicitly telling any future employer, "you will probably have me for a couple of years, then either you will realize that I am not that good, or I will get bored and leave. Either way, you will have to replace me". For a young executive, six years in one company may feel like (do the " air quotes" and roll your eyes with me) *forever*, but that is probably what it takes to build a credible track record.

As mentioned throughout this book, one of the most important insights from my research is that you need to play the long game. Avoid making career decisions for short-term rewards. Instead, keep the big picture in mind and ask yourself what decision should maximise your odds of long-term career success? The Thriving Career framework helps point you in the right direction, but it is also important to note that your focus on **Awareness**, **Bravery**, **Connectivity**, and **Delivery** will need to evolve throughout your career.

An executive career has roughly four main phases. Their length will vary, but we can think of them in successive blocks of seven to ten years – which can be at the faster end in large, global organisations with graduate development programmes that speed your progress, or those that offer many internal mobility opportunities or more frequent promotions.

- **The Formative Years**: In the first part of their careers, professionals need to invest in developing foundational traits and maximise time spent beyond their comfort zone. Identifying and accessing opportunities to develop these traits will be an investment that will reap the highest rewards for their long-term careers.
- **The Growth Years**: In the second part of their careers, professionals must build on their initial foundations to develop a few key leadership capabilities, allowing them to have a larger impact on the world around them. Developing these capabilities will help them build an outstanding reputation and maximise future career opportunities.

		Formative Years	Growth Years	Leadership Years	Legacy Years
ACTIVATE	Awareness	Passive	Active	**PRIORITY**	**PRIORITY**
BET ON	Bravery	**PRIORITY**	Active	Passive	Passive
CULTIVATE	Connectivity	Active	**PRIORITY**	**PRIORITY**	Active
DRIVE	Delivery	**PRIORITY**	**PRIORITY**	Active	Passive

Figure 6.1 Deploy your Thriving Career attitudes strategically over the years

- **The Leadership Years**: In the third part of their careers, leaders must combine their finely honed capabilities to deliver outstanding value to their teams, their peers, and the broader organisation, often on a global scale.
- **The Legacy Years**: In the last part of their careers and lives, leaders will shift their focus to striking a balance between professional obligations that keep them engaged and personal priorities that are fulfilling and meaningful.

During each phase, you will likely need to focus on different parts of the Thriving Career approach to maximise your lifetime career potential (Figure 6.1).

Let's explore how each of these four phases unfolds and what you need to keep in mind as a professional to thrive at any stage of your career.

YOUR FORMATIVE YEARS

During your Formative Years, your biggest focus will be to maximise your learning and build a reputation as someone who gets things done. The two most important dimensions for you to focus on will be **Bravery** and **Delivery**, but you should also start thinking of actively building your **Connectivity** for the future.

If you are about to start your career, I would argue that you should choose the biggest organisation possible. Not only will the brand name be good for your CV, but you should get a lot of opportunities to move around if you are proactive. For your first few years, I contend that it may be better to be a lobby boy (or tea lady) in a large global company such as Apple, Procter & Gamble, or Shell rather than Chief [insert your favourite function] Officer in a start-up. In a large company, you will seamlessly and unconsciously absorb a lot of best practices that will shape how you think about business and organisations. Many things will then become natural to you[1] without you even realising it.

As an added benefit, you might end up feeling like Muzzamil Khider, who confided, "In all my career, I never had a career plan or a big ambition. I trusted the system, and the system took good care of me". Ranjay Radhakrishnan echoed this by sharing,

> As you start your career, you must choose correctly and take advice. I would say never choose just the role, choose the company. Choose a company that is not hiring to just fill a role for today but is hiring you for their (and your) future. While it is important to see who you will work for, and whether you will enjoy working for your boss, it is also important to see who you will work with. Throughout my career, I learnt a lot from my peers and the community I worked with, not just from my manager. Aspects like values, purpose of the company, etc. are now baseline, so there should be a premium for high-quality peers and a community you can learn from. A little competitive pressure is productive, and you learn from each other. This is one of the best things that happened to me at Hindustan Unilever – I got a great start.

Once you are settled in a good company, you should say yes to almost any opportunity that comes your way. It should feel like the training montage in a Rocky movie, except you are navigating organisational charts instead of punching frozen meat. Any extended time spent in cruise mode is a missed opportunity. You should feel "comfortably uncomfortable" throughout your Formative years. Any new transition should stir your gut and trigger some amount of imposter syndrome.

During your early years, you should never feel like you are the smartest person in the room. If you do, you are either in the wrong room or your ego is going out of whack. Seek feedback regularly and

Deborah goes straight for the deep end

At the start of my career, I worked for General Motors part-time as a junior HR staff when a plant HR manager was going off for 10 weeks on his long service leave, so I raised my hand to do his job. At the same time, GM said there was also a production supervisor in the foundry who was going off for seven weeks, and I said I'd do that job too. At 19 years old, I was confident I could do anything. It was only for a few weeks; how bad could I be at it? They were a bit confused, like it didn't make much sense, but they let me do it.

Suddenly, I am on the shop floor with people who wanted to have fistfights, and others who didn't even speak English. At the time, a foundry was no place for a woman, certainly not a 19-year-old woman. I had to get a car to drive to the nearest female restroom, since no other women worked there. It was the dirtiest of operations where they moulded the engines. The working conditions were not great and were very far from an office environment.

GM was quite worried; they did not think this was the place for a young woman to be. They had no idea how this experiment would work and were concerned about my personal safety. I told them I would be fine, but they insisted on installing a security button under my desk. They were most worried about me on night shifts. I had insisted I should also cover them as the night shift employees shouldn't have a different experience because I'm a woman. I certainly had some "interesting" experiences, but it was fantastic. It was only seven weeks so I couldn't do it too badly, but it was a fun experience, and I learned a lot to bring back to my HR job. GM was great about it. If you had a sparkle in your eye and were eager to help, they would find a way to make it work. It is opportunities like this that got me noticed early in the company.

embrace it. People will give you feedback because they care about your future. In general, you should also find that everyone has your best interests and development at heart. Lucien Alziari had that experience early on.

> After starting my career in operations, the company told me they wanted me to move into learning and development. I was 25 and I felt I knew the answer to everything, so I said, 'No, I am not doing that, that's not where the action is.' After a few conversations, they said, 'OK, you don't understand, you ARE going into learning and development' (these were different times). I wasn't happy but I made the move and ended up finding the professional love of my life. I absolutely fell in love with the idea of human development and tying it to the business. That pattern played out two or three times in my early career. I said no to moves, was dragged kicking and screaming into those assignments and ended up being really pleased to have done them. Eventually, I started to listen to people that I trusted, but it took a while for me to figure that out!

You should be in constant learning mode and look for opportunities to move around. At this early stage, you are more likely to be single and mobile, so use that chance while you can. It will only get more complicated later.

Consider moving to a new geography, ideally with a different international culture, including different languages, religions, levels of economic development, etc. The more different from your native culture, the better. Moving from New York to California, or Germany to Switzerland, is good, but probably not good enough to be truly developmental.

Consider shifting to an HR sub-function requiring you to develop a new muscle. If you are analytical and structured, cherish the opportunity to spend time in the fuzzy world of Talent Management or DE&I. If you are a creative, big picture thinker, embrace the opportunity to get into the operational grind of a Talent Acquisition or Total Rewards role.

Explore doing a stint outside of HR, provided it is in a synergistic function that gives you a realistic path back. Natural adjacencies can include Communications (extending from internal to external Comms), Health & Safety (if you are in a manufacturing environment), or Shared Services. You will even get further stretch from functions such as internal audit or even sales.

Foundational Years are also the perfect time to start shaping your persona as a leader. When I joined McKinsey's Canada office as a new consultant, a senior partner left a handwritten note on my desk on my first day that said, "Act like a Partner". I have never forgotten that advice, which should apply to any career. Whether you are in sales, finance, HR, or procurement, act as if it were your business. Make decisions and deliver things for the benefit of the entire enterprise, not just your area. This will profoundly shape how you think of yourself and how others see you. Frédéric Chardot had his own opportunity to shape his early reputation and reflected on it.

> I can tell you I was known for getting the job done in my early years. I was not promoted because I was good-looking or nice to my boss. It was because I was pushing the envelope, never taking anything for granted, and making an impact. For instance, I would confront the French unions, and it was sometimes very difficult. They once kept me locked in a room for 24 hours, but I knew I was doing the right thing for people and the business, so I just took it as an interesting experience.

As a relatively young executive, your colleagues will expect you to be energetic, optimistic, and full of ideas, even if you still lack experience or expertise. You should be a source of energy for others and make people want to spend more time with you. Roberto Di Bernardini took great pride in this, and it served him well.

> In the initial stage of my career, I was a doer, even if I didn't invent anything. I didn't create any new process or good program, but I was very good at getting things done. I was good at taking a recipe and getting exactly the right outcome. I was also very good at connecting with and learning from people who knew more than I did. I was a good listener. One more important thing was that I was smiling all the time. At work, I rarely had a down day. People were telling me I always seemed to be in a good mood, even in bad moments. I transmitted this good mood to people who worked with me.

Stephanie does not take no for an answer

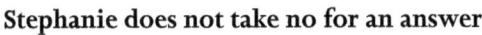

When I started at Nokia, I was placed in the management training programme based in Germany and received a mentor. Since I had already interned with the company in China, they thought I did not really need one, so my mentoring was supposed to be a process formality. However, my mentor happened to be the Managing Director for Germany. They told me he is very busy, so he will probably never have time for me. But I thought that's cool, my mentor is the highest executive in the business, so I must get to know him.

I decided to go to his office one day. At that time, Germany was very hierarchical. I had to go to his personal assistant first, who guarded his office. I said, "Hi, I'm Stephanie, and I want to see my mentor now". She exclaimed, "What mentor, I do not know anything about this". I explained I was told her boss is my mentor, and I would like to see him and introduce myself. She said I didn't have an appointment, and things don't work like this. Basically, she told me to leave but my mentor's office door was open. He heard me and came out to see who was the young girl making so much noise. I said, "Hi, I'm Stephanie. From now on, I'm supposed to be your mentee, and you are my mentor. It's good to meet you". He clearly had no idea, but he took me in and became one of my strong supporters. He said he was impressed because no one ever approached him like that. After that, he became a great mentor, and we met regularly. Everyone looked at me, asking how I managed to get this guy to meet with me given he was so senior, and I was a little trainee. It turned out I just had to ask.

Finally, and perhaps most importantly, take ownership of your career. Don't wait for someone to hand you opportunities on a silver platter. As Stephanie put it, "Don't assume anything; fight for yourself. No one will ask you if you want a promotion, or more money. That is not how life works. You need to take care of yourself". Raise your hand for stretch assignments, volunteer for challenging projects, and make your aspirations known. Even if your company has strong talent processes, be the architect of your own career journey, not just a passive passenger.

In conclusion, the Foundational Years are the platform on which you build the rest of your career. By proactively seeking to develop your business acumen, embracing diverse experiences, cultivating self-awareness, building strong relationships, developing resilience, and taking ownership of your journey, you will be well on your way to building a robust base for your future success.

YOUR GROWTH YEARS

There is no hard rule for when someone transitions from their Formative to their Growth years, but having spoken to many executives who went through that phase, it seems to be the point when the corporate air suddenly rarefies. Early on, opportunities seem to abound, mistakes are quickly forgiven, corporate politics are only a remote concern, and results trump relationships. In the Growth Years, the career funnel feels narrower. Personal constraints become a competing force to professional development. In addition, as you become a manager of managers, the link between your actions and results at the front line becomes looser.

First, let us acknowledge that if you did not start your career in a large global company, the early part of your Growth Years is probably your last chance to change this, assuming you wish to. Some larger multinational corporations will take a chance on executives who have started in smaller organisations, if they feel they have potential to adapt to a large corporate environment. This is what happened to Mieke Van de Capelle, and it transformed her career.

> In my first HR job with Quick restaurants, I started in talent acquisition, but we were doing all kinds of things. They sent a few of us to Hungary, starting everything from scratch. We needed to start up the business, hire the people, get them paid, etc. It felt like pioneering, but I thought it was time to do something more serious.

A recruiter called me about Sara Lee Corporation, and I thought, why would they call me? My experience was still very limited. I realized it would be a big step up for me, but it could be a key turning point in my career. At that moment, my instinct told me it's a very reputable global company with many smart people walking around, where I would be learning a lot more. I accepted the Sara Lee offer to become a local head of HR in Belgium, and that's when it became serious. I felt I learned the trade of HR there and saw what real HR looks like. It was largely a gut feel decision, but if I had not made that move, I would not have been where I am now.

As you progress in large corporations, it can feel like "know-who" becomes as important as, or more important than, "know-how". This is where **Connectivity** should take centre stage as a priority for career development. One CHRO experienced this and, after over 15 years in a large American multinational company, she reached a stage when things changed.

After all these years in the company, I felt things were becoming political. People played games, and it felt like an old boys' club. You would never make it if you were not part of the inside circle. I got lost, as I didn't know how to play that game. I am not American; I speak straight and love to deliver. I don't know how to beat around the bush, talking about things without saying anything. That feeling of discomfort started to grow and, while it was a great company to work for, I knew in my soul I would need to leave.

As a result, she left the company and still feels it was the right decision for her at that time.

In an organisation's "fat belly", the need for performance is even greater because the criteria for measuring that performance become fuzzier, and the competition for opportunities only gets fiercer. More than ever, the principles of **Bravery** and **Delivery** should guide you, and you will get ahead by following your guts, even if others don't get it. Philip Read knew he had to follow his instincts in his Growth Years in Dow when

The company was planning the largest ever foreign investment in China, just off the coast of Tianjin, and they wanted someone to go over and figure out how to staff that. I had always been curious about China, and I was keen to go, but everyone said, 'Don't do it, you are in the headquarters of the company, and you are very well respected. It's all good for you now. There are only downsides to going to China. You'll be out of sight, out of mind'. I did not understand that logic, or maybe I did not care about it. I just thought about what a chance it would be to be in the action, just as China looked like it was expanding onto the world stage.

It was the late 1990s, and China turned out to become the place to be for the next 20 years. Philip's brave bet against the well-meaning advice he received allowed him to boost his career significantly.

In the middle part of your career, you might feel like you have fewer learning opportunities. It is one of the most common reasons executives, who are otherwise happy in their company, tell me they want to look outside. It is the "grass may be greener elsewhere" syndrome. However, this often turns out to be a fallacy. Thriving Career builders will probe deeper. Why do I feel I am not learning as much anymore? How could I better satisfy my needs without changing organisations? What other development opportunities are there for me in my current company? In short, don't always blame your environment for not being challenging enough; maybe the development opportunity is to challenge your own mindset.

This is something Ranjay Radhakrishnan experienced mid-way through his career.

> There was a brief phase when a few of my 'peers' got promoted and momentarily went ahead of me. I was beginning to question myself and whether I was losing out? I had a very open relationship with my then boss. He urged me not to get distracted and explained the benefit of the experience that I would gain by finishing the agenda I had started. 'You must stay long enough in a role to learn from the consequences of the decisions you made and see a cycle through.' He also openly asked me to explore options externally. At first, I did wonder if he implied that this was the end of the road for me, but he said, 'Not at all! Look outside and you will see that we value you more than other companies would. If you decide to stay, then you will stay by choice and will be happy to do so'. That is exactly what happened. I realized I was valued by other companies only for

Roberto reloads his career spring

I got to my first Group CHRO role very early on, at about 33 years old, and it was not a pleasant experience for me. It was for a great and iconic Italian company, but things started to go south from day one. The focus was on massive headcount reduction in a tense social environment with no capital for investment. It was unpleasant, and I left after one year.

It took me 15 years to get into a global role again, when I was promoted to global head of HR for Johnson & Johnson Consumer. I offer my example to anyone asking me for advice. If you have a fast career at the beginning, you may need to accept having lateral moves for a long period of time in your mid-career, before getting promoted again. That is the way the pyramid works. For 15 years, I moved laterally. People would often say, this new job is at the same level of your current job, why should you take it? But the real question is what can you learn from it? Is it something that will put you out of your comfort zone? If you look at my career, I did not waste those 15 years, I was growing all along. I moved from Italy to the United Kingdom, then to the United States, managing Latin America, before coming back to Europe. I changed sector, moving from FMCG to pharmaceuticals. At every step, you need to keep working new muscles. Every time I took on a new role, it was either in a different country or a different sector, and I learned a lot each time I moved. I call this "charging the spring". I was powering up my career spring and then, suddenly, I was promoted to my first big global HR role.

marginally better roles versus my existing employer. I stayed back by choice, finished the job, learnt a huge amount and never regretted my decision.

Taking on lateral or project-based roles is often a fixture of Growth Years. It should be expected and welcome if you are clear about the learning you get. It needs to keep on developing your strategic thinking ability and your ability to have an impact at the enterprise level. Seek opportunities to participate in strategic planning sessions, to analyse organisational challenges from a broader perspective, and to develop a clear understanding of how HR can drive competitive advantage on a larger scale. This will help you display your true long-term potential and, often, get spotted.

One role that can be on offer for high-potential HR talent is that of Chief of Staff role for the CHRO. A few of the HR leaders I interviewed for this book had that experience and felt they benefited greatly from it. It can accelerate your career by giving you a unique exposure to the highest levels of the company leadership and allow you to develop new influencing skills that you will require later. If structured well, a Chief of Staff role could be your on-the-job mini-MBA. Getting paid to learn – it does not get better than this!

If you do change employer during your Growth Years, be wary about the adaptation time, particularly if you come from a long tenure in a single organisation. It will be important to get your mind around your new context and deploy your capabilities and experience in the right way, at the right time. This is something John Holding has learned over the years.

> When you join a new organization, listen, listen, and listen before you act. As Franklin Covey said, 'Seek first to understand, then to be understood.' Don't think you've got all the answers; you must understand the context first. You might have the theory, you might even have the practice, you may have done it before in a similar organization, but every company is unique. It has its own way of how things get done, and it is important to get your head around the informal power networks. Network internally, develop your rapport, get to know people before you convey your vision or plans or risk losing them before you start.

Stephanie gets tapped on the shoulder

After having several country HR assignments across Nokia, I was put on a high-potential list. While I was working in Germany, I had an opportunity to present in front of Nokia's CHRO during a meeting. Shortly after, I was asked to move to New York and work directly with him as his Chief of Staff. That was a big opportunity but, honestly, it was quite uncomfortable for me at the beginning. Up to that point, I had always been in execution roles. I excel at going into the business, creating relationships with business leaders, making things happen in the organisation, and leave when it's working better. Suddenly, I was at the global level, without a big team to lead.

It was my first time as an individual contributor, doing what is often called "ivory tower work". I was supposed to lead HR strategy, and I moderated and facilitated the CHRO's agenda with the HR leadership team on big global topics. I was not making decisions anymore. Instead, I worked on aligning others. Working through others was a completely different kind of work.

Looking back, I know it was helpful for my career because it gave me a new perspective. It made me understand how everything you decide globally has consequences when it hits the ground. I also got to work with all these superstars HR leaders, and I learned to stand my ground. Young Stephanie had to create a strategic agenda, work with them, moderate their discussions, and help resolve disagreements. It rounded me up. However, after a while, I knew it was time for something else. I was ready to be more operational again. Suddenly, I got a call to lead HR for a large group of emerging markets and work on a post-merger integration. They asked if I could move from the United States to Romania, and I was like, yeah, I'm in business again, this is exciting.

Think of it as running a marathon, rather than a sprint. It is worth taking it slower to go further.

In conclusion, the Growth Years phase can be challenging to navigate, but it is also a period of significant opportunity. To thrive in that phase, you will need to fire on all cylinders and showcase heightened levels of **Awareness** and **Connectivity** while still displaying strong levels of **Bravery** and **Delivery**. This is not an easy feat, but being successful in this phase is the key to get into your Leadership Years with great momentum.

YOUR LEADERSHIP YEARS

As your HR career progresses into your Leadership Years, when you may be leading HR for a global division or a Center of Expertise, the need to be a strong partner to the business becomes even greater. Your measure of personal impact and **Delivery** will also evolve. It becomes less about getting things done yourself and more about inspiring, enabling and coaching other senior leaders to do what needs to be done – first and foremost your own boss(es). Leadership by influence, rather than authority, becomes the norm. **Awareness** and **Connectivity** will make your career thrive.

This may also be a time when you might start to think seriously about becoming #1. Many CHROs I spoke with shared that they never really thought about getting the top role until they got to work near the top of their organisation. It can then become "why not me?" We will address the specific opportunities and challenges of a transition to a first CHRO role in our chapter on pivotal career moments, but let's first take a moment to consider what great corporate HR leaders do, which can guide you to move confidently towards your Legacy Years.

As a global HR leader, you are now setting the HR strategy and direction. There may not be anyone else you can turn to, so the buck stops with you. You need self-confidence, initiative, and resilience. Having been a Group CHRO for over 13 years, Jean-Sébastien Blanc has always been very aware of this.

> Becoming a Group CHRO makes a huge difference. Before that, I always thought that somebody could stop the ball if I were doing something wrong. Suddenly, I am the last one in front of the goal. You feel lonely, but you also feel in charge. You feel the pressure, but you

Lucien makes a conscious choice to love HQ

I always enjoyed being close to the business. After an assignment in Dubai with PepsiCo, I realised that, if I was going to have the career I wanted, the most senior roles with the company were in the United States at the corporate HQ (which I called the "puzzle palace"). In Dubai, I focused on how much we sold and whether we were beating Coke – I loved being part of the business. When I moved to the corporate headquarters, I was six hours away from the nearest market, and everything was in hundreds of millions and billions of dollars. The business felt far away.

I needed to replace this with something, so I decided to learn what a corporation was all about. What was the difference between a corporation and an operating business subsidiary? What was corporate governance all about? I also realised that you could learn from failure, but you don't have to be the one who fails. Likewise, you can learn from success, but you don't have to be the one experiencing every success. You can focus instead on becoming a keen student of what is happening around you.

The "puzzle palace" had its share of politics and that was new to me. I had to determine what made people succeed and whether I could do that while staying true to myself. By and large, PepsiCo was pretty good from that perspective. Another huge benefit of being at headquarters was that I worked on truly strategic issues. I remember being in a meeting with four CEOs at the same time – the CEOs of Quaker and PepsiCo, the heir apparent to the PepsiCo CEO, and Indra Nooyi, who was president and went on to become CEO. I was surrounded by these very high-octane individuals and worked on strategic, high-impact stuff. I loved it.

also have fun. You build a strategy, you build a team, you have the power to act with a full scope.

However, he also qualifies this with a warning that "when you are at corporate HQ, in most cases, you create new work. And the more corporate people you have, the more they will create work for others". One way to balance this as a global HR leader is to keep things very simple and rely on your team to turn your direction into concrete action. According to Farnaz Ranjbar,

> Whenever my team asks what our HR strategy is, I say we only have one strategy and that's getting things done to support the business. That is our roadmap, so let's stop talking about it and just drive strong execution to our commitments.

Farnaz's approach to guiding her HR team by setting the direction and letting them run for it makes a lot of sense, because many CHROs I interviewed feel they never have enough time with their own teams. As you get close to the C-Suite, you are going to spend a lot more time with the Board and other stakeholders, leaving you permanently starved for time. Laura Garza has acutely experienced this and shared,

> I remember every time I needed my former CHRO bosses, they were saying I am sorry, I am with the lawyers or with the Board, I have no time for you. I thought, my goodness, they're so boring. Now, as CHRO, I can totally relate. I can see my team wants to talk to me, but I am moving from crisis to crisis, from social media to employment law to anything. That means I never have enough time with my team. You need to have very good HR people who will do the right thing end-to-end without you even watching. You may have a few minutes for them here and there, then you move on because the Board or the other senior executives need you.

As a result, your relationship with the Board will be key to your success and needs to be managed through a mix of art and science.

The dynamics of dealing with the Board might seem complex, but it does not have to be. Most of the CHROs I spoke with mentioned that this is a critical piece of their role, but Geoff Lloyd is the one who put it most simply, and entertainingly.

Ranjay learns to develop resilience

I realised over my career that further progression is not just defined by the skills and competencies you develop. Those get taken for granted beyond a certain point. Your progression is also defined by the leadership acumen you develop – the ability to exert influence and create impact. However, the resilience you develop is what helps you sustain success – certainly as a CHRO. These are three legs to the progression stool, and if one of these legs is underdeveloped, you will fumble.

When you become a CHRO, it's a very lonely job and your resilience will be tested like never before, which is something I wish I had known and better prepared for. You need to simultaneously deal with multiple orbits: the CEO and their leadership team, the Chair and the Board, the Remuneration Committee (RemCo) and their advisors, your HR leadership team to name a few. You are always handling multiple orbits in multiple ways, and you are quite alone in that. Very often, you're the only one who the Chair, the RemCo Chair, or the CEO can talk to. Most of the time, you can talk to no one. As a result, you need a strong resilience toolkit and practice. You must recover fast because the next difficult meeting is waiting at your door. The faster the speed of recovery, the more rhythmic and matured your recovery techniques are, the more successful you will be.

I keep telling high-potential HR leaders: it's not about whether you will become a CHRO; it's about whether you will be a successful CHRO for long enough. When I became CHRO for the first time, I was ignorant enough to say I didn't need an experienced CHRO as a mentor. I was totally wrong. You need a CHRO who has "been there and done that" in your wisdom council because you are never prepared to handle the multiple orbits and have this level of resilience. Sure, you are prepared to do the technical aspects of the job and handle some of the leadership aspects, like influencing the CEO and Chair, but you're never prepared to handle everything.

I don't have a combative attitude towards the Board. They have a job to do; it's a very difficult job, and I'm there to help them as, ultimately, I work for them and the investors. The CEO and the CFO also have a very difficult job, and if they do it well, everybody benefits. If they do it badly, everybody is in trouble. One of my CEOs told me, 'We haven't got 70,000 employees, we've got 70,000 families to support'. I have never forgotten those words. You must approach things with a positive mindset and think, 'How can I get the best for everybody here?' Board members are there because they are bright, and they will easily spot if you are a bullshitter or a careerist, so I just turn up and try and do my job as well as I can. I find that people react well to that. Some CHROs may get drunk with the idea of hanging out with the Chair or spending time with RemCo. But they're not your friends. You're not going to go on holiday with them. You must remember your position and what you need to deliver: a happy executive team, a happy Board and a successful business.

One opportunity you will get as a senior HR leader, particularly if you become CHRO, is the ability to contribute well beyond HR and help shape the company's overall strategy. This has been the source of great satisfaction for many CHROs, and they embraced it eagerly. This is one of the key reasons Myriam Beatove Moreale picked her second CHRO role with Randstad after Cargill. She shared,

> Being part of my company's Executive Board allows me not just to be an HR leader, but a business leader – shaping the strategic direction. It enables me to contribute broadly to decisions and support leaders and people in being at their best. You need to make strategic choices that truly stick. That means looking at how the organization works today and how it should work in the future, then defining the business model that supports that shift. From there, you can understand the roles and responsibilities, the leadership capabilities and behaviours that are required for the strategy to be successful. That's exactly the role a CHRO plays in these discussions. It's not just about HR; it's about driving business impact. That's where I want to play, and that's where I get my energy. That's also why my background in finance, strategy, and HR has been so valuable – it helps me connect the dots across disciplines and contribute where people and business truly intersect.

Finally, as CHRO, you need to keep an eye on the horizon because if you stay in the seat too long, you may block the way for others. This ties in with managing your own succession and transition to the next generation. That answer will be different for everyone, but Hugo Martinho is one who is very intentional about his own horizon. He openly shared,

> I am very clear on my future, and I share this with my team and even with our shareholders. I will not stay beyond five years in my CHRO role (assuming I can make it that long!). I think companies need to reinvent themselves, and there are cycles. Some of my predecessors have stayed much longer in the position, and I don't think that is right. Companies need new leaders to bring new ideas because human nature makes us become complacent. We start losing the innovative thrill. I gave myself five years, then we will see what happens.

Tatsuo Kinoshita is a leader who had a similar experience and managed a thoughtful, planned transition. He shared,

> After five and a half years as CHRO of an e-commerce company, I knew the time had come for me to pass the baton to the next person. We hired externally a female leader 10 years younger than me with a background at Cisco and Dell. Like me, she had a passion for contributing to develop a Japanese company. Her hiring took 18 months, but it was well-planned, and she became my natural successor, so I was confident to move on.

As a counterpoint, even the most thoughtful and foresighted HR leaders can be surprised by unexpected opportunities, as Stephanie Werner-Dietz experienced.

> I stayed in Nokia 25 years because I loved the company. I never answered external calls, and I did not write a CV for 25 years. Two and a half years into the Nokia CHRO role, a head-hunter called me about another company. She told me, 'You are only 50 years old, are you going to stay in this role for 15 years? Don't you want to get out of your comfort zone? Don't you want a new challenge, to test yourself in a new environment?' I had always told my people, you need to leave your comfort zone to get stronger, but I realized I was not

applying that to myself. Nokia was my absolute comfort zone. That head-hunter really got me on this one.

As you close your Leadership Years and prepare for the next phase, you may be presented with many options, and the simplest one might be to go golfing full-time. However, as we will discuss next, you should plan intentionally for this transition, building on what truly motivates you so you can continue to maximise your long-term satisfaction into your Legacy Years.

YOUR LEGACY YEARS

For global HR leaders who have dedicated decades to shaping organisations and nurturing talent, preparing for the final stage of their full-time executive career presents a unique opportunity for reflection and reinvention. While going fishing can be a great option, for most of us, it is probably not enough. Having personally retired once already, I know that planning for your Legacy Years is critical and needs to be anchored in a great level of **Awareness**. It can be complex, uncertain, and you usually only get one chance to get it right. Many aspects come into play, such as:

- **Financial**: Obviously, you need to feel that you and your significant others will be financially secure. On the other hand, the danger is that you save too much and skimp on living. The book *Die with Zero*[2] can give you some thought-provoking perspectives on this.
- **Emotional**: Breaking away from a 30+ year executive career is an emotional step that cannot be underestimated. How much of your persona is tied to your employment and job title? Next time you sit next to someone on a plane, and they ask what you do, how comfortable will you be to tell them "I do nothing"[3]?
- **Physical**: Health and well-being are likely to become increasingly important in your life, and preparation for this should start as early as possible.
- **Sexual**: OK, this one is clearly for another book, but let us not forget it is part of what makes us human.
- **Social**: Many studies have shown that the extent and breadth of social connectedness correlate with life span. If you regularly and meaningfully connect with others, you will live a longer and likely happier life.

- **Spiritual**: In this broad category, you may include spirituality if you are of a religious inclination, or simply a quest for meaning and fulfilment. In essence, you need to know what will get you out of bed every day, when your email box is almost always empty in the morning.

While still busy as a full-time CHRO, Natalie Bickford has thought about this quite a lot. She cautioned,

> People advise me not to step away from executive life too young because then it's a long road. If I'm honest with myself, I also know that my ego is quite tied up in my work. I love it when I'm out with my husband and people assume for the first half an hour together that I'm a housewife, then they patronizingly say, 'And what about you, do you work at all?' I love that. I recognise that, after you step down, the world changes. People stop returning your calls quite quickly when you are no longer useful, so that transition needs to be orderly and well-planned.

As Natalie alluded to, you need to use your **Awareness** to face your deep-rooted fears. Common ones are "I fear people will forget me", "I fear my life is running out", "I fear losing my cognitive abilities", "I fear I will run out of money", and "I fear I won't matter anymore". There will be more. Dig deep, be brutally honest with yourself. List down your biggest fears and share them with the person closest to you. Get their views and discuss implications. You can then start peeling the onion on addressing those concerns with activities that set you up nicely for the next 5, 10, or 50 years.

When designing your "afterlife", you still need to set long-term objectives. The North Star for your soul. Most executives only have a vague idea of what this might look like as they often don't have the bandwidth to explore the idea in detail beyond "I want more time for myself", "I will learn to play guitar", "I will get healthier", or "I want to give back". While these are well-meaning intentions, they lack specificity. More importantly, they might only reflect where you are in your life at that point, with your current frame of reference. They are, often, simply a subconscious rejection of what you don't like about your current situation, e.g., "I am not at home often enough", "my blood pressure is too high", "I never get to spend time with my kids", or "I wish I had more time for hobbies". Things change and after learning to speak Spanish or finally getting to spend 24 hours a day with your spouse, you might realise that you want different or more things for the long-run. On that point, it may not be you who decides this is not sustainable, but your spouse. Many executives have shared with me that, after years of frequent travel and late nights in the office, being home all day every day has quickly become unsustainable for their spouse who have their own lives, and home, perfectly under control without you, thank you very much.

First, you need to plan way ahead. If you are facing retirement, say within the next 12 months, and do not already have a clear idea of what that may look like for you and your family, you are under-prepared. This is something Charles Bendotti kept in mind throughout his career. He shared,

> I prepared myself for 25 years for the day corporate life would come to an end. I never saw anything from Philip Morris as something I truly owned. For example, when I was an expatriate in Hong Kong living in an expensive villa rented by the company, I would regularly remind my family: remember, this is not ours. We enjoyed the beautiful view, the nice car, and the business class travel but never forgot they weren't ours. That mindset gave me a real sense of freedom. I come from a background that taught me nothing comes without hard work, so I've never been driven by status or money. I appreciate them, of course, but they don't define me. When I turned 45, I made the decision that within ten years, I'd be done with corporate life. So, when I left Philip Morris at 50, I was mentally ready.

If you know Charles, you might appreciate that he is a very passionate and spiritual person who enjoys endurance sports and reads a lot, so his interests are very varied, which always helps. He added,

> It might sound silly to some, but I reconnected with God, not in a religious sense, but by opening myself to something greater. It took a lot of inner work to reconnect with spirituality and rise above the focus on material things, career, and success, to see if there's something higher. In HR, you sometimes must make difficult decisions that deeply impact people's lives, and you learn to protect yourself emotionally. Now, I try to reconnect with my own emotions,

 **Rob gets off his bike for one more meaningful challenge**

When I retired from Corning, I knew I was going to do something, but I did not know what that would be. I was at a point in life where it was mostly about who you are and how you want to spend your time. I always wanted to go to Tibet, so I got my visa and visited monasteries. While there, I thought about what I wanted to do next and decided I would like to be a part of something meaningful and bigger than myself. It had to be with people that I got energy from, who I want to spend time with when I get out of bed in the morning.

I had happily retired from Corning for over a year, cycling and getting fitter when I was approached for a new CHRO role with a family-led company. I thought if I'm going to do this, it needs to be something different. I would want to create a new benchmark for how you are treating people, the types of leaders you are developing and the culture you are creating.

I sat down with the CEO and talked to him about how you develop high-value leaders concerned about more than the financial bottom-line. I talked about what it takes to build an organisation people are drawn to and want to work in. I said, "If you don't want that stuff, that's totally cool – I am doing some consulting, I ride my bike a lot, and I play my guitar, I am all good". However, the CEO loved my vision. He said, "We are a family-led organisation, and we want to be different in how we run our business".

While the company only operates in North America, I agreed to join because it gives me a real sense of purpose. I had turned down a couple of Fortune 500 offers, and I have no regrets. I want to see if I can work with an organisation with the right values and not be driven by a quarterly P&L. I want to create something special.

my true self, and offer that presence to others who might need it or value it. I feel free and I simply let people come to me.

One best practice for transitioning to your Legacy Years is to keep your options open for as long as possible. One way to do this is by simply recognising what option will not work and staying open for anything else. Some people will retire and leave the door open to another CHRO role, while others will move on to other things. Mieke Van de Capelle has reflected on this and shared,

> I don't think I will do a fourth CHRO role. You can never say never, but I feel I've seen a lot, and, at one point, there is a risk that you will think you have seen it all before. You need to remain open to looking at problems differently. You also need to practice what you preach. In HR, we talk about continuous learning and avoiding obsolescence, and I always believed there is an expiry date on executives. When you're too long in a role, you must make room to get a new set of eyes on what you're doing and bring a different perspective. It is mandatory not just for renewal and rejuvenation but for keeping your organization on its toes. Over the years, I've had to part ways with people who were oblivious that they had become obsolete or blockers. I have always been clear that this is not going to be me. At this stage of my career, I have also become far more of a giver than a taker. I enjoy that tremendously, but I must also stay mindful of my own continuous development and growth. I won't go into consulting because I know I would be dramatically unhappy simply giving advice. I also think I'm too young just to be sitting on Boards. I know it is much work, but I enjoy being in the action.

We will specifically address the transition from CHRO to a Board role as a pivotal career moment in our next chapter. At this point, let us simply recognise a variety of things fall within the broad "Board role" category. At one end of the spectrum, you have the independent non-executive director role for a publicly listed organisation, which comes with a lot of regulatory constraints, good financial remuneration and a great deal of public exposure. At the other end, there are advisory Board positions, often for start-up/scale-up businesses, or non-profit organisations, that may not be remunerated but offer a lot more flexibility, growth and opportunity to be hands-on. In between, you have private Boards for family-led or private equity-backed businesses. You must recognise the variety of opportunities and responsibilities that come under the wide Board umbrella, before deciding whether one of those may be right for you. As Phil Read explained, after an operational career, you need to be thoughtful about what comes next.

> I have deeply felt the weight of responsibility in my job over the years. It is a privilege but also unremitting accountability. To be done well, any role needs to be done whole-heartedly. As we think about future roles that we might play, including Board roles, it is important to understand what level of accountability we want at each stage of life.

Finally, almost as important as *what* you will be doing once you transition from your executive role is *how* you manage this transition. Having spoken to many executives who went through the process over the years, I could see three clearly different models emerge.

- **Professional progression**: In this mode, executives strive to carry the momentum of their professional life by transitioning to non-executive roles or building their own advisory business. They typically view this as a natural extension of their executive career and often start these new roles in parallel to their last full-time role.
- **Confident serendipity**: In this mode, executives know well what they do NOT want to do but will not actively try to shape what comes next. They are happy to let people and opportunities come to them, being confident that they are leaving their executive career with a solid reputation and a broad network of relationships that will bring good opportunities to them.
- **Purposeful reinvention**: In this mode, executives decide to pro-actively reinvent themselves in a role that will leverage, but be quite different from, their executive career. This will typically involve becoming a teaching faculty, a coach or getting involved in not-for-profit organisations and generally being of service to others. It may not come with an income stream but must be a source of meaning.

The most successful leaders pick their "legacy model" with their eyes wide open. Whatever you choose to do and how you go about it, the need to remain meaningfully engaged and intellectually stimulated is likely to be critical. It is also a time to soothe your soul. Ranjay Radhakrishnan sees it as shifting his life "from a portfolio of responsibility to a portfolio of joy", which is a beautiful mindset for that stage of life.

NOTES

1 The danger, of course, is to eventually take them for granted and face a rude awakening when moving to smaller or less mature organizations.
2 *Die With Zero*, Bill Perkins, 2020.
3 I first fully retired at 46 years old, and this scenario happened to me often. I would love to see the confusion on people's face when I told them I was doing nothing. While I was at peace with it, I would enjoy watching the five stages of career grief that would often play during our ensuing conversation – from disbelief ("No way!"), curiosity ("How did you swing that one?"), envy ("I wish I could do it too"), doubt ("I would never be able to do this because of [insert a reason])", and finally – after some co-creative soul-searching – to hope ("I must start planning for it too").

Mastering pivotal HR career moments

Seven

To be good at HR, you should have been fired at least once. You need to understand what that feels like.

Thomas Stassen

Throughout my career as an executive recruiter, I got the chance to speak to many HR leaders about their career issues. I have observed that a few lingering issues kept on coming back, often linked to key points of transition or opportunity. In this chapter, we will explore some of these most pivotal moments. They may not "make or break" your career entirely but negotiating them smartly will certainly help improve your chances of success, and happiness, in the long-run.

How do you recognise these pivotal career moments? I would compare them to the concept of moments-of-truth in service businesses, which can drive or destroy customer confidence. They will be high stakes and make your guts churn. Famous examples in the customer service sector include when your luggage gets lost after a flight, when your credit card gets stolen, or when you find bed bugs in your hotel room. Those are rare but emotionally charged incidents. Pivotal career moments are similar. You will be presented with a difficult choice or situation, and you will struggle between competing arguments to decide what to do next. Crucially, how you handle these moments can make a big difference in your HR career trajectory, so let us look at a few of those and apply our Thriving Career wisdom to help you navigate them successfully.

CENTER OF EXPERTISE ROLES – A BLESSING OR A CURSE?

Center of Expertise (COE) roles in HR are critically important for any organisation, as Amanda Rajkumar highlighted.

> I believe they are equal to the business partner teams. I've always beefed up COEs, which can create a healthy tension with HR leaders

in the business partner functions. You want both sides of any HR function to be strong, highly capable and innovative, working in harmony, in a symbiotic relationship.

So, while COE roles are clearly important for the business, are they critically important for your career?

For Human Resources professionals aspiring to leadership positions, a career trajectory is rarely a straight line. It often involves navigating a landscape of diverse roles, each offering unique growth and skill development opportunities. Among these, the COE role presents a compelling case for strategic career advancement. Some people will see these specialised functions as offering a deep dive into critical HR disciplines, fostering expertise that can be invaluable in ascending the corporate ladder. Others will see it as a mere distraction from developing the leadership skills required for an HR generalist career. These split views were echoed through my CHRO conversations. A share of CHROs argued that developing functional expertise is foundational for a solid career, but an equal number felt that expertise could easily be acquired by hiring the right people and learning from them on your way up.[1] This dichotomy was well illustrated by Darrell Ford who recalled,

> For most of my career, I've done what I called the tick-tock – like the pendulum that swings in a clock. I've gone from COE to operations to generalist assignments, and back and forth, to broaden my skills and my experiences across HR. I've done just about every HR job there is over the course of my career, which rounds me out as the ultimate generalist.

How you look at COE roles will be a very personal decision. CHROs who never went through COE roles felt they did not miss anything. But those who did felt they learned a lot from such roles. I will help break down the issues for you here but, in the end, you will have to decide what might suit you best. If you aim to be a HR specialist, and do not aspire to go broad, then your choices will be relatively easy, and any COE role should be welcome. But if your career aim is, at some point, to become a global HR generalist, read on.

A whole other book should probably be dedicated to the career development of HR sub-functions, which is both critical and subtle, but for now, let us first acknowledge two hard truths with regard to COE roles

1. Not all COE functions are created equal when it comes to accelerating your career trajectory.
2. The stage you are in your career will influence how you should look at COE roles.

Many leaders think of their career as a T-shape development. The vertical branch refers to depth in a proficiency area, while the horizontal branch refers to the ability to deploy leadership skills across a range of sub-functions, including the ability to engage and persuade colleagues from other parts of the organisation. Here is a short sample of a few of the vertical HR areas where you could develop a functional expertise, and how your career trajectory might evolve as a result:

Talent & Organisation: The strategic bet. Here we group functions such as Talent Management (TM) and Organisational Development (OD) as they are often the most strategic sub-functions of HR. John Holding is particularly fond of the OD function to develop a strong strategic view of HR that is closely tied to the business. He shared,

> I think the best CHROs have an OD bent because it is what matters most at Group level. Do the business leaders have the core capabilities to execute on the strategy? Are the organization and the jobs designed right? Are the senior people working as a high performing team? Are the skills in place across the business? Do you know the most important roles in the business, and are succession plans dynamic, reviewed and actioned? Is there a sound talent strategy in place?

If you happen to be in a Group TM or OD role while a large M&A project is taking place, it can be a great help for your career. Tripti Jha shared that experienced leading the Group Talent function in Novartis.

> One of the advantages of heading the end-to-end Talent agenda is that you work with the CHRO, the CEO, the entire executive committee and the Board. I was privileged to work a lot with the Board of the company, with the nomination and remuneration committees on all key appointments and talent issues. One of the projects the Sandoz Chairman asked me to help with was to set up the Sandoz board as

we prepared for the spin-off from Novartis. I helped build that board, working with the Chair and it was a great exercise and opportunity to set up a high calibre Board from scratch.

Such strategic roles will, almost always, be worth your consideration as career accelerators and you should welcome an opportunity to spend time there.

Total Rewards: The smart investment. Total Rewards is perhaps the quintessential COE where skills and knowledge can distinguish great from merely good performers. One reason for HR leaders to welcome a rotation in Total Rewards towards the end of their career is to get exposed to executive compensation. This experience is sometimes seen as critical for aspiring Group CHROs and will give senior Total Rewards leaders early exposure to working with Boards.

An early Total Rewards experience can also be foundational in driving practical HR discipline as Tanuj Kapilashrami experienced early on in HSBC.

> To be a great CHRO, being a generalist aggregator is not enough. In the early stages in your career, you need to fill technical gaps, and your skillset needs to be rooted in the technical specialism of the function. In my early career in HSBC, everyone wanted to be an HR business partner because that was the sexy thing at the time, but I took an opportunity to do an assignment in Hong Kong in Rewards. It was fantastic because in those days it was a very technical job, full of excel spreadsheets and pivot tables. Unlike today, technology was not great, so I learned a lot from it.

Total Rewards roles have the potential to pigeon-hole their practitioners and limit their career options, but the highly analytical nature of the work will suit many who do not aspire to the softer side of HR.

Talent Acquisition: The honey trap. Talent Acquisition (TA) is sometimes seen as the poor cousin of HR sub-functions when it comes to career development. In fact, in my 2025 HR Career Survey, this was the sub-function with the lowest career satisfaction level (12% below the HR average). It can be a very process-heavy function that does not naturally open doors to broader HR roles or other sub-functions. In addition, much like engineering or sales roles, if you are very good at your TA role, you become a precious organisation resource and there will be limited incentives for the company to move you around. While it can be an exciting area, with a measurable impact and good exposure beyond HR, you might easily get pigeon-holed there.

If you want to build a generalist HR career and are offered a move to a TA role, make sure it is strategic in scope and intent, which is what Deborah Borg experienced mid-way through her career in Dow.

> The company said if I wanted my career to progress, I needed a COE experience. I didn't really want to do that, as I felt it was too far away from the action. However, they said 'you want to drive change, right? We need to transform the way we recruit' and they sold me a regional recruiting role as an opportunity to run my own internal business. It was very formative to be able to build things at scale, which helped me later in my CHRO roles. It gives you a different set of questions to ask, things to look out for. For example, I can spend a lot of time personally interfering and intervening in people's careers, but I can only do that for a handful of people. How do you get to *everybody*? How do you find the Deb in Australia who no one knows? What mechanisms can you put in place that let's this great but invisible talent find their way through the organization?

People Analytics: The bold move. The People Analytics sub-function is still emerging in many organisations and is driven largely by technology development and the rise of new AI-led capabilities. It can be a source of great learning for HR professionals in the early part of their career, and many CHROs interviewed mentioned this is likely to be a key skill for HR practitioners in the future. While it is not yet as prevalent as the other HR COEs, I believe young HR professionals today should consider a rotation in People Analytics and get exposed early to what will be considered mainstream HR in the next decade.

Ingolf Thom is a proponent of HR leaders embracing their analytical side more proactively. He advised to

> Discover the analytical side in you. It is increasingly important for HR professionals to have an appreciation for data and analytics, not being afraid of numbers, but embracing them. HR needs to use data to make decisions, and historically we were not the strongest at it. As an HR professional, you need to speak the language of your client organizations, which in many industries is numbers. Don't come with

fluffy bullet points on PowerPoint but bring evidence and show trends you analysed. You need to have your act together when it comes to analytics and not be afraid of it.

A stint in the People Analytics function may give you that edge that will make you stand out.

Now let us also examine how your career stage will influence how you should look at COE roles.

- In your Formative years, there is essentially no bad choice, and any COE role will be an opportunity to learn something new. The only pitfall, if you don't plan to build a specialist career, would be to do the same COE role twice in a row. You would risk getting pigeon-holed into that specific sub-function of HR. To be sure, it is perfectly OK to do so by choice, but only if it happens intentionally.
- During your Growth years, the choice becomes trickier. Taking on a COE role risks disrupting your trajectory, unless (1) it is part of a clear development plan and the role has a clear logical next step and/or (2) it is a clear growth opportunity, for instance by giving you your first global role or your first exposure to HQ. If neither of those scenarios is in play, you should be wary of making a lateral move into a COE role without a clear path beyond it.
- In your Leadership Years, if you are determined to becoming a global CHRO, there are only two COE role that, in my view, possibly make sense as a final step to get there: the Group Head of TM (to get exposure to the entire C-Suite and the Board) and the Group Head of Rewards (to round up your profile, particularly if it has a strong focus on executive compensation). Any other COE role will probably be only a derailer or a placeholder role while you are passed over for CHRO succession.

If you aim to be a generalist, the case for and against COE roles as a means to develop your career can be equally strong. Ultimately, you will have to decide what is best for you based on where you are in your career, and what is your North Star.

On the For side

- You may get surprised by how much you learn from it. It happened to Tatsuo Kinoshita when he was appointed as a COE head for the

Ingolf loves moving around the HR operating model

To be successful in HR I believe you must explore the entire operating model, and I was fortunate that my career went this way. COE roles teach you important things you won't get from other parts of HR. COE experiences taught me how to see the big picture, strategise with the business, and set corporate governance. How do you define a process or solution that will be readily adopted in all sites around the world? How do you design, deploy, and govern it? How do you introduce it, communicate it and roll it out?

I always found COEs to be the place where the future is created. When you are in the field, you deal with tactical, day-to-day problems. In a COE, you learn to think long term. You engage with business leaders on their people priorities, monitor external trends, talk to leading consultants, and see the bigger picture. It also teaches you project and change management, which often is not the strongest HR skillset. Work in a COE gets done differently than in business partnering or operational roles in the field. Knowing how to navigate and deliver in these contexts is critical if your aim is to become a good CHRO or global business partner. For anyone who is mid-career and wondering about a first COE opportunity, I would always advise to try it out.

I have seen it can be a humbling experience for individuals coming from a business partner role where you are responsive to the needs of a leader or a leadership team. Suddenly, you are responsible for a set of processes used worldwide and their continuous improvement. It's a different way of getting work done and it is important to have that experience in your toolbox. For example, a Total Rewards role is important to understand how incentive systems really work and how a Board of Directors looks at remuneration. What are the KPIs in your short-term incentive programme and how do you link incentives to business strategy? How do you explain that to an organisation? You need have an appreciation for numbers, for statistics. You need to embrace it as part of your toolkit, and an experience in Total Rewards gives you that sort of mindset and capability.

HR Operations of GE Japan. "I was not convinced initially, because I always felt more like a business guy, and I am less interested in corporate shared services. I thought I would give it a try and see what I could learn, and it turned out to be fantastic. That job helped me understand technology, and that is something I have used for the rest of my career, especially as CHRO of the Japanese e-commerce company Mercari. It also taught me how to establish global operations and helped me build a lot of connections as I could work with other regions".

- If you do a COE role early in your career, you will develop skills that will serve you well over the long-run. This is what happened to Monique Carter in her first company. "The CHRO in Comet told me I had the potential to be her successor one day, but, first, she asked me to become the company's head of Centres of Excellences. In those days, it was a broad mandate dealing with culture, engagement, management development, operational training, and talent management. My first reaction is that I didn't really want to do it, I thought it was going to be too slow and not connected with the customer, which I enjoyed. I had to be persuaded this was a good idea, but I did it and really enjoyed it. It was the first pivotal moment in my career".

On the Against side

- As a generalist, you can probably build deep technical skills quickly if you surround yourself with the right people and are smart enough to ask the right questions. This is something Allison Pinkham strongly believes in. "At a young age, I was taught to look beyond obstacles, and focus on working harder, preparing more and leveraging all the resources I could to accomplish any goal. For example, I was originally told I needed to lead Total Rewards at some point in my career to become a CHRO. However, my view is that if you have high learning agility, strong business acumen, and a great Head of Total Rewards you don't necessarily need to have led Total Rewards before becoming a CHRO. It's about surrounding yourself with an exceptional team and having a strong desire to learn".
- Not every company and culture is created equal when it comes to the construct of COE roles. In some companies, these roles will

be the cornerstone of HR career development while in others they might be administrative and largely toothless. Use your **Awareness** to read your context when making your career decisions, as Hugo Martinho did in Schindler. "A few years ago, the company offered me to be Group Head of Talent and Development at HQ in Switzerland. I felt that was not for me. These Group COEs roles are far from the business because of distance and time difference, and because Schindler is very decentralized. I felt I needed to be where the action happens. Self-awareness and organizational awareness are very important for us to have clarity when we make career decisions, so I turned that COE role down".

COE roles can offer a valuable pathway for HR professionals to deepen their functional expertise, develop strategic thinking, hone process management skills, and leverage data for impactful decision-making. However, it is crucial to be aware of the potential disadvantages, such as the risk of getting siloed and the possibility of getting disconnected from the business. By strategically selecting COE roles that align with their career North Star, Thriving Career builders can leverage these specialised functions as a calculated climb towards impactful and fulfilling leadership positions. The journey to becoming a successful HR leader can certainly involve embracing specialisation, but never at the expense of a holistic understanding of the business and the people it serves.

A FISH OUT OF WATER – ROLES OUTSIDE OF HR

In the dynamic landscape of modern business, the role of the HR professional has evolved from administrative oversight to strategic partnership. For those aspiring to senior leadership roles, including the coveted CHRO position, the strategic decision to spend time in roles outside of the HR function can be a powerful driver for career advancement. It can also be a death trap. While such a move presents both opportunities and potential pitfalls, on balance, the prevailing sentiment among seasoned CHROs suggests that the advantages of gaining cross-functional experience can outweigh the risk and turn you into a more holistic and impactful HR leader.

If you are simply considered for such a stretch assignment, it is already a positive sign for your career. Charles Bendotti, who has clear views on the topic and spent half of his career leading business, looks at it in a pragmatic way. He shared,

> I have massive respect for the HR function and its importance, but if you never get the chance to take on even one role outside of HR, something's off. It usually means people didn't see you as versatile enough or agile enough beyond your domain. How can you become a truly well-rounded leader if you've only ever seen one side of the business?

It does not mean that you must accept that assignment, but if no one ever considered you for a role outside of HR, it might be a sign that you need to work on your business acumen or, at the very least, your reputation.

Many of the CHROs I interviewed shared that they had been considered for roles outside of the HR function at some point, especially during their Formative Years. One executive, who was picked in his Leadership Years, was Frédéric Chardot. When working in LVMH, he was tapped on the shoulder and explained,

> Late in my career, I got offered the opportunity to leave HR and drive commercial transformation globally. I always say to people, whatever you decide, it must be your own choice. I just said Yes and decided in five minutes to leave HR without knowing if I would come back. I had the intuition it was the right thing to do. Suddenly, I didn't have my HR community to back me up. You want to know who's doing what? Sorry, you don't have access to the org chart or the HR systems to check things out. It was exhausting but it was fantastic. We had a strong impact on the business, and it was so successful that I was promoted to lead global transformation at Moët Hennessy. I really enjoyed that job, but transformation roles require you to have so much energy and drive as you are moving mountains on your own. Your 'tour of transformation' can't last for too long. After 3 years, I started to realize I was missing HR. Yes, you can have great impact as a business leader, but I was losing my impact on people, so I chose to go back to HR.

One of the safer ways to do a role outside of HR is to do it in your early years, as part of a rotational programme. Not only will the career stakes be lower, but it will shape you as a HR leader for the rest of your career. This is something Janice Deskus experienced early on, and which marked her for life. She recalled,

The Hamilton Standard (now a division of Raytheon) CHRO came to me one day and said he wanted me to leave HR. I was shocked! He said the best HR people know the business and he wanted me to learn it. I joined Hamilton's Operations Management Development programme that was almost exclusively for engineers. It was a two-year programme with one six-month assignment as a foreman on the shop floor. I was maybe 25 years old, and here was little blondie girl from HR getting into the plant. I remember how much the hourly folks hated this program; they called us the golden children. There were about 50 unionized men, all over the age of 45. I remember saying, 'Listen, I don't have a clue what you people do out here, but I hope you can teach me how to add value'. This showed humility and a willingness to learn rather than a know-it-all approach I think they were expecting.

When her rotation came to end, it was Janice's turn to be in for a surprise.

When I left six months later, they rolled me in a chair to the middle of the group and gave me two presents. The first was a training certificate for my 'Introduction to Reality', which was the course they said they had put me through. The second one was a plaque they made me swear on that I would always keep it in my office. It was a Velvet Hammer Award because I was soft and sweet but also knew how to be tough. They made me put my hands on both plaques and swear that, as I became a 'big shot' in my career, I would always have these in my office, so I would remember how they contributed to my growth and wouldn't forget where I came from. They are in still on my wall today and one of my greatest sources of pride.

When evaluating roles outside of HR, it can be helpful to distinguish between getting another related functional experience, such as leading Communications, Transformation or even Strategy, and running a commercial business or operations, which may be a more significant career risk (but a source of great learning, if you succeed). In addition, it is important to consider whether this is a rotation as part of a development plan to make you a more well-rounded HR leader, or an outright career shift designed to re-orient your career. All scenarios can lead to success, but you need to have upfront clarity so you can weigh the risks of making such a move against the potential rewards.

Hugo uses his HR tricks to turn operations around

Mid-way through my HR career with Schindler, we had an issue in Singapore, where our operations had been one of the world's most underperforming. Suddenly the Asia Pacific president asked me to take over. He said, "We tried so many things and nothing seems to work. We have nothing more to lose!" He strongly believed we had a people issue and trusted I could handle it.

I decided to take up the challenge, even if that meant going two levels down in job grade. Life should not be about rank but having new experiences and building capabilities, and that Singapore GM role offered me the chance to run a P&L and be accountable for an operation. I never saw that as a demotion. What is more important? A little bit more money in the bank or the chance to create a new future? Of course, it was a huge risk because many others had failed but I felt that if my bosses invested in me, they should have some belief I could do it.

I never worked so hard in my life because the situation was indeed critical and in operations you are only as good as the numbers. At the beginning, the CFO was worried because she knew the HR guy was coming to run the business. She expected a disaster. However, because I'm not a financial or technical person, I saw things in a different way, and believed profitability would come if you made the right decisions. Some of those decisions cause a lot of grievance with HQ because I completely changed our strategy and not a single management team member survived the first year. I also used simple HR tricks. For example, I showed the team how Singapore performance compared (badly) to Hong Kong, which hurt their pride. I redesigned variable compensation, which nobody used to look at, to focus on delivery. With changes like this, suddenly quality improved because people started being part of the solution. As a result, in three years, we doubled the size of our business, and tripled profitability. I thoroughly enjoyed it.

When it comes down to leaving HR to lead a business, there are two schools of thoughts. Leaders like Charles or Hugo feel that it can be a tremendous experience to add to your credibility with the business. Charles put it in a particularly vivid way and shared that

> People often confuse business acumen with business credibility. To earn credibility with a line leader, you need the scars. You need to have been on the same battleground. It's just like in the army: some go to the front line, others stay back and cook. Yes, they're all part of the same unit, but when it's time to fight, you'll always trust the one who's been under fire, not the one who was stirring the pot in the kitchen.

The counterpoint to this argument is that if you leave HR to run a business, you might not get a chance to really stand out. Several CHROs were offered the opportunity to run business but turned it down after careful consideration. Usha Kakaria-Cayaux put it best when she explained

> Several times in my career, I had an opportunity to move out of HR and work in the business. I always said thanks but no thanks. For example, a few years ago I was working for a great regional CEO who told me, 'I'll give you a GM job tomorrow if you want it. I know your skills and you know the business, so you will be successful'. However, one mentor advised me, 'Sure, you can go be a GM, and you'll probably be a good one. But you don't know if you will be a great one. You'll probably just be part of a group of a hundred other good GMs in the company. However, right now you stand out, because there are few HR leaders who are commercial, and you act like a business leader not an HR leader. The question is, will you stand out as a general manager?' It was a good question, and it scared the heck out me, not because I wanted to stand out, but because I wanted to make a difference. It didn't necessarily deter me, but it made me think. How will doing a business role enable me to have greater impact *and* grow professionally? Should I step out of a place where I disproportionately add value? Or amplify my impact in an area I can differentiate myself in and help to elevate the HR function based on having started my career outside of HR.

In the end, led by her strong **Awareness**, Usha concluded that the best way to stand out might simply be to stick with being a differentiated HR person and be at peace with it. Ranjay Radhakrishnan, who is always very thoughtful on such topics, echoed the same idea.

> I landed in HR by accident but chose to stay by design. A few times in my career I was offered to go work outside HR and I always refused. I genuinely love HR, and I've always loved it. I will never know whether I did the right thing or wrong thing, but I know I did the happy thing. I've seen many people who are brilliant functional experts become average general managers. If you know what you're good at, if you know what you are happy doing, why would you want to go and start doing something else? Because you have a desire for hierarchical progression and want to be somebody? Sorry, I don't want to be somebody else.

FORESEEING AND HANDLING POTENTIAL CAREER ACCIDENTS

Despite your best efforts at career management, it is likely that, at some point, you will face a potential "career accident", i.e., a difficult situation where you encounter a tough choice and might feel forced to make a move. We have already touched on some of those instances earlier in this book but let us review some of the most common causes of career accidents, so you learn how to spot them early to potentially prevent them. If not, then get ready to act.

- Getting pigeon-holed into a sub-area of HR too early. This is the curse of competence. Being good at something usually means you will get more of it, and you can unintentionally box yourself in. Use your **Awareness** to manoeuvre around this potential pitfall.
- Being put in a situation where your values are compromised. HR leaders with a spike in **Bravery** will always stand for what they believe in. If you find yourself in a situation where, despite your best efforts, you cannot change your context, do not compromise. It is time to step out.
- Tying yourself too closely to a single sponsor. It can be easy to be lulled by a sense of complacency when you are following a rising star. It may even get you very close to the top but, at some point, the music may stop. Never skimp on **Connectivity**, even if you feel that things are going great. It will be your career insurance policy.

- Getting bogged down by the politics of middle management. If corporate politics is not your game, stick to your skills in **Delivery** as a key differentiator. And if you see that the corporate culture does not value this anymore, it is time to change your context.
- Getting on the wrong side of a corporate restructuring or a post-merger integration. Things happen; you cannot always be on the winning side. My advice here is not to get too jittery. Too often, I see executives starting to send out CVs when a deal is announced. Why the rush? If you are a talent, the organisation will surely find a way to retain you. You may not get a perfect role at first, but you should play the long game.

If, despite all your efforts and best intentions, you have just lost your job unexpectedly, despair not. It is time to move from passive opportunity generation to active job searching. Focusing on Career Health is still important, but now you need surgery.

First you need to cover the basics – update your CV, brush up your executive branding profile on LinkedIn and social media, activate your networks and make your recruiter contacts aware of your situation (see Arnaud's Take for a deep dive on best practice recruiter management). There are plenty of consultants and literature out there to help you with this.

In parallel to these short-term initiatives, think through your options strategically. Be realistic that, when you are actively looking for a new role, you lose some of your bargaining power. It is not so much about what you are interested in doing any more, but more about who will be interested in what you can do. Do a stock-take of your experience and your capabilities: who is most likely to find value in your experience and, therefore, in hiring you? The closer you stay to your existing industry and latest role, the higher your chance of success. Trying to change too many degrees of freedom at once might be stretching yourself too much and delay finding a new role. For example, as I live in Singapore, I am often contacted by executives from the United States or Europe who have lost their jobs and want to explore whether it is time for them to get their first Asia experience. My answer is invariably that it will be very hard. If you have never worked in a region, but want to move there, aim to move internally first. It is very unlikely a new employer will take a risk hiring a new executive straight into a new geography where they have never worked.

Be proactive and data-driven. Which sectors are your primary targets? Which ones are growing? What are the most relevant companies for you to target in those sectors? Who are the key people you need to get to know in those companies? If you have followed this book's advice on **Connectivity**, you should already have a built-in list of former colleagues and university alumni who could be good contacts for you. You should already have initiated a relationship with them. Now is the time to ramp things up and check in to see how they might be able to help you.

Lastly, when presented with a new job opportunity, do your due diligence. Then do some more. I personally recommend reverse reference-checking. Just as a potential employer will want to speak to your referees, you should want to do the same. Think about it – would you buy a new house without speaking to the neighbours first?

We can learn from Yolanda Talamo, who took great care in selecting her next organisation after getting on the losing side of an acquisition. She shared this great example:

> When I interviewed to join SABMiller I wanted to make sure that the culture was right for me. After I met the hiring manager, I asked if I could speak to more people in the business before I made my decision. He looked at me funny and said, 'Are you asking me for more interviews that are not needed?' I had to explain that I really wanted to make sure I made the right call, because I was burned once before. He seemed to love the idea and organized a trip for me to Colombia and to Peru which were the largest businesses of the entire company worldwide at the time. I visited the business, spoke to the general managers and the HR heads, and toured the breweries. When I came back, the hiring manager jokingly asked 'Are you pleased? Do you need to speak to more people?' I eagerly said that I was very pleased to accept the offer. After I joined SABMiller, he kept on sharing the story with everybody. I became 'the girl who asked for more interviews.'
> I don't regret doing it. Sometimes you need to be sure, even if you must ask for unconventional things, like more interviews. It turned out to be a great fit, and the next few years were great for me. I integrated very well and fell in love with the company and its culture.

If you don't feel as comfortable as Yolanda formally asking for additional meetings, you should do your own confidential reference-checking. To be clear, I am not talking about scrolling through anonymous Glassdoor reviews but having targeted, individual conversations. A few clicks on LinkedIn should allow you to quickly find several former executives of the team, function or BU you would be joining. I find that people are generally very happy to help and generous with their time … if they had a good experience. If people don't respond, or you get only very generic, non-committal opinions, keep in mind that in reference-checking exercises, what is *not* said is almost as revealing as what is openly shared.

ARNAUD'S TAKE

Let us discuss how to optimise your interactions with professional recruiters, primarily those working in external search firms. In fact, the principles are essentially the same for dealing with in-house TA executives. Always remember that you are building a relationship with people, not with institutions and recruiting talent moves freely and often between search firms and internal TAs teams. What goes around comes around and it simply pays off to be helpful to everyone.

External recruiters should always want to get to know HR leaders, simply because they will hope to get business from you at some point. They may not lose much sleep over helping you get a job, but the notable, and most important, exceptions will be the HR search boutiques as well as the HR practice of bigger firms. These are the recruiters you should want to get to know for your own career, and they can be different from the people you use to hire for your organisation, even if they are in the same firm.

Be discerning on how you spend your time with recruiters. You could spend an inordinate amount of time networking with them and turn this into a near full-time job. However, this may paint you as a so-called "stalker". Focus on the firms that have the best reputation, and the consultants with whom you have personal chemistry. Please do not talk about Firm A to a consultant in Firm B. You ideally want each recruiter to feel like they have a unique, privileged relationship with you.

As mentioned earlier, be constructive with any recruiter who contacts you. They have elephant memories and, most critically, they have a database. You don't want to be labelled as unhelpful. You cannot always tell who might get your profile into a short-list. Even the most junior person in a recruiting team might make or break a future candidacy. Be engaging with everyone and be generous with information when they call you to get your views. It will pay back in the long-run.

If you are actively looking to generate external career opportunities, an important preliminary step is to do your homework. Do not expect recruiters to do the thinking for you on where and how you should look. Too many executives have come to me looking for a job asking me "Who do you think will value my background?" I am sorry, but it is your career, not mine. That is for you to figure out and tell me how you think I can help.

Before you start speaking to recruiters, make sure to have your story ready. What are you looking for? What are your red lines or constraints? How do you think about compensation? For example, beyond sharing your current compensation or your broad expectations, be ready to articulate how important compensation is at this stage of your life, how you think about fixed vs variable, how much financial risk are you prepared to take, etc.

Make sure to include in your outreach the internal TA leaders of the companies you are targeting. Yes, it might hurt your ego to reach out to people who may be more junior than you and to ask for a favour, but beggars cannot be choosers. Importantly, try first to find out who the real hiring decision-makers are in each company. TA executives can be anything from a mere mailbox passing on CVs, to a strategic business partner and major gatekeeper in hiring decisions. Try to figure this out, so you can be strategic in how you approach each company.[2]

As an HR leader, you should have been part of dozens, if not hundreds, of hiring processes for your own companies. You will have worked with some great candidates, some who are a nightmare, and anyone in between. Leverage that experience when the tables are turned and be the candidate you wish you could hire. Think of the few candidates who have most impressed you and how they behaved during the hiring process. What words come mind to describe them? Here are some that would make my list: approachable, authentic, decisive, forthcoming, pragmatic, professional, and responsive. The list goes on, and you can make your own. As a candidate, think of systematically displaying these behaviours when dealing with recruiters, in search firms or in-house. Their experience with you as a candidate will make a lasting impression, whether you get the job or not.

Be transparent and forthcoming with information. A recruitment process is in essence a dating game. A dance, followed by a negotiation, and – perhaps – a deal. It can be tempting to play your cards close to your chests, trying to learn more about the other party's needs and intentions while disclosing as little as you can. This may, however, paint you as a difficult, perhaps even dishonest, candidate. I would always advise full transparency. For instance, in some U.S. jurisdictions, it is illegal for a recruiter to ask for your compensation. However, besides the legal principle, do you have a valid reason for holding back that information? If not, just volunteer the data, and it will be easier for everyone.

If you are not genuinely interested in a role, say No early in the process. Candidates who go all the way through the process and turn down an offer at the last minute are disruptive. This always reflects badly on them, no matter what reason they give for turning the offer down (the blame is often shifted to their spouse). It will usually result in a big red cross on their file for future roles handled by that recruiting firm. Do yourself a favour, if you have a sense that a role is not right for you, declare it as early as possible in the process. If the recruiter insists for you to "please keep an open mind and just go meet the client for coffee" then you can be satisfied you have done your part. No one should be surprised if you decline the role in the end.

Lastly, recruiters are experienced at picking up red flags. Personally, I am always wary of candidates who are interested in any job that comes their way, who have not done thorough research in the client company, or who have not consulted their family about a possible relocation. I even had an HR executive once proudly tell me of all the offers she got and turned down. I asked her why she did this. She smiled saying she simply wanted to know how much she was worth. In my experience, those are signs that a candidate is not serious. Such red flags will erode trust both for the recruiter and the hiring company. So, think like a HR person (!) ... what would you worry about if you were your own candidate? Address any of those issues early and openly.

MANAGING THE TRANSITION TO YOUR FIRST CHRO ROLE

Not everyone will aim to become a global Group CHRO but getting into such a visible and sought-after role can feel like the pinnacle of one's HR career. This pivotal moment often results from a lot of hard work and does not happen by chance. Most companies put a great deal of time and attention into selecting their C-Suite executives and the CHRO role is no exception. If you are considered for a CHRO role, take comfort in the fact that you do deserve to be at that point in your career.

One useful data point is that, across the 45 CHROs interviewed for this book, about half of them got their first CHRO role through a head-hunter, while the other half were either promoted internally or accessed that opportunity through a personal connection. This means that, despite my previous admonitions that head-hunters won't be much use in your career, they are quite important to transitioning to the CHRO level, especially if you happen to have a diverse demographic profile, which is often a key selection criterion in external CHRO hiring.[3]

Besides what we covered in our earlier chapter on Leadership Years, for the purpose of demystifying this pivotal career moment, we will discuss two critical areas:

- How should you decide what CHRO role to pick when presented with an opportunity?
- What to expect when you get into the role and prepare to hit the ground running?

Transitioning to your first CHRO role is a critical career step and doing it in the right company is important. Building on the **Awareness** that you should have developed through your career, make sure to do a thorough due diligence, pick a company that will fit with your motives and offers a context that will maximise your chance of success. Mieke Van de Capelle recalled what it took for her to pick her first CHRO role.

> As a senior HR leader, I could never work for a company that is high on centralization and control. That's not who I am. I always wanted to work in empowering organizations, making sure that accountabilities were drilled down as low as possible, de-layering, simplifying.
> You need to be mindful about what you stand for and whether that matches the company culture. Otherwise, you're just fitting a square peg into a round hole.

One of the special cases of first CHRO appointments is the "big fish in a small pond" scenario, when you are offered to step up to your first CHRO role in a smaller, sometimes much smaller, organisation.

This can be a very hard decision to make as it gives you the chance to have a bigger personal impact but on a relatively small scale. A couple of our CHROs took up such an opportunity. It is fair to say it mostly did not work out as they had hoped. They were back on the corporate ladder a couple of years later. It does not mean it could not be right for you, but you should apply caution when assessing the future potential, and the culture, of a smaller business.

Many of the CHROs I interviewed transitioned to their first CHRO on an internal promotion, where they were familiar with the context. This is obviously a less risky transition as you will have the advantage, and some of the disadvantages, of being a relatively well-known quantity to the selection committee. Stephanie Werner-Dietz experienced this first-hand in Nokia and got the chance to push back on her first CHRO promotion that required a relocation until the timing was right for her family, thanks to her strong **Bravery**.

> I remember I was helping my Nokia CHRO do succession planning for his own role, and we had put together a great list. As the management team was reviewing this list, my name came up, and I was added. I was shocked. I had never planned to be a CHRO, and I was not sure if the timing was right since my daughter was still small, so I decided to hold off. After several months, the opportunity came up again, and everything worked out well in the end both for the company and for my family. When I left Nokia a few years later to become CHRO at ArcelorMittal, I remember the CEO said in my farewell speech 'Stephanie is going to a steel company, which is very appropriate since she has nerves of steel!'

Once you have been selected for the role, you might want to invest in getting someone to coach you on what to expect, as most of the CHROs I interviewed shared that they were scarcely prepared for the demands of the role. Yolanda Talamo was aware of that potential gap when she stepped up to the CHRO role at Heineken and proactively worked to close it.

> It is important that you get support in transitioning to your new role as CHRO. I got consistent advice from many people to find a coach. I hired someone from an executive search firm who I felt comfortable with, and it was the best decision I could take. She taught me how to find answers in myself. She helped me so much.

It takes a lot of **Awareness** to realise that getting to the top is not the end of the journey, but only a new beginning.

Once you get appointed in the role, you will surely want to hit the ground running. Don't! The first thing you should realise is that, more than for any other transition in your career, it is urgent for **Delivery** to wait. You should spend your first few weeks taking things in, especially if you are new to the organisation. Even if you are going through an internal promotion, you should start by asking questions and deciding what kind of CHRO you want to be.

Having spent the first decade of her career as a business consultant, Athalie Williams knew that she would have to go back to her roots when she stepped up to the CHRO role at BHP.

> When I got into my first CHRO role, I remember thinking about it as if I were in a consulting role. You go into a new client, and you don't necessarily understand their business, but you can bring structure and process. I knew I had to put those in place to get to the outcomes the business needed. I drew on the knowledge and expertise around me to create the conditions for us to be successful. I thought this would be my contribution. I would not suddenly become an expert in coal or in business partnering, but I could help the team understand the roadmap and make sure that we had the right processes in place to deliver.

As we discussed earlier, managing your relationship with the CEO and the Board is key to your success as a CHRO, and this should start as soon as you get selected and appointed. Charles Bendotti recalled his selection process as CHRO of Phillip Morris International.

> One Board member asked me, 'Charles, what kind of CHRO will you be, the CHRO of the company or the CHRO of the CEO?' I paused and said, 'That's a very good question. If you're asking, I imagine you expect me to say: the company's CHRO, not the CEO's.' Then I added, 'I will always do what's right for the company. But in return, I also expect never to be put in a position where I'm caught between the Board and the CEO. If you have something to say to my CEO, speak to him directly.' In the same way, from the beginning, my CEO and I agreed on full transparency. I committed to always telling him when I agreed or disagreed but when we walked into the Boardroom, we would speak with one voice. I also told him, 'If the Board asks

Leanne opens her mind to her potential

I never thought I wanted to be a Group HR head. When I was in Diageo, the CHRO had been in his role for 13 years and I felt I was so different from, and less experienced than, him. I told people I didn't aspire to that job, but one colleague said, "Actually you would just do it your own way and that would be enough". That was a chink of light for me. Then, one day I had a conversation with the Diageo CFO, who I had worked with years before and had always been a big supporter of mine, even though we'd had some big debates and disagreements. In that conversation, he casually asked, "What are we going to do to put you in the best position possible for the Group HR Director job?" The word that stood out to me was "we". What are WE going to do. Suddenly, somebody was alongside me. Driving home that evening my mind was blown that he believed this could be a good idea. There was nothing certain at all, of course, but that conversation gave me a sense of momentum.

The company went through a transparent selection process, including looking externally, over about a year. I brought an unusual mix of skills beyond HR and that's what, I think, got me the job. The CEO could see that I was first and foremost coming at it through a business lens and could bring change and transformation because I was not hindered by old thinking. I think that is what made the difference.

When I left the Group HR Director role at Diageo two years later, people thought I was insane and, in many ways, I was. I think I was too young to know I should have stayed. I didn't really understand at the time that these jobs are big commitments, and you must live up to them. I didn't understand what a mess I created until I started to step down. Once I started talking to my CEO about leaving, I couldn't stay. Something was broken in the relationship. I feel I let him down and I would have wanted to take that back if I could.

for my view, I'll say we got aligned, but I'll also share my personal perspective if needed.' His response stayed with me. He said, 'That's exactly what the Board expects. I may be the CEO today, but I'm also a Board member and tomorrow I might be Chairman. I expect senior executives to tell the Board the truth, both today and tomorrow.' We agreed and built a strong, trusting partnership for many years.

Similarly, Johanna Söderström recalls being called into the Dow CEO's office at the end of a lengthy CHRO selection process to hear the verdict.

I came in and he said, 'I value your business mind and your views on people, and I would like to work with you as our new CHRO'. I just got up and gave him a huge hug. He looked at me and said, 'I take that as a yes?' I smiled in agreement, then I said 'Thank you for your confidence, now I also have a few things I would like for us to agree on. It is OK if you change your view, but this is important to me. You will always hear the truth from me; I am not going to filter things from you more than needed to cut to the chase. If you ask for someone to sweet-talk you, it will not be me. I will discuss matters with you very respectfully and behind closed doors as needed, but I will always talk straight to you. You should expect nothing less from me because that is what makes me honest and authentic.' He agreed and commented 'how refreshing' so that became our playing field.

Both Charles' and Johanna's stories illustrate well the constructive tensions that CHROs need to manage across a range of demanding stakeholders, but those who show both **Awareness** and **Bravery** will thrive.

In summary, no matter how successful you have been as an HR leader throughout your career, your first CHRO role will likely bring you a lot of surprises and unexpected challenges. However, with some strategic preparation, and some help, you can get ready for them.

GETTING ON BOARDS

I often speak with HR leaders who aspire to transition to Boards role and find that it can be a difficult thing to do, as few Boards value having a current or former HR professional among them. Board members, who are usually former C-Suite leaders themselves, often feel they can do "the people thing" themselves and simply hire external consultants on technical topics like remuneration. I am afraid the loudest calls for having more HR people on Boards are often largely only heard from HR people themselves. Yet, there are many examples of CHROs who have successfully managed that transition, so it is certainly achievable. Perhaps more than any other career transition, this one needs a great deal of long-term preparation. Think years, not months.

Traditionally, Board discussions have revolved around financial performance, strategic direction, and risk management, with the people agenda sometimes relegated to a secondary concern or delegated to sub-committees. Several leaders I interviewed highlighted the need for more CHROs to be on Boards because decisions related to CEO appointment and executive compensation are some of the most visible, and sometimes controversial, decisions that a public company can make. An experienced former CHRO can help guide that process. However, while there is a growing recognition that human capital is a critical asset for any company, there is still a long way to go for HR leaders to have a natural seat in the boardroom, like finance or legal leaders do.

If you do get to join a Board while you are a sitting CHRO, there will be a lot of benefits, which Myriam Beatove Moreale got to experience.

> Being a CHRO and an independent director fuel each other. From a Board perspective, I learned to take a distance, to ask powerful questions and to influence. That fuels my executive role because I can apply some of that to steer my team. I know how to create the framework and the guardrails to set the direction then I want my team to lead it because they will learn from it. In the other direction, the executive role helps me to stay relevant in my independent director role.

Johanna Söderström echoed that sentiment and shared,

> I am convinced that I have managed to get conversations to a different level on the Neste Board because I bring current and fresh understanding of what it means to be on both sides, Board and management, for instance with our responsibility towards stakeholders. From the management side I think more holistically. What Board members seem to forget sometimes is how much work they create for the organization that might not be needed. By putting

Leanne strategically builds her Board portfolio

As CHRO of Burberry, I was very exposed to Board meetings, including committee work. By that stage, I really could see the criticality of the Board environment and I was interested in it, but I felt I still needed to work on myself. To do this, I went on the Board of a small company called Go Ahead, which was in the FTSE, but was very small. I did it because I was really interested in their business which was in trains and buses, a public service.

I was very intentional in thinking about my first Board role and knew I should not think about "where is this in the Footsie". You've got to ask yourself whether you are really interested in the business, because these roles are a long-term commitment. It was a small Board, and I thought I'd learn a lot from that because I could have a broad contribution. With my HR background, I became the Chair of the Remuneration Committee, but we were all on all the committees, since there were only five of us on the Board.

Later, this led me to an opportunity to join the Compass Board. There were many things that really appealed to me about it, but what really attracted me was that is a people business, with 600,000 employees. That was brilliant because they were not recruiting me to be a potential RemCo Chair, but because the people side of the business was so important. I loved that. It is also a very interesting, very diverse Board and a growing business.

out a simple request, they can kill the machine. We need to engage at the right level, because the more management gets in the weeds, the more they will drag the Board there. I do think it makes us all better to be able to sit on both sides.

To make yourself attractive to Boards, you must put yourself in the shoes of a Nomination Committee Chair. What would make them want to hire you? What would be your unique value proposition? Proactively defining your niche is something that Johanna is very passionate about.

> You must think about your brand. Are you known as someone who can help move things forward at a strategic level? Are you known for your ability to really work with people and build relationships? Board members have worked with so many difficult people in their lives, and they don't want that anymore. They want to contribute and deliver on their duties and, of course, have the difficult discussions but do not have the appetite to work with Board colleagues who are known to be difficult. You must think about your reputation and understand early on if you need to work on changing it. You need to do your own soul searching and hold up the mirror about who you are and what you want to be known for. Are you approaching things with a constructive mind or are just trying to poke holes and be negative?

Johanna applied this strategy to her own case when she got into the pipeline to be elected for her first Board role. She shared,

> I took stock of good Board members that I had come across in my role as CHRO. I realized they were good in my books because of the kind of questions they asked and how they asked them. Then I thought about the ones who were the opposite, and didn't contribute or who would even be considered destructive. Those talked mostly about themselves, about what they had seen and done before without context to the company or its situation. When I started on the Board of Neste, I realized my signature as a board member could be driving true talent conversations as a strategic enabler, and the international business acumen I had built over 20 years with Dow. It's not as evident for CHROs to bring something new to a Board as it is for a CFO, a CEO or a big BU president. For a CHRO to truly be considered Board-ready,

they must have their specialty, their niche. I know mine is the global reach and having talent and transformation as strategic enablers. Of course, I also have the mega DowDuPont merger and spin experience and speaking four languages do not hurt either. Everyone has their niche, and they must be able to articulate what that is.

In thinking what kind of Board member she wanted to be, Johanna described the infamous airport test, which is a simple but powerful hiring criteria for high-pressure jobs: if you were stuck in an airport sitting next to this person for several hours, how would that make you feel? How much would you enjoy their company? So, ask yourself, how would you do in an airport test sitting next to a Board Chair?

Many of the CHROs who are on Boards are often CHRO++, meaning they have had other non-HR experiences in their career. Often, they started as business consultants and developed a track record and reputation as broad business leaders, not just HR professionals. As Mieke Van de Capelle put it, it is best to have several arrows in your quiver, particularly when it comes to contributing broadly to business strategy. She explained,

> I don't think anybody who is a one trick pony can land a Board seat. There are tremendously strong HR people who are extremely business savvy and have an innate understanding of how human capital contributes to business performance but, sadly, that's not the case for everyone. As a result, you don't hear so many HR people sitting on a Board. You don't want someone too narrow on a Board, because you talk risk, strategy, financial performance, and you need to contribute on a full spectrum of topics. When I interviewed for the Board I sit on, I was asked for my views on the overall company performance. The conversation naturally gravitated on the business, on the footprint, on performance, on the evolution of the margins, on some of the strategic choices around the distribution model. It was a business conversation.

To target your first Board role, it may be helpful to aim for sectors with a strong people side to their business as they will often put more value on an HR skillset. Companies in service sectors, such as retail, consulting, logistics, or hospitality, will tend to be better bets. As an additional factor, you should pick your first Board role carefully, as it

 **Tanuj makes sure she does not get boxed in**

When head-hunters occasionally called me with Board opportunities, I always said I have two clear criteria. I wanted something which had big retail presence in the United Kingdom, because I was very conscious that Standard Chartered is not a high street retail bank, and I missed that buzz. I also wanted a business which had a very strong purpose and heritage. So, when a large U.K. retailer called, it felt right.

When I got appointed on the Board, I spoke to a mentor who said, "It's a great opportunity for you but will you be sitting on the Board as an HR person or will you be there as a seasoned, experienced executive who understands banking?" He pointed out that when CHROs get on a Board, they often narrowly box themselves, talking about diversity or employee retention. He said, "You have worked in five different markets, you understand risk, you understand supply chain disruptions, you understand regulation in a broad way. Don't box yourself in". This advice has been very important to me and that is what I have done.

I never let myself be constrained by my job title. In fact, in the first couple of Board meetings at Sainsbury's, when topics like diversity or employee engagement came up, I restricted my contributions, which was so difficult to do. Everyone expected me to be in my swim lane, but I didn't want them to box me in. On the other hand, when we had supply chain disruptions, or regulatory issues, that's where I would leverage my experience. We think about risk so differently in banking. Our understanding of risk is very mature because we manage it in 50 different geographies with 50 different regulators. The Sainsbury's Board probably wanted somebody with an HR background; in practice, even if you get a seat based on that definition, what you choose to do with the opportunity is up to you. I understand transformation, the use of technology, digital issues and that's where I try to contribute.

will often set the tone for future non-executive opportunities that will come your way. I once had a candidate who was very keen to get on a Board and was offered to be an independent non-executive director for a business in receivership, held 50/50 between a family business and private equity investors. He was put in the middle to mitigate the acrimonious relationship between shareholders with widely different objectives. He decided to do it because he really wanted to put a Board role on his CV but had to grind his teeth for three years through a reputational mess. He could not wait to step down once his term was over. Unfortunately, ten years on, he has not managed to get any other Board role, and I suspect one of the reasons is that this first Board role stained, rather than enhanced, his track record.

The path for CHROs to Board roles is not without challenges, but the increasing recognition of human capital as a strategic differentiator presents some opportunities. A high level of **Awareness**, and an honest self-evaluation of your suitability, as well as a strong track of **Delivery** for the business, will set you in the right direction. The boardroom awaits those who can transcend the traditional boundaries of their function and demonstrate their value as strategic business leaders with a profound understanding of the human element of business success.

ARNAUD'S TAKE

Landing a Board role is not an easy thing to do. Not many are called, even fewer are chosen. However, it helps if you are realistic about what you are trying to achieve. In my experience, you first need to define what type of Board you are aiming for. Here is a selection of your potential options:

- **Public company Boards.** This is the gold standard, and usually what people hope for because it comes with prestige, visibility, and decent compensation. They are also the hardest roles to get and with the highest reputational risk for you. Their Remuneration (RemCo) and Nomination (NomCo) sub-committees will be the most obvious fit for someone with an HR background. You will likely hold the status of Independent Director, be expected to uphold strict standards of governance and act on the interests of all shareholders. For such Boards, because of ESG[4] or regulatory requirements, having a diverse background may be a significant advantage. Your time horizon will depend on the jurisdiction you operate in, but you often will be

expected to roll off the Boards after a few terms, e.g., three times three years, or lose your independent status.
- **Private equity-backed Boards**. On these Boards, you would be selected and appointed to represent the interest of a specific investor. As such, you will not be deemed as Independent. To fit the representation needs of a P.E. company, you would likely need to have a strong relationship with them and have demonstrated that you understand well that you can drive performance towards the operational and financial standards expected by that P.E. investor. Your required time commitment and potential operational involvement may also be greater than for other types of Boards. Your term horizon on the Board will be that of the investor you represent.
- **Family-led company Boards**. On the Board of a private, family-led business, you will most often be expected to contribute your domain and strategic expertise, with limited external exposure. Accessing these Boards will often be through a personal connection with one or more family members, and your time horizon may be long, provided you can hold the trust of the family.
- **Non-profit Boards**. Joining the Board of a non-profit organisation can be a great way to ease into non-executive life while still actively working on a full-time executive role. Non-profit Board roles typically have a strong focus on fund raising and your own brand and networks will be a strong factor in getting you appointed. Depending on the size of the organisation, you may get limited to no remuneration and therefore it is best to aim for organisations that serve a cause for which you are passionate[5] and get intrinsic motivation.
- **Advisory Boards**. Smaller and/or fast-growing organisations, particularly early-stage technology companies, are always eager to bring in advisory expertise, especially if this does not involve increasing their cash burn. On these Boards you will be expected to contribute your experience and to actively coach the Head of People as they scale up the organisation. Your compensation – if there is any – will likely be in shares rather than cash, and you might also be expected to invest in the business yourself.

Once you understand the breadth of potential opportunities, you need to deploy your **Awareness** and ask yourself: which one am I interested in and why? There are generally four broad drivers: getting

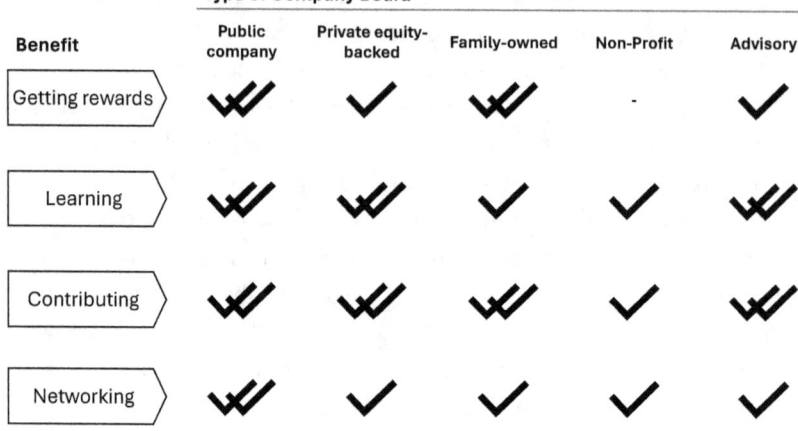

Figure 7.1 Mapping of Board opportunities

rewards (gaining short or long-term wealth), learning (getting exposed to new ideas, becoming familiar with new sectors), contributing (having a chance to give back, applying your experience), and networking (making new business relationships, boosting your visibility). All those reasons are valid, but it will pay off to ask yourself which one(s) is most important to you, as it might guide the type of Board role you want to prioritise. Figure 7.1 offers one practical way to think through this.

For instance, if what truly motivates you is to contribute your experience and make a difference, then any Board will probably give you this: big or small, public or private. However, if financial rewards are a serious consideration for you, non-profit Boards are unlikely to be a fit and P.E.-backed or advisory Boards will only work if you are fine with taking risk and getting most of the rewards as equity, leaving it to the back end.

If you get a chance to join a Board, it is probably well worth a try and remember, as discussed earlier, not to get boxed in. As for the rest of your career, be a leader of business before you are a leader of HR.

NOTES

1 Let us acknowledge that the set of leaders interviewed for this book has an inherent bias, given that they all ended up in the ultimate HR generalist role as Group CHRO.

2 This is something search consultants can help you figure out, even if they don't specialize in HR. If they cover a certain industry, they will probably have some experience working with your target companies as clients and can help tell you about their hiring culture and processes.
3 For specific data on this, check out my LinkedIn channel where I regularly publish statistics and demographics on senior HR appointments globally.
4 Environmental, Social, and Governance.
5 As a side note, everyone is generally excited to help non-profits that involve causes such as children, animals, the arts, sports, or economic development. On the other end, non-profit organizations that aim to help the sick, the old or the dying always find it harder to attract Board members. It may be something worth keeping in mind as you evaluate where to apply your skills to make a true difference.

Your career (re)starts here
Eight

> If you decide that you want to do something, you will find a way. In the words of Yoda, do or do not – there is not try.
>
> Monique Carter

Up to this point, we have examined in depth what has helped successful CHROs go through their careers and their lives, but what do these insights mean for you? Activating **Awareness**, betting on **Bravery**, cultivating **Connectivity**, and driving **Delivery** have worked well for these HR leaders and help deliver great professional outcomes for them, now let us detail how you can take these insights and apply these practices to your own long-term career development.

Let us build YOUR own Thriving Career.

ASSESS YOUR CAREER HEALTH

Every journey starts with a small step. You might be in your early years as a professional or a couple of decades into your career as a leader and face professional uncertainty. As a leadership advisor, I have been privy to many conversations with leaders who struggle with career issues and are looking for thoughtful guidance. Unfortunately, there is often limited help available. At one end, there are many outplacement firms and a plethora of career coaches who will help you polish your CV or practice your interviewing skills but will usually not be invested in your long-term success. At the other end, there is an army of recruitment firms, big and small, who get paid to fill positions but will not pay much attention to your career unless they think they can get business from you in your next role. This last point can be particularly frustrating for HR leaders looking for honest career advice, as there is no incentive for recruiters to give unbiased feedback, beyond merely making you feel good.

To help leaders at all levels take stock of their career, you will find in this book's appendix a simple Career Health self-evaluation tool. It will help you test yourself against our Thriving Career framework. One purpose of this tool is to give a somewhat quantitative basis for what is often a vague answer to the question: how well is my career going? More importantly, the Career Health self-evaluation tool challenges you to think concretely about what you may need to start doing today to build your career for the future. In essence, it is simply an excuse to start a conversation – with yourself and with others – about where you are and where you want to go with your career. You can then start turning these insights into both strategic and tactical actions.

You might find the impact of the Career Health self-evaluation tool more profound than it might initially appear. The key is to go beyond the obvious and be honest with yourself. To do this well, it is best to allocate some quality "me time" to it – at least one hour of uninterrupted thinking time, preferably away from work, alone and with your favourite beverage on hand. An inspiring panoramic view might help as well, and the people who got the best out of the exercise have done it during a vacation (a real one – away from the kids!) or on a retreat.[1]

Score yourself to get an indication of your current Career Health level. Your overall final score will be anything between 12 and 48 and here is how you should interpret it in aggregate, before you dig into the specifics of each dimension:

- Score of 40 or more – Well done, that is a solid level of Career Health, at any tenure. You probably won't need too much corrective action, besides a couple of small adjustments at the margin. You will likely be able to handle those yourself. Go to the sections in this book that address these specific areas and get some inspiration for what you should do next.
- Score 30–39 – That is pretty good and probably means nothing is seriously broken. It is likely that a couple of areas will be on the weaker side, so you need to decide how much you want to work on those to improve your future career prospects. Discuss those with a peer or mentor first. Getting external advisory help might be useful to help you structure some interventions.
- Score 25–29 – You are in the danger zone, particularly if you feel that your career is performing relatively well today. You might have fallen prey to a "performance/health" mirage, lulled by a sense of complacency that things seem to be working out in the moment. This might be a warning sign, and I recommend you spend time

doing some soul-searching, on your own or with some help, to determine if and how you can improve things before it is too late.
- Score 24 and below – You are likely in a difficult career spot and must make a conscious choice. It is possible that you might simply not get to build a Thriving Career from here and need to settle for operating at a more transactional level of career management. If you are at peace with this choice, that is perfectly OK. However, if you do want to strive to improve your career prospects, you may still have options but will probably need a lot of help.

As with any external assessment, remember that your Career Health score does not define you. YOU define you, and get to decide how healthy your career is, based on your own understanding of the career drivers we discussed throughout this book. Take some time to digest the results. Discuss them with trusted friends. Adjust them if you need to. The most important thing is that they should spark some soul searching to help you decide what to do next.

GET AN EXTERNAL VIEW – YOUR LIFE 360 ASSESSMENT

Another powerful tool we can use to help refine our understanding of the state of our career is a Life 360 assessment. This is similar in nature to a 360-feedback exercise you might get at work, but it goes beyond. It aims to map the interplay between your professional and personal self in a holistic way. It helps surface hidden patterns that may help, or hinder, you as you look to build your Thriving Career.

The purpose of the Life 360 assessment is to paint a holistic picture of the state of your career today, with a view towards the long-term. It consists of a series of structured stakeholder interviews across the professional and personal environments you operate in. You could conduct these interviews yourself; however, it is usually best to have a third-party do it if you aim to get honest answers and unbiased insights. Contributors to your Life 360 should be about five to eight people for a holistic view, including a selection of:

- Your current direct boss(es) (HR and/or Line).
- One of your boss's bosses from the business.
- One or two HR peers in your current company who are in roles like yours, but in another part of the organisation, e.g., other COE heads if you are in a COE role.

- The person you consider to be your biggest detractor at work.
- The person who cares the most about you at work.
- One or two of your closest significant others. It should include your spouse and anyone whose life would be directly impacted by any future career decision you make. Children allowed, but probably no pets!
- Anyone who has had a major impact on your life within the last couple of years, including personal mentors.

Does looking at this contributor list make you slightly uncomfortable? For example, do you feel it might be awkward to ask your superiors to help with this exercise? Or your spouse? If so, it may already tell you something about the state of your relationships. One particularly important contributor is your biggest detractor. You might hesitate, at first, to ask them, but in my experience, they are often happy to contribute and usually do so in a helpful way. This was reinforced in my conversation with Tripti Jha who shared that "we are often most grateful to people who supported us, but I am also grateful to people who are my biggest critics because you always learn something from them. It's important to be learning from their views". You might be surprised with the results of such an exercise.

Table 8.1 highlights some of the questions that a Life 360 exercise should aim to address. Not every contributor will have a concrete view on every topic, but by the end of the exercise, you should have an exhaustive picture of how others see you in action.

Getting answers, even if only directional ones, to these questions from third-party feedback during a Life 360 assessment will help cross-check and validate your own Career Health self-evaluation. Analysing these insights, where the largest gaps are to your ideal target, will help you prioritise your areas of intervention.

As an example, I recently conducted a Life 360 assessment with a leader in the United States. In her late 30s, Melissa is a Senior Manager at a technology company on the West Coast and has been getting passed over twice for promotion to a Director-level position in the last couple of years. She took the Career Health self-evaluation and immediately recognised that she has a **Connectivity** issue, together with a lack of clarity on her long-term career objective (**Awareness**).

Table 8.1 Issues to address in a Life 360 assessment

Thriving Career Attitude	Questions Your Life 360 Exercise Should Aim to Answer
Awareness	• How well do you know yourself, and how well do others know you?[a] • How well do you understand the professional and personal context in which you operate? • What internal and external challenges would you need to overcome to achieve your career objectives?
Bravery	• How do others see you behave in the face of professional adversity, particularly when compared to your peers? • How much learning agility have you demonstrated? • What is your track record in seeking, listening to, and acting on feedback?
Connectivity	• How strong are you at building meaningful personal and professional relationships? • What is your most effective relationship-building style? • How much curiosity and adaptability have you demonstrated when operating in unfamiliar cultures or environments?
Delivery	• What is your professional reputation? What are you best known for within your organisation? • How strong is your track record of delivery as a leader? • How do your business colleagues rate your business acumen? • How strongly do others perceive you as a trusted advisor?

[a] Savvy HR practitioners will recognise this as the Johari window. The framework can be usefully applied to career management and reveal blind spots and hidden patterns that can have a profound impact on how you make future career decisions.

We took stock of Melissa's career situation through her Life 360 assessment, and several patterns emerged for her, both of underlying issues and potential solutions. Over the course of several discussions, we unpeeled the onion of her upbringing as an immigrant in the United States with insecurities that pushed her to always want to prove herself by outworking others. We discussed her difficult relationship with her parents, as well as their financial issues when Melissa was growing up, and how it tainted her view of success and team management until today. We discussed the potential pitfalls of Melissa's very high work ethics and strong task orientation when it came to building strong relationships with colleagues (the hidden cost of

Table 8.2 Melissa Life 360 assessment results

	Self-Evaluation Score	Areas of Strength	Developmental Areas
Clarify your purpose and objectives	2	• Has gotten better in the last year at striking the right balance between work and life	• Needs a clearer rationale for wanting to move up in the organisation
Know your motives	3		• Wants to get everything done but may think she can do it all herself. Need to prioritise more
Establish your priorities	3		
AWARENESS	**8**		
Enjoy being comfortably uncomfortable	4	• Listens well to feedback and to others	• Needs to learn that she cannot do everything herself
Seek to learn from feedback and failures	3	• Good at working in high-pace, high-pressure environments	• Needs to show that she can manage through influence and in ambiguous situations, as would be required of senior leader
Have the courage of your convictions	4	• Very protective of her team, not afraid to speak out and step up for her for them,	
BRAVERY	**11**		
Appreciate unfamiliar cultures	4	• Strong at building close-knit teams, which is important to her	• Can appear pushy which creates frictions with others
Cultivate meaningful mentors	2	• Has traditionally built relationships and gained respect by outworking others.	• Needs to show she can better manage up and laterally to show her upward potential
Nurture a positive people ecosystem	3	• Not afraid of hierarchy. Strong and regular access to her SVP	• Need to expand relationships beyond her current Division
CONNECTIVITY	**9**		
Behave as an owner	2	• Has shown great drive and initiative.	• Needs to solve problems more for the long-term rather than in the moment. Chase more long-term solutions
Build a reputation for getting things done	4	• Strong reputation at getting things done when the accountability is clear. Always overdelivers	
Act as a trusted advisor	4	• Becoming better at leading from the back and letting her people take the front	• Too much focus on tasks does not leave enough time for relationship-building at work
DELIVERY	**10**		

151 **Your career (re)starts here**

a high **Delivery**). We uncovered how the lack of chemistry with her direct boss would likely hamper her in the short-term, but how she should cultivate the direct access she has to several senior vice presidents (SVPs) in her organisation (**Connectivity**) to build a more well-rounded reputation beyond "give the hard work to Melissa and she will always get it done".

Building on these deep personal insights, Melissa could then move on to applying some of the techniques we detail later in this chapter, including developing her own Mentor and Sponsor Maps, within and beyond her current organisation. She also led more conscious work on her executive brand to increase her visibility and leverage more public-speaking opportunities. From these early interventions, she could start to think more broadly about her personal definition of success as a whole person and look more confidently into her professional future.

THE ROLE OF CAREER THERAPIST

In the evolving landscape of career development, a new role is emerging that goes beyond traditional career coaching – the career therapist. While career coaches typically focus on tactical career advancement strategies, resume crafting, and interviewing skills, career therapists go deeper into the psychological foundations of your career journey.

A career therapist helps executives diagnose and address long-term career issues that may be hindering professional growth. They focus on understanding the root causes of career challenges rather than just treating the symptoms. Much like a psychotherapist works to uncover unconscious patterns affecting mental health, a career therapist helps identify unconscious biases, self-limiting beliefs, and behavioural patterns that may be sabotaging your Career Health. Imagine discussing moments of vulnerability from past jobs, perhaps times when feedback stung or opportunities slipped away due to indecision or fear of judgment. Each experience unearths insights about who you are as a leader and where you might go next. It's akin to an athlete breaking down their video footage, not just celebrating victories but dissecting failures for lessons learned.

The career therapist approaches your professional life holistically, recognising that career decisions are influenced by your values, motivations, personality, and life circumstances. They help you develop greater self-awareness – one of the foundational attributes we discussed in this book – by exploring questions like: what truly motivates you? How do your early career experiences shape your current decision-making patterns? What unconscious fears might be holding you back from taking different career steps? They help you develop the wisdom and courage to take the right career risks.

Traditional career coaches might shepherd you through your next job rotation, promotion, or recent redundancy. In contrast, career therapists focus on long-term Career Health and ultimate satisfaction. They help you align your career choices with your authentic self, ensuring that your professional journey reflects your core values and purpose. A career therapy session looks very different from a career coaching meeting. The career therapist creates a safe space for exploration and reflection. In a world where careers are increasingly non-linear and require continuous adaptation, the career therapy approach may be your key to a truly thriving professional life.

If you are interested in working with a career therapist, or perhaps in becoming one yourself, here is the job description.

KEY RESPONSIBILITIES
- Facilitate structured reflection on career purpose, motivations, and priorities.
- Conduct in-depth assessments to understand clients' career history, patterns, and unconscious biases.
- Help identify and overcome psychological barriers to career growth.
- Facilitate Life 360 assessments and Career Health evaluations and provide insightful analysis of feedback.
- Help design personalised long-term career programmes that address both tactical and strategic aspects of career development.
- Guide executives through career transitions with a focus on maintaining psychological well-being and long-term satisfaction.
- Provide ongoing support to help clients design, implement, and adjust their career strategies.

SAMPLE PRE-REQUISITES
- A degree in business or management, ideally complemented by a qualification in psychology or counselling.
- Business acumen and understanding of executive leadership challenges.
- Proven experience in executive coaching, leadership development, senior-level recruitment, or talent management.

- Good knowledge of psychometric assessments and feedback methodologies.
- Excellent listening skills and the ability to create psychological safety.

A career therapist is an independent professional, akin to a psychotherapist who would be exclusively focused on career management issues. They play a role at the crossroads of organisational psychology, career counselling, talent management, and employee well-being.

Whether you decide to work with a professional, or on your own, let us now look at specific interventions you can apply to work on each of the four foundational pillars of our Thriving Career framework.

WORKING ON YOUR AWARENESS

If Awareness is an area where you feel you need improvement, I have some news for you: it is both the easiest and hardest pillar to meaningfully improve on. It is the easiest because it depends entirely on you, so you have full control of the levers. These levers will include how much self-awareness you have, how much clarity you develop about your purpose in life and at work, and how well you understand the personal and professional context you operate in. However, it is also the hardest area to move the needle on, precisely for the same reason – you and your mindset are the key to any meaningful change. How you choose to see yourself, see the world, and define success will be key to excelling in Awareness. We all have deep-seated beliefs, and they can be hard to challenge, let alone change. However, the prize is worth the effort, because if you lack Awareness, you are building your career on shifty foundations.

To start working on your Awareness, you need to keep in mind these key action points and questions to answer.

1 Spend time thinking deeply about your professional purpose, your Why, which will need to be somewhat congruent with your personal purpose. Do some soul-searching, seek input and feedback from the people who know you best, and potentially from a coach. Go over this every few years as a "purpose check" to revalidate whether anything has changed, in your environment or in your soul.
2 Think about what your professional objective(s) might be. What does the best possible professional outcome look like for you, now? How realistic is it and what would it take for you to get there (i.e., what might you need to sacrifice)?

3 Make a list of what motivates you, across work and life. What gives you the most energy and gets you out of bed in the morning? See if you can spot patterns and peel the onion to get to the core what these means to your future career choices. Make a prioritized list of those motives, so you are ready to respond quickly to any trade-offs. Once again, seek input and feedback from the people who know you best, particularly in your personal life. I recommend refreshing this list at least once a year as a matter of best practice and ensuring that you get full buy-in from your significant other(s) on what your priorities will be.

One extra piece of Awareness you can work on is an explicit stock-take of the various professional contexts you might face – and which ones are most likely to suit you. This would include

- **Ownership context**: Are you more likely to be best suited for large corporate environments, start/scale-up companies, non-profit organisations, government, family businesses, etc.?
- **Decision-making context**: Are you more likely to thrive in a decentralised, entrepreneurial environment or in a more hierarchical, structured environment?
- **Organisation culture context**: Will you be more successful in an organisation that values consensus and relationship-building or one that values performance and results?
- **Growth context**: Are you going to be more effective in a company that is on an expansion and investment path versus one that needs higher levels of efficiency and rationalisation?

Taking these steps towards Awareness will ensure that you have great career clarity on where you are, where you want you go, and how you might get there. It will greatly simplify any decision you need to make when evaluating a new opportunity.

WORKING ON YOUR BRAVERY

As we have witnessed through many career stories, showing Bravery is key to unlocking developmental learning and building a strong reputation as a values-driven professional. This will be fundamental to your future career-building efforts, and the earlier you can start displaying Bravery, the more beneficial it will be for you in the long-run.

Over the course of your career, you may be asked to participate in internal leadership development programmes or external recruitment processes that will involve an in-depth leadership assessment. Whenever you are asked to conduct such an assessment, you should insist on getting to see the results[2] and ideally spend time with the assessment consultant to do a thorough debrief and get their views on your leadership profile. Relating to Bravery, the specific top 3 leadership competencies that you should get their read on are[3]

- Learning agility
- Personal resilience
- Dealing with ambiguity

If you have not yet conducted such a leadership assessment, it may be worth investing in doing one for yourself. The best ones will provide a qualitative view, along with some quantitative results, at least directionally, and help you benchmark your competency level against a sample of your peer population.

If you work with a career therapist, they can help you conduct a specific leadership assessment related to the various dimensions of Career Health with a particular focus on the Bravery element. This takes the form of a series of case-based situational assessments where you will be presented with hypothetical business cases that will involve ambiguous problems, incomplete and evolving information, inconspicuous but unavoidable trade-offs and generally difficult decisions and recommendations.

WORKING ON YOUR CONNECTIVITY

Strong Connectivity is a career asset that will serve you well and likely help you across other areas of your life. In his seminal book *The Tipping Point*, Malcolm Gladwell highlights the Connector's role in social phenomena, essentially acting as a people hub. It would be easy to brush this off as an innate and rare personality trait – much like Raymond Co seems to have displayed since his university days – but in practice, anyone can nurture that attitude through intention and conscious discipline.

Your starting point should be to understand the universe of stakeholders who might play a role in your future career. Before we get into its mechanics, it is worth detailing four types (actually three plus one) of stakeholders that can play a role in your career and how you can recognise them:

1. **The Advisor.** You go to them for their experience and insights when faced with a tough decision, a difficult challenge, or when you want a long-term perspective on an issue. They have often faced career challenges like yours and can offer life-tested recommendations.
2. **The Hugger.** You go to them for a sanity check, positive reinforcement, or when you need an energy boost. They are often close personal friends, family members or former colleagues who are familiar with your professional trajectory and aspirations.
3. **The Challenger.** You go to them for a third-party perspective on issues or when you seek to evaluate alternative career paths. They often have varied industry or functional experience, such as consultants, and/or a track record of challenging conventional thinking.
4. **The Sponsor.** You go to them to open doors and access opportunities, or when you need personal introductions. They will usually be senior people in your current or former organisations, especially on the business side.

The first three – Advisor, Hugger, and Challenger – are Mentor archetypes. They will be a source of wisdom for you, much like the personal Board of Directors that Usha Kakaria-Cayaux and Ranjay Radhakrishnan have built throughout their career. While the first two may be obvious, it might be worth expanding on what a Challenger is and the value they could bring to your career. I can think of no better illustration than the one Natalie Bickford gave me, who considers one of my former Spencer Stuart colleagues as a useful mentor to her. She explained,

> I have relationships with many head-hunters because I work with them a lot, but I believe I have made myself unpopular with several of them by not taking the roles they offered. However, there is one head-hunter whose opinion I value a lot. We met when we were both very young, and we go for lunch at least once a year. When you get to be my age and in a senior position, there aren't that many people who knew you when you were 25. There is some value in that because you can't bullshit them, and they can talk to you however they want. Those relationships are truly valuable.

The fourth stakeholder type – the Sponsor – is a somewhat different type of animal. It is someone who can actively make something happen for your career. They might recommend you for a job, open the door to a new company or simply introduce you to new relationships. In almost all cases, they will be more senior than you and able (ideally, also willing) to do something for you. A Sponsor can also be a Mentor, but you should be clear in your own mind which role you expect them to play when you interact with them.

To actively work on your Connectivity, I recommend developing and maintaining two separate stakeholder maps to support your career development: a Mentor Map and a Sponsor Map.

A Mentor Map lists your current mentoring relationships against their archetype – Advisor, Hugger, and Challenger – together with a short action plan. It is simple in principle but can be illuminating in practice. Table 8.3 presents my personal Mentor Map, with names removed to protect the innocent.

Once you have taken stock of your mentoring relationships, you can determine where you need to allocate your efforts. Do you need to create new relationships to cover some white spaces, or do you need to deepen existing relationships, maybe by speaking more frequently? Your aim should be to build a relatively diversified portfolio that you can leverage depending on your future context or challenge.

In addition to the Mentor Map, you should develop a Sponsor Map, which is a list of senior leaders who may play a key role in advancing

Table 8.3 Example Wisdom Map

Name	Role	Contact Frequency	Relationship Strength	Last Contact	Contact Plan
• WY	• Advisor	• Daily	• Strong	• Daily	• Ad hoc
• PP	• Advisor	• Quarterly	• Medium	• June	• Lunch in October
• MH	• Advisor	• Weekly	• Strong	• June	• VC in July
• PB	• Challenger	• Monthly	• Strong	• May	• VC in July
• VH	• Hugger	• Quarterly	• Medium	• June	• Lunch in October
• TS	• Advisor	• Quarterly	• Medium	• May	• VC in September
• DM	• Advisor	• Annually	• Emerging	• March	• Call in January

your future career. As mentioned, some of your Sponsors might also be Mentors. Your Sponsor Map (example in Table 8.4) might include people who

- Already know you, e.g., your boss's boss(es), senior colleagues you worked with in former companies.
- Should know you, e.g., current Board members of your company, your company CEO.
- Do not know you, but you would like to be on the radar of, e.g., the CEO or CHRO of other companies you admire or plan to target.
- You can access relatively easily and might help in the future, e.g., prominent alumni from the schools you attended or companies you worked for.
- Are specialist recruiters in your domain or industry.

Once you have built those two stakeholder maps, they are your call-to-action. How confident are you that they are strong enough for the future? Are there any glaring gaps that should be addressed? What will you do to maintain those relationships or, even better, deepen them? What is your action plan to expand to new ones?

It can be helpful to share those with your significant other or anyone else who can give you constructive feedback on it. The key is to use it as a starting point for reflection, turn it into intentional and concrete action steps, and keep things dynamic over time.

Table 8.4 Example Sponsor Map

Name	Company	Title	Relationship Objective	Last Contact	Contact Plan
• John A	• PepsiCo	• BU President	• Get to know	• N/A	• Meet at NYU alumni reunion
• Jordan B	• Spencer Stuart	• Managing Partner	• Get on radar	• N/A	• Get introduced through Susan
• Jane C	• PepsiCo	• Board member	• Get to know	• N/A	• Cold call email asking for a meeting in NY
• June D	• P&G	• Regional HR Head	• Intro my credentials	• March	• Follow up from March meeting
• Jim E	• Heineken	• COO	• Strengthen ties	• April	• Lunch in White Plains in July

WORKING ON YOUR DELIVERY

There is no way around it – business acumen starts with financial savvy. As an HR leader, you should be able to read your business P&L or any internal financial report and have a good idea of what is happening without someone explaining it to you. It is not about becoming a Chartered Financial Analyst, but you should know enough to be reasonably dangerous. If you don't feel confident in your ability to understand the numbers, it is time to schedule some learning sessions with a buddy in the finance team. No question is too stupid to ask. If you don't understand the answer, probe until things become clear.

If you feel you are lacking some fundamental understanding of accounting principles, consider enrolling yourself in a managerial accounting class. This is often the most suitable programme for HR professionals as it connects the fundamentals of accounting to behavioural science by dealing with topics such as performance management, incentives, variance analysis, and decision-making. It will challenge your analytical and quantitative spirits in a thoughtful and immediately practical way, unlike a pure Accounting 101 class, which is likely to only put you to sleep.

Beyond financial savvy, a broader knowledge and understanding of key business principles around marketing or operations will also be very important. In most cases, these can be absorbed on the job by attending as many non-HR meetings as you can and paying great attention (pro tip: do not bring your mobile phone with you. Be present and attentive). However, if you feel that this is not enough, several CHROs I interviewed for this book highlighted that obtaining an MBA has been a great help in developing their broad understanding of business. It may be a full-time MBA or an executive MBA depending on your current career trajectory. If you target an executive MBA, you should explore getting sponsored by your company and, if they are reluctant to invest in you, it is perhaps a sign that they don't see in you the potential you feel you have.

One way to do a simple self-evaluation of your Delivery when it comes to your relationship with business is to determine your "HR zone of influence". Think of the quarterly business reviews, annual sales kick-off meetings, and other strategic planning exercises that the business holds regularly. How closely involved are you in those meetings? How relevant are you to the business? Figure 8.1 introduces an easy way for you to self-rate.

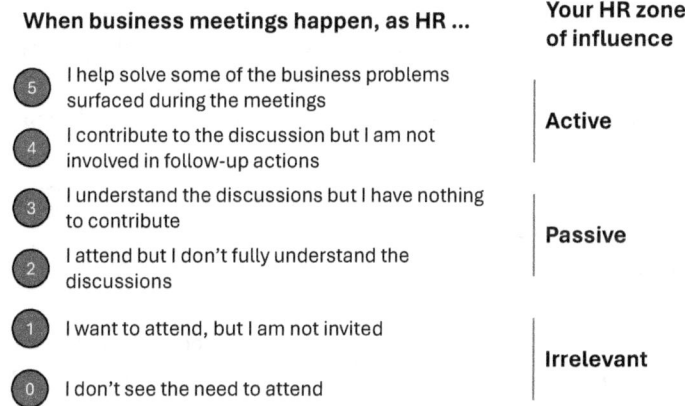

Figure 8.1 Determine your HR zone of influence with the business

Strive to always be in the active zone and be seen as a natural value-adding sparring partner for the business leadership team. One additional point to keep in mind is that you need to deliver for the broader business, not just for your boss. As Archana Bhaskar put it,

> Human Resources is about being in the service of business, not the leader. The moment business leaders see is that it is not about 'my' view or 'his/her' view, but what would benefit the business, they are much more willing to take you along.

At first sight, this might appear counter to the idea that you need to build a trusted relationship with your boss. In practice, when done well, it will gain you a lot of respect.

The idea of building trust with your boss, and generally with anyone you work with, should be central to your work. On this, I have found *The Trusted Advisor*[4] book to be an evergreen reference. I was fortunate to be trained on its methodology in both McKinsey and Spencer Stuart leadership programmes, and I always found its Trust Equation to be extremely useful. While it is geared primarily for an audience in professional services, its ideas apply broadly and any professional in a generalist or business partnering role will find it immediately applicable.

Another important way to work on your Delivery is to determine your reputation in your current company. It is not easy to get an unbiased view, and this is where a Life 360 exercise with a career therapist can be valuable. The key questions to answer are

- What are you known for? What do people systematically come to you for?
- What truly makes you stand out compared to your peers? What are you unusually good at?
- What are your blind spots?

Once you understand your baseline, you can decide how you should work to shape it. Reputations, like trust, take a long time to build and can be damaged easily, so it is important to be very intentional.

You may, at some point in your career, find yourself in a situation where, for whatever reason, your reputation is not what it needs to be. This is when you need to think hard about whether you need to change yourself or change your context. For example, you might be an average fit for an investment bank, but a rock star for an insurance company. If you feel you can't win the game, maybe just change the game!

The idea of building your reputation is nothing new and relatively common sense. However, as we will discuss next, while it is a necessary condition for long-term success, it is likely not sufficient, and you will need to think more broadly. You will need a strong *executive brand*.

BUILDING YOUR EXECUTIVE BRAND

To truly boost your career-building efforts, there is one more piece of the puzzle that you should think about working on. We skirted around it throughout this book, but now that you have a good understanding of all the elements of a Thriving Career, we must address it head on – you need to think about your executive brand.

Executive branding is the conscious process of aligning your personal self (who you are in everyday life), your professional self (how you show up at work), and your digital self (how you come across on social media). If you have followed this book's advice, your **Awareness** will have helped you define your career North Star. This should be the guiding force for your executive branding strategy. It involves intentionally aligning your "three selves" towards your overall career objectives (Figure 8.2). If you can achieve this, these

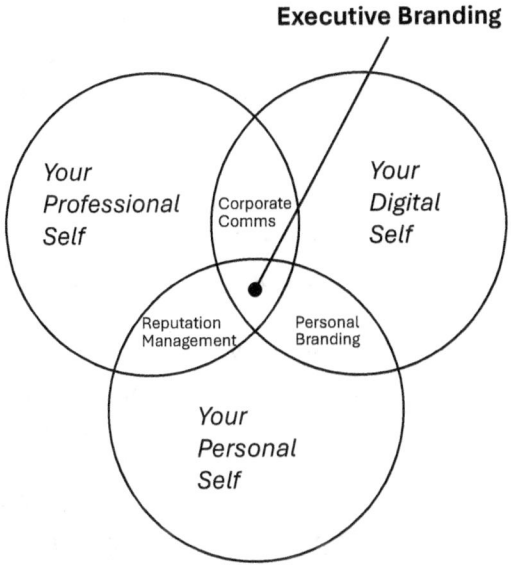

Figure 8.2 Executive branding aligns your "three selves"

three personas will support and reinforce each other, and you will have built the best possible platform for a Thriving Career.

Executive branding goes beyond managing your reputation, which is a function of how you behave and what you achieve at work. It is also more than corporate communications, which often simply amounts to posting your company's latest annual results or corporate event pictures to your followers. Finally, and most importantly, it is much bigger in scope that the "personal branding" trend of the last few years, which is largely focused on making people look good on social media platforms by claiming expertise that may, or may not, be backed by their actual experience.

For career purposes, an executive brand focuses on the "consumer" of your brand: senior executives and colleagues with whom you want to create a meaningful and lasting impression. In essence, it amounts to a promise about who you are, how you will interact with them, and what you can do for them if they work with, promote, or hire you. Think of any product or service you might buy as a consumer. Why do you trust a certain brand versus another? What benefits, tangibles or intangibles, have you come expect from that brand? The same principles apply to you as an executive. What would any senior executive, or recruiter, come to expect if they decide to work with you? Carefully and intentionally crafting these messages and backing them up with evidence of your actual capabilities and experience will help you stand out.

Like consumer branding, you can think of executive branding as a marketing process. Your prior work on **Connectivity** and a comprehensive set of stakeholder maps will come into play and needs to be aligned with your executive branding plan. It needs to address

- **The people you are "selling" to**: Who are the key senior executives in your current company you need to target? Who are the key executives in other companies who should know what you stand for?
- **How you position yourself**: What are the needs of these senior executives – explicit or implicit – and how can your executive brand help meet these needs? What evidence do you have to support what your brand stands for?
- **The channels you reach them on**: Will you just passively "influence" on social media? What work-related interaction opportunities will you leverage? How will you proactively call some of them?

This may sound coldly analytical, but the exercise can reap major rewards. For example, one famous luxury goods CEO (who shall remain unnamed, but I can safely say most ladies would aspire to own that company's products…) hired a marketing agency to help build her executive brand ever since she was a mid-level executive. Fast-forward 20 years, and this executive became a global functional head in a top 5 global consumer goods giant, then a Group CEO in a $20B company. Now, to be sure, hard work played a big part in her success, but a lot of very intentional efforts on executive branding – building an amazing reputation and hundreds of thousands of social media followers – certainly helped as well.

While you may, or may not, want to hire your own marketing consultant to help you, let me give you with a few fundamentals on the topic so you can get going on your own, as summarised in Figure 8.3.

For career purposes, a strong executive brand will aim to achieve several strategic outcomes, across the offline and online worlds, for you: visibility (know you exist), familiarity (feel a sense of intimacy), credibility (trust in what you can do), and relevance (feel the need

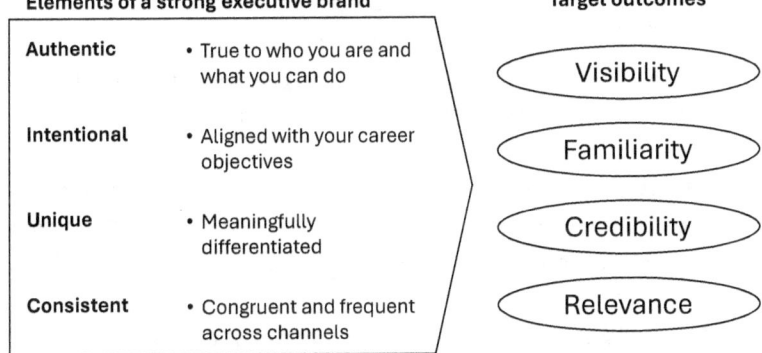

Figure 8.3 Fundamentals of executive branding for career purposes

to work with you). There is no shortcut to achieving these objectives. It takes a lot of patience and hard work. Think years, not weeks.

To get there over time, you will need to pull four interconnected executive branding levers.

- **Be Authentic**: Brands cannot be faked, at least not over a long period of time. Save yourself the trouble of having to create the perfect persona. Be genuine to who you are, with your own strengths and weaknesses. Ensure that your brand promise is backed by your real capability and experience, and it will be easy and natural to deliver on it.
- **Be Intentional**: Executive branding needs to be strategically aligned with your career objectives. It should not involve speaking at any random conference or podcast that happens to invite you or crafting shallow online posts. Be targeted on where you appear. Have a series of core messages supporting each of your three to four brand pillars and stick to those 80% of the time. For the other 20%, it is OK to let loose a bit and show your more casual side.
- **Be Unique**: You should aim to stand out from your peer crowd in a meaningful way. Determine what will be your points-of-difference and develop consistent messaging around them. Ensure that those differentiated brand attributes will be meaningfully relevant to your target stakeholders.
- **Be Consistent**: Think of all the at-work, and online, ways you show up. You need to use consistent behaviours, language, and visuals to

create your own unique *brand delivery*. People who meet you "IRL" should find you aligned with your public persona. When managing social media, do not "post and ghost" – make sure you meaningfully interact with your followers on a regular basis.

The topic of executive branding is broad and probably deserves its own book. We are only scratching the surface here, but this will hopefully give you a sense of what you can get started on.

PUTTING IT ALL TOGETHER – THE THRIVING CAREER METHOD

While all those interventions can be performed individually, the best way to truly boost your career trajectory will be to fire on all cylinders. This can be achieved through an integrated programme structured around your own personal needs, often with the help of a career therapist and, as an option, an executive branding consultant. This holistic approach is the Thriving Career Method (Figure 8.4).

Solid foundations can be put in place across a three-to-four-month period, followed by an ongoing, light touch buddy support system to ensure accountability, with regular touch points for sharing and self-reflection. Figure 8.5 introduces what a Thriving Career programme looks like in practice when conducted with the help of a career therapist.

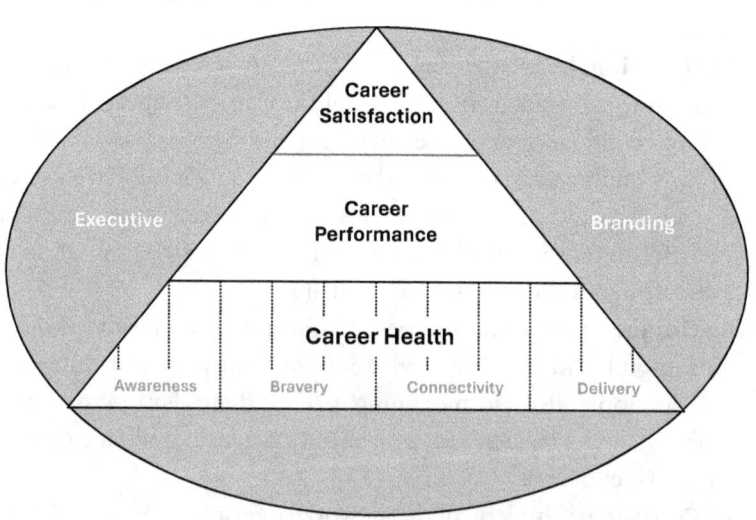

Figure 8.4 The Thriving Career Method

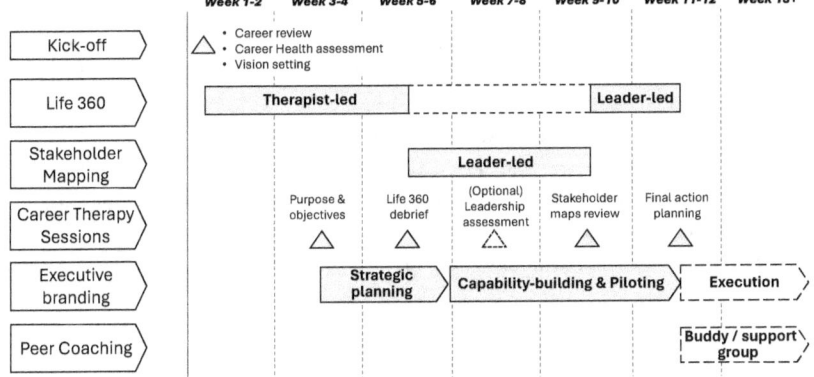

Figure 8.5 Sample Thriving Career programme

The backbone of the programme is a series of career therapy sessions aimed at assessing and improving your Career Health. It is designed around the elements of the Thriving Career Method. The focus of such a programme is different from typical career coaching programmes that are heavily geared towards short-term career performance improvements. In a Thriving Career programme, there will be limited work on helping you rewrite your CV or introduce you to head-hunters. The programme focuses on helping you self-reflect on your career trajectory, identify any unconscious bias that might hold you back, address the root causes of issues, and design an action plan that will serve you for years to come.

Executives find the reflective focus of the Thriving Career programme to be energising and inspiring, giving them a renewed sense of direction and engagement in their career. However, beyond that initial burst of energy, an important success factor is to embed these new behaviours through a peer accountability system. You should identify a peer or buddy who understands the programme and your intentions, so they can challenge you to live up to your commitments. It is best to select them from outside of your current organisation, so you can have truly open discussions in a risk-free environment.

Lastly, my hope is that, after reading *Happy Grow Lucky*, you will not need such an extensive programme, or any external help. I hope that by reading the inspiring, life-tested stories our CHROs shared, you can develop enough clarity on the core principles of Career Health to decide for yourself what will apply to you … and start building your own Thriving Career.

NOTES

1 If you are interested in how to carve out quality "me time" for deep reflection, I recommend *The Art of Retreats: A Leader's Journey Toward Clarity, Balance, and Purpose*, Fabrice Desmarescaux, 2022.
2 As a candidate, you probably will never see the full results, but good assessment firms should provide you with a view of the main findings.
3 The exact label of the leadership competencies might change depending on the assessment tool/firm.
4 The Trusted Advisor, David H. Maister, Robert Galford, Charles Green (2001).

Conclusion
Nine

> Dream more, learn more, achieve more and become more.
>
> Myriam Beatove Moreale

As we draw the threads of our exploration together, we can see that building a Thriving Career is not a matter of chance, but a deliberate journey fuelled by a relentless and intentional drive. We have delved deep into the experiences of 45 remarkable global CHROs, distilling their wisdom into actionable insights that can guide your own professional trajectory. We have examined the foundational attitudes that underpin their success, the winning practices they have deployed, and the strategic approaches they have taken across different phases of their careers. As we stand at the precipice of an evolving world of work, it is crucial to anticipate the contours of the landscape ahead, ensuring that the principles of Thriving Career management will remain evergreen.

At the start of our journey, we began by spotting that career luck is a self-created outcome and distinguished between career performance and career satisfaction. While external markers of success, such as title and compensation, are often visible and easily measured, true career happiness is a more personal and nuanced experience. It stems from the alignment of our professional endeavours with our core values, our sense of purpose, and our overall life priorities. As we move into the workforce of the future, particularly with younger generations who increasingly seek purpose and meaning in their work, the pursuit of career satisfaction is likely to become an even more significant driver for HR professionals.

Similarly, the four foundational attitudes of **Awareness**, **Bravery**, **Connectivity**, and **Delivery** will likely always form the bedrock of intentionally building a Thriving Career. These elements are timeless in their application and will likely continue to guide professionals effectively in the future.

Awareness involves knowing yourself deeply – your strengths, weaknesses, values, and motivations. It also requires understanding your professional environment and the broader context in which you operate. In the next 20 years, as the pace of change accelerates, maintaining this self-awareness will become even more critical. You will need to stay attuned to shifts in organisational cultures, technological advancements, and global economic trends. The tools and techniques for gaining awareness might evolve, but the core principle remains: a deep understanding of yourself and your environment is foundational for intentional career management. I've seen this repeatedly with clients who invest time in regular self-assessment and environmental scanning – they consistently make better career decisions than those who simply react to circumstances.

Bravery is about stepping out of your comfort zone and embracing risks that propel you forward. This might involve taking on challenging assignments, seeking feedback from critics, or advocating for change within your organisation. In the future, **Bravery** will likely involve navigating even more complex and uncertain landscapes. Yet, the essence of **Bravery** – facing fears and uncertainties head-on – will remain unchanged. It will continue to be a vital attribute for those looking to lead and innovate through their careers. I have witnessed countless professionals transform their trajectory simply by having the courage to say "yes" to opportunities that frightened them, whether relocating internationally or taking on projects that everyone else stayed away from.

Connectivity emphasises building meaningful relationships that support your long-term career development. As virtual work becomes more prevalent and global teams more common, the ways you build and maintain these connections may shift. However, the importance of authentic cross-cultural relationships, based on trust and mutual respect, will endure. The tools for networking might change from in-person meetings to virtual platforms, but the need for genuine human connections will persist. Throughout my career across multiple continents, I've found that those who cultivate diverse, authentic relationships consistently outperform those who remain isolated, regardless of their technical expertise.

Delivery focuses on your ability to achieve results and build a reputation for reliability and excellence. In a rapidly evolving world, where artificial intelligence and new technologies constantly reshape industries, having a strong track record of **Delivery** will continue to set you apart. Your ability to adapt and apply your skills in new contexts will be crucial. While specific competencies may evolve with changing business needs, the fundamental principle of delivering consistent value will remain constant. I've observed this pattern repeatedly in executive search: candidates who can demonstrate tangible outcomes, especially in challenging circumstances, eventually rise to the top.

As a final teaser, let me make four bold predictions on how the world of HR will evolve in the years to come, and make the case that the Thriving Career Method will remain evergreen.

- Career paths will become increasingly non-linear. The traditional ladder will give way to a career lattice with more horizontal moves, project-based experiences, and hybrid roles that blend HR with other functions. This will make the **Awareness** attribute even more crucial. Knowing yourself and having clarity of purpose will be essential for making coherent choices in a less structured environment.
- The half-life of technical skills will continue to shrink. The specific HR technologies and methodologies we master today may become obsolete within years or even months. This will elevate the importance of **Bravery** – specifically, the learning mindset that enables continuous adaptation. The ability to embrace new challenges and rapidly develop new capabilities will differentiate great HR leaders from the average ones.
- Organisational boundaries will become more permeable and global. Careers will increasingly span multiple organisations, sectors, and countries. The notion of building a career within a single company will become even rarer than it is today. This will amplify the value of **Connectivity**. The relationships you build and maintain across these boundaries, on a global basis, will become your most valuable career asset.
- The expectations for HR to demonstrate business impact will intensify. As data analytics and automation handle the more transactional aspects of HR, strategic value-add will become the primary measure of HR effectiveness. This makes **Delivery**, particularly business acumen and results orientation, an increasingly critical career differentiator.

As you look ahead to the next 5, 10 or 20 years of your career, remember that while the external environment may change dramatically, the principles of Thriving Career management – **Awareness, Bravery, Connectivity**, and **Delivery** – will likely remain foundational. They are not just tools for navigating today's challenges but timeless principles that will help you thrive in any future scenario. Think of them as your career operating system: the mainframe that enables you to process information, make decisions, and execute effectively regardless of how dramatically your professional landscape shifts.

Your career is a journey that requires ongoing reflection, adaptation, and commitment. By embracing these principles with intentionality, you can navigate the complexities of an ever-changing professional landscape while staying true to your core values and aspirations. This approach will allow you to create your own luck, leading not only to improved career performance but also to deeper satisfaction and a sense of fulfilment.

As Tripti Jha purposefully stated, "It's easy to be an average HR person, but it is very difficult to be a really differentiated one". This book has aimed to equip you with the insights and tools to build your unique and outstanding career by being a strategic leader, a trusted advisor, and a catalyst for positive change in a world that increasingly recognises the importance of its human capital. Play the long game, stay curious, be courageous, connect authentically, and always get sh*t done with purpose. Your Thriving Career awaits.

****

If you found Happy Grow Lucky useful and wish to help share the love, please consider recommending it to two other humans:

1. The one human you care about the most and would like to see thrive through their career, for life.
2. The one human you feel may be facing issues and would benefit the most from the book's insights to (re)start their career.

They don't have to buy the book; you can just lend them your own copy.

Let's have more meaningful career-changing conversations, one human at a time.

Appendix – Career Health self-evaluation

Use the self-evaluation tool below to assess the state of your Career Health. For each category, choose the performance level that most accurately describes your current mindset or practice.

If you want a first reality check, feel free to check on your self-evaluation with your significant other, or someone else you trust to know you well. Do they agree with your assessment? Would they have a different view?

Add up your total score (from 12 to 48 in total) and use the overall scoring scale in Chapter 8 to get a read on where you stand:

EVALUATING YOUR AWARENESS

	Weak (1)	Emerging (2)	Good (3)	Excellent (4)
Clarify your purpose and objectives	I do not have a clear idea of what I want to achieve in my career	I have a long-term career aspiration but not clear idea on how to achieve it	I have a clear idea of what I want to achieve in my career, and some directional views on how to get there	I have a clear idea of what I want to achieve in my career, and what I need to get there
Know your motives	I don't have a clear view of what motivates me, and/or it can change based on circumstances	I have a clear view of what motivates me, and my own personality 'at home', but not as much in a work environment	I understand well what motivates me, and my own personality, but I am not sure on how it should influence my career choices	I have a very good understanding of what motivates me, my personality and how it drives my career choices
Establish your priorities	I feel I can have it all, across my work life and my personal life	I hope I can have it all, across my work life and my personal life but I realise it might be hard to achieve	I know I cannot have it all, across my work life and my personal life but I am not always clear on what my priorities should be	I know I cannot have it all, across my work life and my personal life, but I am very clear on what comes first for me

My total **Awareness** score (3–12) =

EVALUATING YOUR BRAVERY

	Weak (1)	Emerging (2)	Good (3)	Excellent (4)
Enjoy being comfortably uncomfortable	I consistently seek situations that are well-suited to my existing skillset and experience so I can ensure success	I often seek situations that are well-suited to my existing skillset and experience so I can have a good chance to succeed	I often seek situations that I know will be challenging because I want opportunities to develop new skills	I consistently seek situations that I know will be challenging because I thrive on learning and personal growth
Seek to learn from feedback and failures	I am confident in my professional abilities. When failures occur, it is usually through circumstances outside of my control	I am confident in my professional abilities, but I am open to feedback as I know there are things I still need to learn	I am confident in my professional abilities, but I actively seek feedback to continuously improve	I constantly seek to improve my professional abilities by pursuing unfamiliar opportunities and looking to learn from feedback
Have the courage of your convictions	While my professional values are important to me, I am prepared to set them aside if the situation requires it	My professional values guide most of the choices I make at work, and I rarely make exceptions	My professional values are inalienable. I will avoid situations where they may be in jeopardy	My professional values are inalienable. I will work to fix situations where they are in jeopardy and step out only when there are no options left

My total **Bravery** score (3–12) =

EVALUATING YOUR CONNECTIVITY

	Weak (1)	**Emerging (2)**	**Good (3)**	**Excellent (4)**
Appreciate unfamiliar cultures	I feel being in a homogenous cultural environment allows me to operate at my best	I feel getting occasional exposure to different cultural environments can be a source of learning and growth	I sometimes seek some exposure to different cultural environments to learn new things	I often spend extended periods of time in different cultural environments to grow into a more open-minded person
Cultivate meaningful mentors	I do not feel I have a professional mentor who can help guide me	I feel I have at least one mentor who can share their professional experience and insights with me when I need it	I feel I have at least one mentor who knows me well, can give me professional advice and knows my personal priorities	I feel I have a diverse set of mentors who know me well, care for me and can give me advice across my career and my life
Nurture a positive people ecosystem	My professional network is mostly limited to my current colleagues	My professional network includes both current and previous senior colleagues with whom I stayed in touch	My professional network is large, with both senior and junior people, mostly from companies I have worked for	My professional network is large and wide-ranging, across senior and junior people, in various industries and companies

My total **Connectivity** score (3–12) =

EVALUATING YOUR DELIVERY

	Weak (1)	Emerging (2)	Good (3)	Excellent (4)
Behave as an owner	I find it difficult to articulate precisely how my contributions impact the P&L of our business	I can articulate how my contributions impact the P&L of our business in conceptual terms, but not necessarily in monetary value	I can quantify precisely how my contributions impact the P&L of our business	I systematically allocate my work and prioritise my time towards maximising the financial impact on our P&L
Build a reputation for getting things done	I have an idea of what my professional reputation is, but no real evidence for it	I have an idea of what my professional reputation is, based on feedback I have received from my bosses	I know that my professional reputation is good based on consistent feedback I received from others	I know that my professional reputation is strong when benchmarked to my peers, based on impartial feedback I received
Act as a trusted advisor	I generally find it difficult to get close to people in a professional environment	I can usually get colleagues to like and respect me so we can work well together	I usually build close working relationships with most of my colleagues. They feel comfortable sharing their issues with me	I am seen as a reliable partner by my colleagues, including my boss. They regularly seek my views on their most important issues

My total **Delivery** score (3–12) =

MY TOTAL CAREER HEALTH SCORE (12–48) =

APPRECIATION FOR THE 2025 GLOBAL HR CAREER SURVEY PARTICIPANTS

With much appreciation for your support and providing insights for this book through your response to the latest 2025 Global HR Career Survey – my greatest thanks to each one of you.

Aa Sahawatcharin
Aaron Carmichael
Abhay Singh
Abhishek Mittal
Achaibar Gupta
Adam Reidel
Aditi Mahadevan Nair
Aditi Singh
Aditya Mittal
Agnes Commys
Akhil Sharma
Akhilesh Nair
Alan Richard-Hilaire
Alberto Luna de Abia
Aleix Muntal Díaz
Alena Reva
Alessandro Bonorino
Alessandro Pietropaolo
Alex Khatuntsev
Alex Marteau
Alex Moreau
Alexander Jacob
Alexandra Fucik
Alexandra Joos
Alexandre Savary
Alexis Mingasson
Alice Lindenauer
Allan Ko
Alvin Ang
Ambar Mitra
Amelia Generalis

Amelia Lavery
Amit Mittal
Amit Singh
Amna Shoro
Amrita Singh
Amy Hanlon-Rodemich
Amy Walker
Anamika Katoch
Anand Vegesna
Anastasia Shamgunova
Andrea Clayton
Andrea Ferrante
Andrea Isaia
Andrea Koh
Andreas Stroebele
Andrew Griffith
Andrew Kilshaw
Andrew Phuang
Andrew Slentz
Andy Willshaw
Angela Chng
Angeline Oh
Angelo Binetti
Angus MacGregor
Anil Agnihotri
Anisha Pai
Anita Walton-Tilly
Anja Liliendahl Stapelfeld
Anja Michael

Anjali Velayudhan Menon
Ankush Raisinghani
Ann Eliahu
Ann Limcharoenporn
Anna Bisart
Anna Ho
Anna Livingston
Annabelle Thebaud
Anne Frese
Anne Vasconcellos
Annemette Sonderkaer
Annie Bai
Ann-Louise Elkjaer
Anouk de Graaf
Ans Raja Joseph
Anthony Green
Anthony McDonald
Anthony Ward
Antonio Menéndez Sierra
Anu Sridhar
Anu Wadhwani
Aparna Kumar
Arbhorn Sujitjohn
Archer Zhao
Arindam Dan
Art Masarky
Arun Krishnan
Arun Sukumar Kaimal

Ashish Jose
Ashish Patro
Ashley Soupen
Ashok Pillai
Asli Namal Suel
Atul Gaur
Audrey Ng
Ayyappa SK
Aziz Jameran
Bala Sathyanarayanan
Balasubramanian
 Krishnamurthy
Baris Dikilitas
Bastian Becker
Bea Legradi
Bec Munn
Bela Tisoczki
Beng Thiam Ong
Benny Wang
Benoît Barbiche
Bernadette Rolton
Bernard Garrigues
Bertrand Austruy
Beverly Morgan
Bijumon Jacob
Bill Huffaker
Blanca Folguera
Blezilda Ordas
Brenda Wilbert
Brew Baritugo
Brian Butcher
Brian Lambrecht
Brian Smith
Bruce Ball
Bruce Tan
Bruno Couteille
Carina Lovato
 Gillenwater
Carine Garnerot

Carlos Bersoza
Carlos Morán Moya
Carly White
Carmen F. Cortez
Carol Mahoney
Carol Zhang
Carole Diochet Edus
Carollyn Toh
Carrie Chui
Cary Shek
Cashvin Christopher
Cassady Winston
Catie Maillard
Cecile Masquelier
Cecile Umaña
Cedric Brochard
Celeste Hidalgo
Celine Broutin
Celine Gallet
Celine Yeo
Cesar Campos
Chan Foong Peng
Charlene Tan
Charles Belin
Charlie Salameh
Charline Berry
Charmaine Sim
Charu Madan
Chelsea Lee
Chetana Sukumar
Chevy Zhang
Chika Hutauruk
Chris Brock
Chris Porter
Chris Rosenthal
Christal Hngoi
Christian Albrich
Christina Lim
Christina Lu Maxwell

Christina Tan
Christina Yang
Christine Geissler
Christine Song
Christophe Bulard
Christophe
 Wielgosik
Christopher Zyner
Chuck Kemper
Cindy Cheng
Clare Wheeler
Claudia Faessler
Claudia Fischer
Claudio Scalise
Claudio Vespucci
Clement des Robert
Coen Marjot
Colin Daly
Collette Clemens
Craig Cochrane
Craig Murphy
Craig Roberts
Cristian Kaiser
 Caldera
Cristina Croci
Cristina Valmassoi
 Waldenström
CY Yau
Cyl Lin
Cynthia Chia-Lee
Cynthia Lee Mai
Dan Brammadas
Daniele Braga
Danielle Knott
Danielle Savaglio
Danny Zhang
Darren Campbell
David Bowes
David Girardeau

David Karpelowitz
David Kosten
David Milbourne
David Schmit
David Young
   Wook Kim
Davide Inverni
Deanna Koppenhofer
Debbie Shotwell
Deborah Potter
Deepak Bhasker
Deepak Gajre
Deepali Rajani
Deepti Bhanot
Denisa Ptackova
Dennis Armstrong
Dennis Daugaard
   Andersen
Devarshi Deb
Dharma Chandran
Diana Chimienti
Dina Ishwarlal
Dinesh Kalwani
Dirk-Jan Rijks
Diwakar Loshali
Don Schneider
Doris Tao
Doug Beesley
Doutzen Wierda
Dr. Glenn Lee
   Hong Guan
Dr. Mia Mulrennan
Dr. Rich Atkinson
Duncan Skinner
Duncan Thomas
Dunja Heinrich
Edouard Jacquet
Eduardo Amaya
Edwin Tan

Eileen Tan
Eleanor Thorp
Elena Apostu
Eliannah Yeo
Elif Tutum Tuncer
Elisa Cavedagna
Elise Hauge
Elizabeth Ahmed
Ellen Stone
Elvia Morga
Emanuele Celani
Emily McGavin
Emily Moreau
Emmanuel Joffre
Emmanuel Lemoine
Eng-Sing Soon
Enio Gualandris
Eric Goh
Eric Tan
Erica Dias
Erika Abreu
   Laeremans
Errol Douglas
Estelle Wong
Ethan Lim
Eugene Cheng
Eugene Loh
Eunice Fung
Eva Ohlsson
Evan Ho
Evangeline Chua
Eve Baldwin
Ewan Clarkson
Fabienne Enderlin
Fabio Fede
Fabrice Dago
Fabrizio Tripodi
Faizal Zain
Fe Rosal

Federica de Gennaro
Federica Vernero
Federico Balzola
Federico Finzi
Felipe Ferreira
Felix Betancourt
Fernando Tan
Fernando Zallocco
Filippo Monastra
Fiona Plush
Fiona Wong
Flora Tan
Francesco Armino
Francisco Cabrera
   Dávila
Franck Aime
François Guyeux
Francoise Caraguel
Frank Liu
Frank Suyver
Frank Vandewal
Franz-Albert Bell
Frederic Dura
Freya Wang
Gabor Nagy
Gabriele Arend
Gaby Hunziker
Garrett Germon
Gary Goh
Gary Teo
Gautam Dev
Gavin Dow
Geert Aelbrecht
Geetika Tewari
Gena Smith
Geoff Danheiser
George Avery
George Forbes
Georgegina Poulos

Gerald Heritier
Geraldine Butler-Wright
Geraud-Marie Lacassagne
Gerlinde Boback
Giandomenico Maccarini
Gianluca Farinelli
Gina Balagon
Giovanni Chirichella
Gonzalo Ruiz Calavera
Gosia Tomaszów Reinhoudt
Grace Tkach
Graham Almond
Greg Morley
Grégory Rastello
Gualtiero Mago
Guillaume Jouet
Guillaume Rabel-Suquet
Guy Woollard
Gwen Lockington
Gyorgy Endes
Hagen Ong
Hakan Tat
Hannah Atack
Hans Mielants
Hans Peter Knudsen
Hari Menon
Harini Muralidharan
Harmen Nieuwenhuis
Heather Saville Gupta
Heidi M. Glickman, PhD
Helen Vincent
Helena Dreisig
Helena Shen
Hélène Cabasso
Helene Wilson
Hendrik Zell
Henk-Jan Wesselink
Herman Cahyadi
Hernan Darvis Geldstein
Himanshu Saxena
Horst Gallo
Howard Donovan
Ian Heycox
Ian Soares
Idano Di Ciocco
Ilham Maulana
Ilja Rijnen
Illeanne Rukes
Imran Syed
Iñaki Cebollero
Iram Shah
Isha Vatsyayan
Itee Satpathy
Ivan Lim
Ivory Cai
Iwan de Leeuw van Weenen
Jacqueline MacLennan
Jacques Metadier
Jags Mukherjee
James Allibon
James Bell
James Morgan
Jan Bouwen
Jane Lum
Jane Wu Scheibe
Janice Teo
Janice Yee
Jannie Hestehave
Jarko Vlasak Perez
Jason Dolby
Javier Carrero
Jay Thaker
Jayesh Menon
Jean-Christophe Mouchart
Jean-Marie Gourmelen
Jeannie Wong
Jeff Reeves
Jennifer Drysdale-Banks
Jennifer Lucas
Jennifer Nicol
Jenny Kabat
Jens Hovgaard Jensen
Jerald Chen
Jeremy Bingham
Jeroen Bors
Jérôme Dandrieux
Jerome Zapata
Jesse Dirks
Jessica Tan
Jessica Zheng
Jignesh Shah
Jill DeMello
Jill Gates
Jillian Donato
Jim Kennedy
Jim Plumstead
Jimmy Tan
Jo Craig
Joan Burke
Joan Sintes
Joana Liew
Joanna Lim

Joao López
   Villanueva
Jodi Weintraub
Johann Steiner
Johanna Walker
John Li
John Sundaram
John Townsley
Johnathon Ng
Jolanta Bosca
Jolene Koh
Jon Stewart
Jordana Semaan
Jordi Casas
Jorge Yepez
Jos Dessauvagie
Josephine Simeone
Josh Hook
Juan Fernando
   Gallo Góez
Judy Heng
Judy Wong
Juhi Singh
Julene Campion
Julia Gal-Konwalinka
Julie Deenonoad
Julie Koh
Julie Pope
Julio Flores Oré
June Koh
Juseleen Jalil
Justin Schnoor
Jyanthi Elanggo
Kamali Rajesh
Kanchan Chehal
Karen Black
Karen Hutcheson
Karen Tan
Karen Yen
Karine Parent
Karine Scelles
Kate Higgins
Katherine Teo
Kathleen Kee
Kathryn Dolan
Kathy Chandra
Kathy Gentilozzi
Katie Hodgson
Katya Kruglova
Katya Zubritskaya
Kaustav Chakravarthy
Keisha O'Marde-Jack
Ken Wong
Kenneth Kirindongo
Kevin Ball
Kim Robbins
Kimberly Fitch
Kingsley Macey
Kirsty Hagg
Kitty Zhao
Koay Saw Lean
Koichi Noda
Konstantinos
   Karavidas
Kripa
   Krishnamoorthy
Kris Hamner
Kris Sasitharan
Krishnamohan Rao
Krista Skalde-Roy
Krista Weir
Kristian Warner
Kristin Thielking
Kristin Wagner
Kristina Karcic-Ehret
Kumar Abhishek
Kuresha Ramahotar
Laia Estorach Cavaller
Laura Chuck
Laura Spezzaferri
Laurent Aufils
Laurianne Le
   Chalony
Leah Yoong
Leandro Figueira
   Netto
Leanne Goliath-
   Yarde
Lee Guan Ling
Lee Kian Goh
Leigh Stewart
Lesley Tull
Leslie Lenus
Levi Campbell
Li Dai
Liliane d'Ornano
Lily Lee
Lindsay Shirley
Lindsey Burton
Lindsey Cai
Lisa Askwith
Lisa Cloutier
Liz Jewitt-Cross
Lorraine Chua
Luca Battagliero
Luca Citterio
Luca Di Maio
Lucille Lou
Lucy Tan
Luigi Maria Fierro
Luis Correa
Luke Lim
Machar Smith
Mads Kuld Pedersen
Magda Setoguchi
Mai Linh Julia
   Schielke

Maikku Virtanen Weber Hartmann
Maite Cuadra Sacristán
Manisha Kadagathur
Manolo Cuervo
Manuel Sanchez Vivas
Manuel Scotto
Marc Roos
Marc Verspecht
Marcela De La Barreda
Marcin Przeworski
Marcus Seelbach
Maria Antoniou
Maria Fernanda Páez Villegas
Maria Rivadeneira
Mariane Boldori
Mariya Trifonova
Mark Daldorf
Mark Deayton
Mark Musgrave
Mark Reid
Marta Ilbak
Martha O'Connor
Martial Maury Laribiere
Martin Appel
Martin Cepeda
Martin Corfe
Martin Garnes
Martin Paz
Mary Lemonis
Masha Vis-Mertens
Massimo Malaguti
Mateen Thiruselvaam
Matteo Villani
Mattijs Mol
Maung Lin
May Anne Bird
Mayank Rautela
Mazen Mazraani
Meaghan Hunter
Meg De Keukelaere
Meg Langan
Meg Stevens
Megan Walker
Mehul Mehta
Melanie Bovero
Melanie Eisinger
Melanie Tan
Melany Sulaiman
Melissa Bruno
Melissa Park
Melissa Ribeiro
Meng Hwee Teoh
Mern Yee Tai
Michael Boyle
Michael Charpentier
Michael Haag
Michael Knierim
Michael Koops
Michael Pedersen
Michael Roberts
Michelle Kiernan
Michelle Kwait
Michelle Ong
Mihaela Andronic
Mike Clarke
Mike James Ross
Mike Wukitsch
Miklos Magyar
Mila Perez
Milena Hansen
Min Chia Chang
Mirna Zerekli
Mohit James
Mohit Rajkumar
Mona Garland
Monette Lasala
Monica Chia
Monica Navascues
Monica Swandayanie
Morten Bechlund
Morven McLean
Mustafa Alzoubi
Nadeem Ashraf
Naj Wright
Naresh Kumar Pinisetti
Naseem Khan
Natalia Mikulich
Natalia Natinoh
Natalia Navin
Natalie Wintermark
Neal Yang
Neetu Bhatnagar
Nelly Ruer
Niccolò Nitti
Nick Avery
Nick Hudgell
Nicki Hickson
Nicolas Seguin
Nicole Pelengaris Patel
Nicole Poon
Nidia Knight
Nina Kreyer
Nora Schoenthal
Ola Arvidsson
Olga Revutska
Ollie Roberts
Ovell Barbee
Pablo Alonso
Pallavi Kapoor

Palmy Keerati
Pamela Teo
Pancanita Manalu Rao
Paolo Codazzi
Paolo Emilio Testa
Parviz Dhamodiwalla
Pascal Billaud
Pascale Van Hoecke
Patricia Enright
Patricia Lam
Patrick Burguet
Patrick Higgins
Patrick Johnson
Patrick McGurk
Patrick Wilhelmi
Paul Richard
Paul Trudel
Paula Erickson
Paul-Peter Feld
Pedro Casaño
Peter Attfield
Peter Kornerup
Peter O'Sullivan
Peter Vosch
Peter Xiao
Petros Tottas
Philipp Bastian
Philipp Kurtenbach
Philippe Apostolides
Pierre Petrissans
Pierre Stassin
Pip Penfold
Poh Meng Quek
Poolvithajakij Punlop
Pragati Negi
Prakash Thangachan
Prashant Parashar
Praveen Menon

Queen He
Rachael Fitzpatrick
Rachel Cox
Rachel Zhang
Rachna Nazir
Rachna Sampayo
Radjes Somaroe
Raf Lamberts
Raghu Chandrashekar
Rahul Kalia
Rainbow Chan
Rajan Krishnakumar
Rajiv Burman
Ranjith Menon
Rashmi Somu
Ravi Bali
Ravi Gopalan
Rebecca Holland
Rebecca Hone
Rebecca Munoz-Matla
Rebecca Vostri
Regan Taikitsadaporn
Remko Verheul
Renata Guimarães
René Bujard
René Pennings
Renee DeFranco
Renita Brammadas
Ricardo Sanchez-Moreno
Richard Barnes
Richard Laidlaw
Rick Young
Ridha Imansyah
Rikke Bräuner
Rishi Dadlani
Rishi Donat

Rishi Kaul
Rob Hendriks
Rob Luijten
Robert Frank
Robert Hicks
Robert Mikaelian
Robert Mostert
Robert New
Robert Rigby-Hall
Roberto Mar
Roberto Ponte
Robin Hamel
Rodolphe Boschet
Rohit Kaushik
Rohit Zutshi
Ronald Tay
Rory O'Byrne
Roshan Niwunhella
Ross Pollack
Rowan Bell
Royce D'Costa
Rubén Alejandro Ramírez Torres
Ruchi Tenani
Ruth Gellert-Neale
Ryan Cheyne
Saba Adil
Sabrina Fenoglio
Saeko Nakamura
Sally Cullen
Sally Tang
Sam Diwakar
Sam Khanna
Sam Oliver
Samanta Todaro
Sameen Khan
Sameer Nagarajan
Sampat Aratti
Sandeep Mookharjea

Sandi Sadek
Sandip Kulkarni
Sandra Yap
Sandrine Bianchi
Sangeetha Rajalakshmi
Sanjeeb Lahiri
Sanjeev Kumar
Sanjoy Shaw
Santhipharp Khamsa-ard
Sarah Barron
Sarah Chun
Sarah Houghton-King
Sarah Lim
Sarbari Basu
Sasha Diskin
Satya Pasi
Saurabh Jain
Savita Mittra
Scott Schoneman
Scott Woody
Sean Hurley
Sebi Chacko
Sehr Ahmed
Seng Huwi Ng
Sergio Barra Aguirre
Sergio Boscarol
Shahed Ashraf
Shahzad Umar
Shannon Lyndon-Lugg
Shantanu Dash
Sharmain Chin
Sharon Foo
Sharon Frost
Sharon Ho
Shelly Rajpal

Shereen Bong
Sherin Varghese
Sheyla Gabulle
Shirley Tjan
Shishir Jha
Shubhashri Singbal
Shuchika Sahay
Shyam Upadhyay
Sid Pednekar
Sigrid Neeskens
Silviu Bozdog
Simina Simion
Simon Hand
Simon Hunter
Simon Kelner
Simon Smith
Simon Viggers
Simona Bertinotti
Simone Reynolds
Sirius Ma
Sitwat Husain
Sjoerd Cooijmans
Sofia Verissimo
Soni Ignatius
Sook Mun Yip
Sophie Coles
Sophie Dashwood
Sophie Toumieux
Soumitra Das
Soumya Babu
SP Ang
Steen Hjortholm
Stefan Hermans
Stefan Salzer
Steffen Berkenkopf Laib
Stephane Durand
Stéphane Milhet
Stephanie Hamilton

Stephanie Liang
Stephanie Moles-Rota
Stephen Golden
Stephen Liu
Steve Carroll
Steve Kalicharan
Steve Lim
Steve Lin
Sue Black
Suhrid Chaudhuri
Sunil Kesavan
Surabhi Sanchita
Sureash Kumar
Suryakant Pandey
Susan Graham-Bryce
Susan Lim
Susan Vaughan
Susanna Swann
Susanne Felscher
Susie Gleeson-Byrne
Suzan Morno-Wade
Suzanne Soh
Svetlana Gurevich
Swe Swe Aung
Sylvia Arifin
Takehiko Aoki
Tammi Pirri
Tania Nag
Tanya Lulloff
Tanya Watkins
Tao Ma
Tarek Beram
Tasnim Tudor
Tatiana Filipe Joao
Tekla Szabó
Theresa Lui
Thomas Mulder
Tiffany See

Tim Lynch
Tim Toterhi
TM George
Toby Hough
Todd Korlesky
Tom Kucinski
Toni Hautakoski
Tony Sivaa
Trish Ball
Trui Hebbelinck
Trupti Mohan
Udayan Dutt
Ujjwal Sarao
Ute Driyono Tanusaputra
Valentine Holder Beaucamp
Valerie Hayden
Valerie Nizard
Valerie Robert
Vanessa Iloste
Varsha Mulani
Vasil Stoyanoff
Vassia Kontouli
Veronica Zhao
Veronika Ivanovic
Vicki Ng
Victor Ubeda Roncero
Victoria Bethlehem
Victoria Lim
Victoria Tay
Vijay Prasad
Vinaya Hebballi
Vineet Gambhir
Vinita Menon
Vivien Roussakis
Vladka Kozakova
Wayne Searle
Wei Ren Goh
Wendeline van Loon
Wendy Mullen
Wendy Ng
Wesley Vestal
Wije Mookiah
Wouter Van Linden
Wytinne Cheng
Xavier Güell
Yana Khaldi
Yann Journo
Ying Michael Wang
Yinn Ewe
Yinyin (Sharon) Shu
Yves Demaeght
Zach Toh
Zahina Bibi
Zakaa Farhat
Zakaria Rbii
Zulfa Zulkifli

For Product Safety Concerns and Information please contact our EU
representative GPSR@taylorandfrancis.com
Taylor & Francis Verlag GmbH, Kaufingerstraße 24, 80331 München, Germany

www.ingramcontent.com/pod-product-compliance
Lightning Source LLC
Chambersburg PA
CBHW051611230426
43668CB00013B/2064